KINGLAKE-350

Adrian Hyland lives in St Andrews, in the foothills of the Kinglake Ranges, and teaches at La Trobe University. His novels *Diamond Dove* and *Gunshot Road* are also published by Text.

ADRIAN HYLAND
KINGLAKE-350

TEXT PUBLISHING MELBOURNE AUSTRALIA

The Text Publishing Company
Swann House
22 William Street
Melbourne Victoria 3000
Australia
textpublishing.com.au

First published in 2011 by The Text Publishing Company
This edition published 2015

Cover design by Imogen Stubbs
Cover photograph by Thomas Chambers
Page design by WH Chong
Typeset in Granjon by J & M Typesetting
Maps by Guy Holt

Printed in Australia by Griffin Press, an Accredited ISO AS/NZS 14001:2004 Environmental Management System printer

National Library of Australia Cataloguing-in-Publication entry:
Author: Hyland, Adrian.
Title: Kinglake 350 / Adrian Hyland.
ISBN: 9781922182920 (pbk.)
            9781921834738 (ebook)
Subjects: Wood, Roger.
            Police—Victoria—Kinglake—Biography.
            Black Saturday bushfires, 2009.
            Wildfires—Victoria—Kinglake.
            Forest fires—Victoria—Kinglake.
            Natural disasters—Victoria.
Dewey Number: 363.37099453

This project has been assisted by the Commonwealth Government through the Australia Council, its arts funding and advisory body.

**For the invisible heroes
and for those who are still suffering**

Contents

People who appear in the book

Kinglake police

Leading Senior Constable Roger Wood (acting sergeant on February 7)
Senior Constable Cameron Caine
Sergeant John Ellks

CFA: Kinglake

Captain Paul Hendrie
Linda Craske
Trish Hendrie
Kelly Johnson
Di MacLeod
Phil Petschel
Carole Wilson
Kinglake Tanker One
Dave Hooper (crew leader)
Paul Lowe (driver)
Rod Elwers
Aaron Robinson
Steve Nash
Kinglake Tanker Two
Steve Bell (crew leader)
Ben Hutchinson (driver)

CFA: Kinglake West

Captain John Grover
Deputy Group Officer Chris Lloyd
First Lieutenant Karyn Norbury
Kinglake West Tanker One
Karen Barrow (driver)

Kinglake West Tanker Two
Frank Allan (crew leader)

*Department of Sustainability
and Environment (DSE) firefighters*

Tony Fitzgerald
Aaron Redmond
Sean Hunter
Natalie Brida

Abbreviations

CFA   Country Fire Authority

D24   the unofficial term for the Victoria Police communications centre (it was originally intended to be housed in corridor D, room 23 of police headquarters but then shifted to the room next door: the name D24 stuck)

DSE   Victorian Government Department of Sustainability and Environment

SES   State Emergency Service

Vicfire   the CFA's radio communication network

VKC   the callsign for Victoria Police network control

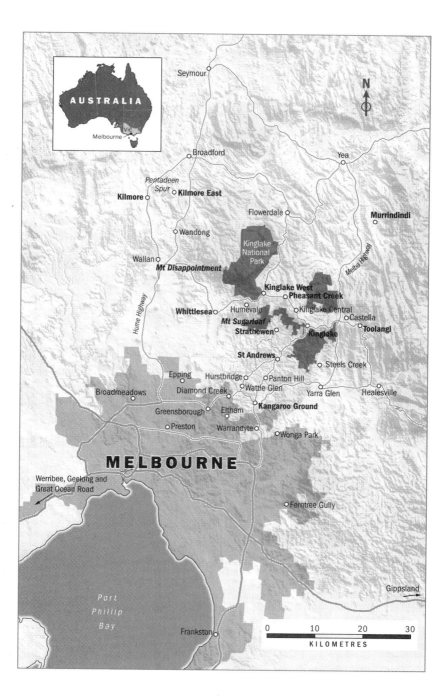

This awful catastrophe is not the end but the beginning. History does not end so. It is the way its chapters open.

St Augustine

GIRLS AND HORSES IN THE FIRE
(Kinglake, 7 Feb 2009)

Nothing will come between them,
those girls and their horses;
not wind or rain, nor pillars of fire.
If a hand should flick a match
amongst leaves or trunks implode
with the weight of heat, or lightning
blast the wasted trees, still they'd run,
these girls, through conflagrations,
wreathed by flames and embers.
Girls who run towards horses in fire,
may you find your home in the equine stars:
Pegasus, Equuleus. Hush, sleep now.

Lisa Jacobson

AUTHOR'S NOTE

Thousands of people were involved in the Black Saturday disaster; hundreds of heroic deeds were performed. In focusing on the actions of a handful of individuals, I have attempted to produce an account of the day that will stand as a tribute to them all.

UNCHARTED TERRITORY

We were lucky at first.

At the end of January 2009 the State of Victoria sweltered through three successive record-breaking days of 43 degrees-plus heat. In Melbourne the mercury climbed to 45.1 degrees Celsius, the third-hottest day on record. Birds fell from the sky, bitumen bubbled underfoot. The air conditioners roared from Werribee to Frankston, and sweaty citizens flocked to the beaches. And at first, apart from small outbreaks in bushland at Delburn and Bunyip State Park, the threat of fire remained latent.

But the long blast of heat, the culmination of twelve years of drought, was a critical factor in what followed. It gave the fuel in the forests that final nudge, drying it out, pushing it closer to ignition point. Even thick logs and rainforest gullies, which under normal conditions would not burn, were parched and ready to contribute their stored energy to a conflagration. A spark was all the bush would need.

There was a brief respite for the city of Melbourne itself at the start of February, as a sliver of cold air from the Southern Ocean drifted in and briefly cooled things down. But the synoptic set-up remained in place, hammering the rest of the state with one 40-plus day after another. Weather forecasters, scientists and fire chiefs were horrified at the potential disaster they saw building, and the warnings issued by the Bureau of Meteorology became increasingly strident.

On February 6, Premier John Brumby's earnest features filled the Friday evening screens.

> If you don't need to go out, don't go out…If you don't need to travel, don't travel. Don't go on the roads…If you can stay at home, stay at home. If you've got relatives who are elderly, if you've got friends, if you've got neighbours, please call on them. Ring them…It's going to be a terrible day.

A weather balloon released four hundred kilometres to the west in Mount Gambier at 4 am the next morning detected high-altitude winds blowing at eighty to a hundred kilometres per hour. It was an ominous indication that they would descend and lash Victoria later in the day.

Fire chief Russell Rees had the disasters of Black Friday (1939) and Ash Wednesday (1983) in mind when he compared the weather forecast with some of the 'classic fire days' of the state's history and said, 'The weather predicted is in fact worse. We are in uncharted territory.'

The next morning the *Age* carried the prescient headline:

The sun rises on our 'worst day in history'.

Black Saturday. Our luck was about to run out.

HOME FRONT

Roger Wood rolls over, drifting up from the bottom of a deep blue dream. He groans. Somewhere outside there's a bubble of voices, kids laughing, up and about at the crack of dawn. It feels that way to him anyhow; he worked until 2 am last night, got home in the small hours. He's tempted to catch a little more shut-eye but then he remembers about today. Not a day to be lying in bed.

A screen door slams, a dog barks. He draws himself up, stretches, steps into the shower. When he comes out into the living room, still buttoning his police uniform, seven-year-old Darcy looks up from the couch, laughing. His arms are full of wriggling guinea pigs. 'Dad…'

'Morning, mate.'

'Hey Dad, if we leave, I'm taking 'em with me, okay?'

Roger smiles at that. Last time they evacuated because of the weather, Darcy took the guineas with him and they had babies. Maybe he's hoping it'll happen again.

Jo, his wife, and nine-year-old Tiahn are at the table. Kasey, the eight-year-old, comes in from feeding the chooks. He joins the family for a bowl of cereal, adds a handful of strawberries from the garden. Jo's been on the go for hours, battening down the hatches, watering, soaking, covering up, preparing the garden for what threatens to be a day from hell.

'Should we feed the horses?' asks Tiahn. At her age, horses are never far from her mind. The equine population on the property fluctuates depending on what old strays they've brought into the fold. There's eight of them at the moment, ranging from a Shetland to a Clydesdale, and a pair of rescue pigs acquired from Edgar's Mission.

He looks outside. 'Nah, not yet.' The wind is already bristling the paddocks, stirring angrily, whipping up the dust. 'It'll just blow away. We'll feed 'em tonight.' He looks towards the dam. The day's going to be a shocker, and the fire-fighting tank has been out of water since the pump down there started playing up. He has to go to work soon; he won't be here to help out if a fire comes.

He checks the clock. Time for a few quick repairs? Emphasis on the quick.

He steps out onto the veranda, pauses for a moment to look around. His home is an eight-hectare property on the outskirts of St Andrews, in the foothills of the Kinglake Ranges, about forty kilometres from the centre of Melbourne. He bought the farm twenty-five years ago, when he was only twenty-one. He and Jo raised their family here and you couldn't imagine a better place to do it. The kids can run wild, feel the wind in their hair, the grass under their feet. Roger has always loved horses, and he's passed that on to his kids: sometimes they spend all day galloping round the farm, taking long trail rides up through the surrounding hills. Birthday parties, family gatherings, he'll hitch the trailer up to the tractor and take them on hay rides, laughter eddying in their wake.

Roger and Jo have been together for thirteen years. Good ones, but not without grief. Their first child, a boy named Jesse, was diagnosed with a malignant rhabdoid tumour at eleven months, and they watched over him helplessly until he died four and a half months later. Roger and Jo both know the value of their relationship, their family.

The three youngest go to school in Strathewen, nine or ten kilometres away. It isn't the closest option, but they chose it because it's a tight-knit little school, nestled in the bush and blessed with beautiful gardens and caring teachers; more of an extended family than a school. The oldest boy, Dylan, has just completed Year 11 at Eltham High. On weekends the family might wander down to the market, meet up with friends, maybe enjoy some Thai food, catch a bit of country music at the pub.

There'll be no socialising today, though. Roger has to get to work, and in this weather there won't be much of a market anyway. There won't be much of anything except this withering bloody heat. The forecast is the worst he's ever heard. The worst anybody has ever heard: temperatures in the mid-forties, ripping northerly winds, humidity barely registering.

Mid-forties? Can that be right? Coming on top of the three days over forty a week ago—and the twelve years of drought before that— it is a day to strike fear into the heart of anybody in rural Victoria.

Wood jumps into the four-wheel-drive and heads down to the dam. Starts up the pump, a Honda twin-impeller, which runs for a few seconds then dies. He tries again. Same result.

Damn. Fuel blockage. He's got neither the time nor the tools to fix that right now. He can't be late for work, not today. He drives back up to the house, finds Jo out on the veranda.

'Get it going, Rodge?'

'Sorry, hon; no time.'

She isn't impressed; he knows that look. 'I'll try to nip down some time during the day, make sure you got water.' He checks his watch. 'Gotta go.'

He puts on his equipment belt, retrieves the Smith and Wesson .38 from the safe, slips it into its holster. He climbs aboard the Pajero and heads north-east towards Kinglake.

*

As Roger Wood drives up the thirteen-kilometre road that locals call The Windies (with a long *i*, because it winds) he finds his thoughts drifting towards fire. Naturally enough, since the day feels like it's on fire already.

He thinks, as he sometimes does when making this ascent, what a bugger of a place it would be to get caught during a bushfire. The road is a death trap, literally: he's seen a lot of death on it. It's narrow, full of hairpin bends, often blocked by landslides and fallen trees. There's almost nowhere you can overtake. You've got a sheer drop to your left, fifty, a hundred metres in places, an even steeper slope climbing away to your right. The vegetation is thick and varied—red box and peppermint gums on the lower slopes, towering mountain grey gums in the upper reaches. It would pump out an unbelievable amount of heat if it ever went up. Some of those trees are fifty metres tall; the radiant heat alone could kill you from hundreds of metres away.

The road is dangerous even without the added complication of fire. He's attended a stack of accidents along its serpentine bends and narrow lengths. They had a weird one not long ago. A group of leathery motorcyclists roared up the hill en masse, raced through Kinglake, completed the great loop back down the Melba Highway. It wasn't until they got back to their outer-suburban homes that they noticed their mate at the tail-end of the column was missing.

Somebody eventually spotted the missing bikie at the foot of a mountain grey some twenty metres from the road. God knows what speed he'd been doing, but he'd missed the turn, sailed through the air, collected the tree. Wood ended up sliding on his backside as he went to check the body. Stone cold, of course. So steep was the drop, they had to get the State Emergency Service to winch the poor bugger out.

Another time the Country Fire Authority attended a burning wreck and found a bloke dead in the driver's seat. Tragic, but not particularly urgent; until somebody noticed that the hole in the windscreen looked man-made. They searched the scrub and found the passenger fifty metres away—still alive.

Today, however, Roger Wood completes the trip without incident and cruises into the main street.

Kinglake started out as a rough and ready timber, mining and farming community, named after Alexander Kinglake, an English author whose contributions to posterity are an out-of-print history of the Crimean War and a town he never saw. These days the majority of the population works off the mountain, making the long haul down The Windies every day. They're drawn here by the cheap land and the beautiful environment. You can buy a cedar kit-home and put it on a big bush block, live a life you couldn't buy for a million bucks in Melbourne: wake up and smell the eucalypts, listen to the kookaburras chortle on the setting sun. An ideal place to raise a family or see out your days.

It's a town of frozen winters and log fires, of red-earth potato farms and pick-your-own berries. It's a town where Aussie Rules football rules. The Whittlesea Country Music Festival is on this weekend. You can guarantee a lot of the locals will have made the thirty-kilometre drive down the mountain for it despite the heat— and despite their eclectic makeup: farmers and greenies, university lecturers and labourers, tradespeople and teachers, musicians and shop assistants. They have their little run-ins from time to time, but the differences are mostly balanced out by a powerful sense of community.

And the town has one thing going for it that is unique, something that doubtless contributes to that sense of community: the Kinglake National Park, 22,360 hectares of luminescent fern gullies and water-falls, kilometre after kilometre of walking tracks and nature trails.

Take a tramp along those trails and chances are you'll come across one of the subtle wonders of the bush: a ring of yabby holes that give away the location of an underground lake, an orb weaver suspended in mid-air, a currawong call that is in fact a lyrebird mimicking a currawong.

The vegetation is as rich a display of nature's plenty as you'll find on Earth. On the lower, more exposed slopes, red box and narrow-leafed peppermint gums predominate. On the more sheltered south- and east-facing slopes, magnificent stands of mountain ash up to seventy metres in height are common. There are specimens in the Wallaby Creek catchment that, at over ninety metres, are among the tallest trees in the world. The understorey varies enormously, with patches of bracken and blanket bush, musk-daisy, hazel pomaderris, blackwood and silver wattle.

The locals are proud of their forest and inspired by it. Many of them make their homes along its shadowy perimeters, and on any day of the week you see people—ordinary joes, dads home from work, kids at hand, mums with four-wheel-drive prams—just wandering around, soaking it up. You might get seventy observers on a freezing winter dawn for the annual lyrebird survey, hundreds of visitors on a Saturday in spring. The National Park is what makes the district a unique, peaceful place to live. When it's not on fire.

Acting Sergeant Roger Wood pulls into the police station and opens the office. He's on his own this shift, in charge of the police station and the town itself while his superior, Jon Ellks, is on leave. His radio call-sign is Kinglake-350. The date is Saturday, February 7, 2009.

FIRE PLAN

Roger Wood's working day starts out no differently from hundreds of others over the past five years. He checks the messages on the phone and the equipment in the strongroom, reports in to the police communications centre, D24.

'Kinglake-350 to VKC Wangaratta. Stats for the day: One up—Code Two—Wood the member on till 1800.'

'Thanks Kinglake-350.'

'Roger and out.'

'Roger, Roger.'

A brief smile. How many times has he heard that one? 'You have a good day now.'

Although he's a long-term local, Wood only joined the Kinglake staff five years ago. Early in his career he spent six years as a beat copper in places like Preston and Broadmeadows—some of Melbourne's more challenging suburbs—but he was out of general duties for a long time after that, with fourteen years in the Victoria Police Mounted Branch. At Mounted he did everything from breaking in horses to driving the transporter. The most satisfying aspect of the job was search and rescue. You never knew what to expect. You might get a call in the middle of the night from anywhere in the state, usually somewhere rough: a bushwalker lost, a skier in trouble, a school group overdue. Load up the horses and away you'd go. He experienced the full gamut of police operations during those years, or as much of it as you saw from the back of a horse. As well as the bush work, there were demonstrations and riots; crowd-control operations—not the least risky of them at the footy, where they copped the job of escorting the umpires on and off the field.

Roger Wood loved the Mounted Branch, but it was more than an hour's drive away, too far for a man with a young family. Sergeant Jon Ellks, the officer in charge of the Kinglake district, had known Wood for twenty years and was pleased the day he rang up and asked if there were any vacancies on Ellks' patch.

'Pain in the arse, he was, from the day he arrived in Kinglake,' says Ellks. 'But in the best sense. He wanted to know everything. If there was something he didn't know, he'd ask. And if I didn't know, he'd say, "But we have to find out." And I might say, "Rodge, mate, it doesn't really matter," he'd say, "No, no, no—might come in handy some day."'

That was how Wood approached the job from day one. He's steeped himself in the culture of the district. He knows the back roads, the black spots, the short cuts. He knows who is likely to own the little plantation in the scrub, who'll be driving home drunk, which kids are in trouble at home. If he's called to a disturbance at the pub, chances are he knows exactly what's going to happen— who'll be there, how they'll react, how it'll end up—before he walks in the door.

Having done time in some of the roughest postings in Melbourne, he is perfectly capable of bringing force to bear if there's no other option. But he's come to realise that more often than not there are other options. Michelle Marshall, proprietor of the Toolangi Tavern, comments that there never seems to be trouble when Wood is around. 'He just radiates confidence,' she comments. 'Never seen him use force. He doesn't have to.'

If there's one thing that everybody interviewed for this book agrees upon, it is this ability to inspire confidence. There was the man with the psychiatric problems who took to calling D24 in the middle of the night, saying he was having troubles but he'd only see 'that Woody feller, thanks'. The mother who rang him to report her son for theft because she knew he'd get a fair deal. One woman, whose first and only meeting with him came when he booked her for speeding and driving an unregistered vehicle, commented: 'He was so charming about it, this big, handsome fellow, explaining what I'd done wrong, saying how he knew I'd learn from it. Far as I was concerned he could have booked me all day.'

On February 7, with Jon Ellks on leave, Wood is acting sergeant. But the values Ellks has always instilled into his team—personal commitment, strong community relationships, an intimate knowledge of the region—are Roger Wood's values too, and they will save a lot of lives before the day is done.

As Wood goes about the morning rituals, he keeps an eye on the sky and an ear on the radio, listening in particular for any indications of fire. There are none yet, but from experience he knows they tend to come later in the day. The police are about as ready as they can be. They've met with the other emergency services organisations on the mountain—the Country Fire Authority, State Emergency Service, Ambulance Victoria, Department of Sustainability and Environment—and done what they could to alert the community.

If he has time, though, he might take a wander up the main street later. Wouldn't do any harm, show some presence on a day like this. Gives people reassurance just seeing the uniform. He knows just about everybody he's likely to encounter: a lot of them are friends. Andrew from the video hire. Brad, the printer. Laur, who owns the sheepskin shop. At Cappa Rossi's Pizza, Isabella and Rossi have even named a pizza after him, the Woody Special.

His latent concerns are intensified when a woman with a couple of kids comes in and tells him she's worried about the weather. You can tell she's not a local soon as she walks in. She says she's only just moved up the mountain, doesn't have a fire plan. Doesn't quite know what a fire plan is.

The Country Fire Authority recommends that every household in a bushfire zone should have a written fire plan, a document that ensures the household is as ready for fire as it can be. It covers matters such as preparing your property (surrounds trimmed, gutters clear, hoses at the ready and so on), evacuation plans, strategies for defence, emergency contact details. One of the many benefits of having a plan is to make it more likely that each member of the household will know what the others are doing: lack of communication during a bushfire can be fatal. Another is that drawing up the plan encourages residents of the fire zone to think seriously about fire—which direction is it likely to come from, what happens if the kids are home alone, which personal objects would I be shattered to lose?—something that, otherwise, surprisingly few of them do.

This woman is no Robinson Crusoe. The government's been pushing the policy for years but despite that, research by the Bushfire Cooperative Research Centre suggests that only 20 to 25 percent of households within the danger zone have taken the trouble to produce a written plan.

'Should I be worried?' the woman asks.

Strewth. Wood scratches his head. She lives in one of the most fire-prone communities in the world; it's been hit by fire time and again in its 130-year history; today is the worst forecast *ever*, she doesn't know what a fire plan is—and she's asking if she should be worried?

There is a standard police procedure in these situations: do nothing other than recommend that members of the public 'activate their fire plans'. Anything else, any specific suggestion, could go pear-shaped and leave the force open to litigation. You suggest to a person that she stay—you could be held responsible if she dies. You suggest she goes, she gets caught out on the road—same thing. But he looks at her standing there, thinks about the weather, the slope, the parched bush. Thinks about his own family down in St Andrews.

'If I were you, ma'am, I'd take the kids and get off the mountain. Early. Like now. Go down the city somewhere, visit a friend. Lot of safer places than Kinglake on a day like this.'

The woman looks a little taken aback. 'You really think it's that bad?'

'What I'd do if I were in your shoes.'

She nods, picks up a barefoot boy who's playing with a rack of pamphlets. 'Okay, that's what I'll do then.'

She leaves, and he never sees her again. But when he casts his mind back over the conversation, days later, he prays that she took his advice.

*

The Bureau of Meteorology might have issued hundreds of warnings during the days leading up to February 7, but how much attention the residents of Victoria paid to those warnings is open to question.

We heard them, but they were just words: we'd heard them all before. They rose out of the radio or off the screen, drifted about for a while; settled into the woodwork or floated off into the ether. You'd see the Premier, John Brumby, draw down his solemn eyebrows and you'd think, oh yeah, but he's a *politician*. And those public servants: only trying to justify their fat wages. We hadn't had a decent fire in almost thirty years.

That's how it was for people all through rural Victoria. At the start of summer, some talking head would get up there and give you the guff about fires and threats and preparations. Every year's going to be 'the worst ever'. What are you supposed to do? Scuttle off down The Windies every time the weather warms up? Go and see *Shrek Ten* at Greensborough Plaza?

The CFA's gold standard for warnings is a day of Total Fire Ban, when it's an offence to light a fire, or even use a welder or grinder, out in the open. There's been hundreds of those in the past; nothing's ever happened. The long-term locals don't look too worried. Really, what are the odds of getting hit? A million to one?

That's a generalisation, of course, and unfair to a lot of people. There were those who prepared, and prepared well. They activated their fire plans. They *had* fire plans. Some left early, others arranged their defences: they primed the pumps, laid out the hoses, gave the property a final clean-up.

But there were many more who did few if any of those things.

There were some, even in positions of authority, who suspected that major conflagrations were a thing of the past. We were so much more sophisticated now: we had sky cranes and water bombers, improved communications, bigger, better trucks. And of course, we had the internet; the CFA website gave you regularly updated summaries of all fires reported across the state. If there was any danger, surely the authorities would let you know? There was even talk that the drought itself had made a megafire unlikely: that after twelve years' desiccation there simply wasn't enough fuel left to sustain a monster fire.

And if by any chance a fire does come, you know the routine. Let the main front pass; give it maybe ten minutes, then nip outside, start up the pump if you've got one. If not, a mop and bucket should do the trick—there was that fellow in Anglesea on Ash Wednesday back in '83 who saved his entire street with a mop and bucket. Extinguish the spots; remain vigilant: watch for further outbreaks.

Way to go.

NEIGHBOURHOOD WATCH

Heat waves and fire threats notwithstanding, Roger Wood still has routine jobs to attend to. Like any town, Kinglake has its share of trouble-makers and he's on first-name terms with most of them: occasional drunks and dopeheads, men and women on the edge of the law. They're part of the local subculture: grow a little weed, pick up something that's fallen off the back of a truck (the trucks of Kinglake must have very loose tailgates, judging from the amount of stuff that falls off them). Men in lumber jackets and elastic-sided boots disappear into the bush with hunting bows, come back with a deer on the roof and a whiff of dope on the breath.

But they're harmless enough for the most part. There's even a kind of camaraderie between crims and cops.

That's one of the things about living in a small town. In a place this size you have to get along. It's simply not possible to maintain arguments, divisions and grudges the way you could in the suburbs. You live cheek-by-jowl, make allowances, get to know each other, discover you have more in common than you knew. When trouble comes, you help each other out.

Sometimes weird stuff happens. It's the combination of isolation and the wuthering, gloomy forests: they might attract tree-huggers and naturalists, but they also attract trouble. Those lonely mountain tracks make a good place to dump cars; bury evidence or bodies. They have a certain appeal for suicides: less chance of some busy-body coming along and spotting the hose attached to the tail-pipe. A year ago a group of wannabe-jihadis decided it was the sort of place to test your home-made bombs. They had the poor judgment to do it near the property of a CFA volunteer who promptly phoned the Kinglake police. They're now doing time in Port Phillip Prison.

Today might be a bit unpredictable, Wood thinks. Things can get strange in the heat. On the one hand, a lot of the usual trouble-makers can't be stuffed tearing themselves away from the air conditioning and the plasma screen. On the other hand, some guys get a little troppo after a few cooling ales. The two kind of cancel each other out.

A welfare check at Flowerdale is the first job: he receives a call from a father, anxious to know how his daughter is faring. She's been having trouble with her partner, hasn't responded to his calls.

Wood goes straight out to the car. Domestics are a heavy proportion of the work out here, and he doesn't like even the hint of one. He drives out to Flowerdale, forty kilometres away, and finds the woman at home. She's fine. They have a chat at the screen door.

'Maybe you ought to make more of an effort to keep in touch,' he suggests. The woman concurs, but when he gets back to the car he calls the man himself, just to reassure him.

Driving back to the station, he comes across a feller he knows broken down at the service station. Paul Grieve is the partner of Jane Hayward, principal of his kids' school. A police car isn't a taxi, but you can't leave the poor bugger out on a day like this. He gives Paul a lift back home.

Another job comes up: a firearms inspection at a Mr Singh's. The Singhs own a broccoli farm just out of Kinglake. He knows the family: decent people, immigrants who've worked hard, done well. There's been a bit of trouble recently because they've been firing guns to scare off the birds; managed to scare the neighbours as well. They've sorted it out now, though.

Wood finds Mr Singh at home and checks that the weapon is safely stored. It is. He has a chat with the gentleman, learns more about the house, which he finds fascinating: the building is made from polystyrene sections. Even today it's incredibly cool.

That's one of the things he likes about this job: there's always something to learn. You meet people, listen to their stories. Sometimes the information comes in handy; other times—well, it's still interesting.

As he steps outside he is buffeted by a gust of hot, violent wind.

He feels uneasy, something playing on his mind. He's driving back along the Kinglake road when it surfaces: the woman and the fire plan. He advised her to get off the mountain, but is his own family much better prepared? That bloody pump.

He checks the clock: a bit after eleven. Time for an early lunch? Everything seems quiet.

He takes a run back down to the family farm. A quick hello to Jo and the kids, but he doesn't have time to hang around. He grabs some tools from the shed, drives down to the dam, pulls the pump apart and in ten minutes has it back together. He yanks the cord. A pause—then it starts. Beautiful: running like Herb Elliott.

He races back up to the house, checks the tank, hears the reassuring sound of water splashing into it. Makes a last-minute inspection of his family's defences. He lays out hoses and nozzles, looks over the fittings and connections. Everything seems in order.

BALANCING ACT

As Wood heads down the drive, he pauses. Listens. He's struck by the eerie silence of the morning. The glare is blinding, the air a shimmering haze. The land is seared and withering under the sun's relentless heat. There's a strange smell in the bush, vaguely reminiscent of cloudy ammonia. A flock of choughs are huddled together, so exhausted by the heat they can't be bothered stirring. A pair of wrens—beautiful blue feathers, vicious eyes—dart about, little swoops.

He watches a leaf twist and spin in the morning light. Then another. He follows their zig-zagging flight, sees more join them. Falling leaves: there's been an astonishing number of them lately.

He gets out of the car, crouches down, runs a hand through the litter on the ground. Picks up a handful and lets it fall. Leaves, bark, twigs, crumbled branchwood drift away. The leaf litter is a world unto itself. Wattle seeds, gumnuts, parched bones. A dragonfly's glassy wing. Creatures too small to be seen with the naked eye. Dry leaf mould. Layer upon layer of it, fifteen or twenty centimetres thick in places. All of it crumbling into the great cycle of death, decomposition and birth that is the forest floor. It's thicker than he's ever known it to be. And the rock-hard earth below it hums with stored heat.

The litter is a frightening sight for anybody who's observed with a knowing eye its steady, remorseless accumulation over recent years. It's more than just debris: at this time of the year it's an accelerant. Might as well be petrol.

As he watches those parched fragments trickle through his

outstretched fingers, Wood thinks about the interwoven influences of nature and humanity that have brought the bush to such a state. That simple handful of litter bears testament to years of drought, devastating climate change, an environment, already the most flammable in the world, tormented and stretched to breaking point.

All those falling leaves—what do they mean? The trees are in trouble, they're like a ship on a reef, jettisoning cargo, struggling to survive.

The rainfall in the past year has been the lowest on record: in January 2009 only 0.6 mm of rain fell, the driest start to a year Victoria has ever recorded. The water storage is lower than it's ever been: Melbourne's dams started the year at a fearful 34.7 percent capacity and by now they must be at rock bottom. Groundwater levels, soil moisture, fallen logs and stumps are all severely affected. They're all connected, all indicators of danger: the lower the moisture level in the soil, the more ready the bush is to burn.

The drought reached its nadir in the three brutal days of over 43 degrees a week ago. Eleven consecutive days of 30-plus, conditions not seen in 160 years of white settlement. Temperatures like that cure the land, dry it out, prime it.

And today?

Jesus wept. The worst of all. Scorching heat, negligible humidity: less than 10 percent predicted. The humidity is important. The lower the moisture in the atmosphere, the closer things are to ignition. The wind already feels like a gale blown up from the bowels of hell. And it will get worse as the day wears on.

The McArthur Forest Fire Danger Index is the scale used to measure the threat of fire in the Australian bush. Developed in the 1960s by legendary fire scientist Alan McArthur, it weaves together variables such as wind, fuel, drought, humidity and temperature to come up with a numerical rating that can be applied to any locality. It uses Black Friday—January 13, 1939—as a measuring stick: the index on that terrible day, when seventy-one lives were lost, was set at 100, which scientists believed to be as bad as it could get. A day of

Total Fire Ban, when it is a serious offence to light a fire anywhere in the open, is declared if the index reaches 50.

Today the fire danger index is off the scale. It varies according to local conditions, but in the countryside around Roger Wood's home it's in the 180s. The weather has gone mad, and the bush is ready to explode.

*

Climate has been the driving force behind much of human history. It drove our ancestors in and out of the caves, it propelled the Mongols into Europe, the Vandals into Rome. Its vicissitudes were the reason that empires from the Sumerian to the Egyptian—arguably even the Napoleonic, the Nazi—rose and fell. It allowed humankind to colonise the New World, twice.

Until very recently, humans were outdoor animals with an awareness of weather in our bones. But although we've lived forever in its icy blasts and scorching heat, our understanding of it is still surprisingly limited. We can send a remote-controlled vehicle to Mars, but our best scientists cannot accurately predict the timing of a change in a local wind that will turn a fire about and kill scores of their fellow citizens.

Why? Because the weather is so damned complicated. Even with their staggering computational capabilities, their satellites and multidimensional radar imagery, the experts are giving us, at best, an educated guess. Think for a moment about the phenomenal power needed to shift air masses the size of continents around the globe, or lift enough moisture to deposit millions of tonnes of rain onto the Earth's surface every day.

And the atmosphere—thin blue film of gas it might appear to be from outer space—has a complexity to match that power. Every parcel of air, from a zephyr to a hurricane, is constantly subjected to a battery of influences that include pressure forces, friction, buoyancy, and the deflection of its motion caused by the Earth's rotation, known as the Coriolis effect.

BALANCING ACT

Weather is driven by nature's need for equilibrium. When air ascends in one place it has to come down somewhere else. Simple. But the ramifications interconnect in bewildering ways that have only become apparent with the rise of modern communications: a drought in eastern Australia, for example, could be counterpointed by heavy rains in the southern states of the USA. Low-pressure storms in Darwin will coincide with both a high-pressure system in Tahiti that causes dry weather and heavy rain in Central Africa and the Amazon. They are all connected.

The driver for this eternal flux, the source of all this power, is the sun. The sun's atmosphere is so hot, at some 6000 degrees Celsius, that atoms there can't hold onto their electrons. At its core, the sun, powered by a cascade of hydrogen fusion reactions, maintains an unimaginable temperature of around 14 million degrees. This gargantuan nuclear powerhouse delivers some 175 trillion kilowatt hours of energy to Earth every hour, generating in a day as much power as 200 million atomic bombs.

If the planet was as flat as our ancestors believed it to be, the upshot of that would be relatively straightforward and weather much more predictable. But because of Earth's shape, rotation and tilt, the radiation that streams into the atmosphere is distributed unevenly. It is strongest at the equator, which is why that is the planet's torrid zone, but the equator cannot just keep on becoming more torrid. The equilibrium imperative ensures that the energy that comes in at the equator moves towards the poles. The circulation of the atmosphere and of the ocean currents is the means by which this happens.

This constant energy transfer causes both air density and temperature to vary enormously, to be in a continual state of flux, as weather phenomena large and small—from super-cells to raindrops—struggle to achieve a balance. The instinct for equilibrium is responsible for the wrenching convolutions and sheer variety of our planet's climate: for the Roaring Forties and the Doldrums, the crushing droughts and the sheets of lightning and ice.

Ultimately, it is also responsible for the teeming variety of life on

Earth: for the sleek-backed birds that slip among the manna gums, the nodding greenhood and spider orchids, the fern-filled gullies of the kind that weave their way through the Kinglake Ranges. They are manifestations, all, of climate. And so are the fires that arise time after time and render those varied colours down to a uniform coal black.

INCIDENT CONTROL

It is around midday and Roger Wood is heading for the gate when somebody flags him down.

'Morning, Roger!' Steve Andrews, his neighbour, standing at the intersection of the two properties.

'Morning, mate.' He wipes some of the sweat off his neck. 'Hot enough for ya?'

'Too bloody hot. What do you know about that, Rodge?'

What? He follows Steve's outstretched hand. A column of smoke has appeared in the north-western sky behind him. He raises an eyebrow: that was quick. It wasn't there when he drove down a few minutes ago. Looks a long way off, though.

He listens in to the police radio, learns that a fire has just broken out at Kilmore East. Does a quick mental calculation.

'Should be right, Steve. Good—what?—fifty k's away? Change oughter be here before it gets anywhere near us.' He leaves his neighbour standing there, but as he cruises up the mountain he feels a ripple of anxiety moving in his chest.

*

Some time just before 11.50 am, a fire has been started by a fallen power line on the Pentadeen Spur at Kilmore East. As it races towards the Hume Highway an Incident Control Centre is established at Kilmore. The controllers are briefly hopeful that the highway, a four-lane expanse of bitumen and gravel, will act as a firebreak. But the fire barely pauses as it leap-frogs the Hume along a five-kilometre front and hits the messmate forest on the eastern

23

side. Somewhere in there it begins crowning, roaring through the upper canopy, leaping from tree to tree. It multiplies its intensity by a magnitude of five, then ten. The pyrocumulus cloud above swirls some eight kilometres into the atmosphere. The fire storms through the countryside at a rate two to three times faster than predicted by the McArthur Forest Fire Danger Index.

Fire scientist Nic Gellie has commented subsequently that this astonishing speed and ferocity is changing the way some scientists think about fires, forcing them to question the orthodox concept of fire spreading in uniform ellipses. 'Under the conditions of Black Saturday,' he says, 'spotting, fires merging, and convection columns ruled the fire processes on the day.'

A motorist is travelling towards Whittlesea when he sees the fire coming at him. He turns around, puts the foot down. The fire begins to gain on him. He accelerates even harder; still the fire gains. He swears later he was doing 140 kilometres per hour when it overtook him.

The wind drives the flames up onto the launch-pad ridges. It shatters and snaps the tall trees, whirls the burning fragments into the valleys below or across to adjoining ridges. The experts call this spotting, but that's a feeble term to describe what it looks like to those in its path; maybe 'saturation incendiary bombing' would be more accurate.

Massive winds whip branches and strips of bark from burning trees and whirl them so high they run into winds blowing in other directions. They are chaos in flames, can land anywhere, inflict incredible amounts of damage; particularly dangerous are the long, thin strips of ribbon bark. They burn for a long time and cover enormous distances. The fires that will wipe out farms and wineries along the Yarra Valley are started by debris torn from mountain tops many kilometres away. Fire scientist Kevin Tolhurst estimates that on this day there are embers travelling a record thirty-five kilometres.

One CFA volunteer says later: 'I felt like I was in the middle of a Ridley Scott movie: we were in a gully watching a shower of burning

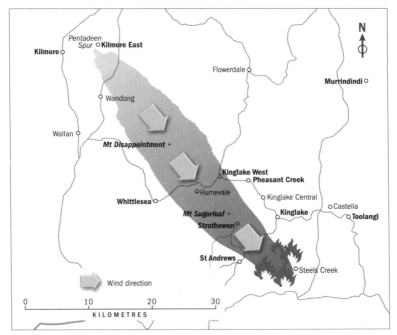

The initial progress of the Kilmore East fire

embers arc overhead, catapulting from one summit to another.'

And those 'embers' can be huge. Later that day a policeman is driving up The Windies with no fire in sight when what he describes as 'a firebomb the size of a caravan' comes whirling out of the sky and lands beside him. He's still blinking in shock as the missile ignites the surrounding bush, starting an instantaneous conflagration that goes racing away.

This process is repeated a thousand, a million times over as the fire careers down from Kilmore East. The front is like a spiral nebula, whirling through space and spraying great arcs of energy in every direction.

RED WIND

Bruce and Margaret Newport, in Chads Creek Road, Strathewen, feel relatively confident of their ability to defend their home. They are well equipped with pumps and tanks, and live a considerable distance from the bush on an Angus beef farm they've kept wet and green in preparation for a forthcoming field day. They are experienced country folk. When the fire approaches late that afternoon, Margaret and the children shelter inside while Bruce patrols the boundaries.

Then he watches in horror as the wind tears the roof from the building. 'The whole thing peeled back like a tupperware lid and came off,' recalls Bruce. 'Beams and all.'

The family survive, but only just.

When many survivors look back on Black Saturday, it is the wind that looms largest in their memory. That hot red blast was the engine that powered the juggernaut.

'It was blowing a bloody gale up on the mountain,' says Roger Wood. 'Never seen anything like it. I was driving a two-tonne Pajero, and when I was out in the open it was rocking like a sailboat in a storm.'

To be in an exposed location in the bush that day was to feel that you were in the grip of a protean force: every branch, each leaf and twig was alive and writhing, straining, breaking loose, whipping away. The grasses bowed and rose as if invisible giants were running through them. One firefighter described a large limb caught up in the power lines, how it made him think of the skeleton of a galleon. As he watched it was torn apart, shattered into fragments that speared fifty metres through the air.

RED WIND

In the Kinglake Ranges it was probably worse than most places because of what fire authorities call the Ramp, where the flatlands rise into the foothills and the slope intensifies wind conditions. The result, local fire managers report, is that winds in the ranges are often twice as strong as statewide forecasts.

*

A big running bushfire is an extraordinarily complex concatenation of events, a synchronicity of fuel, topography, heat, drought and human activity. But it is the wind that causes that frayed conductor on the Pentadeen Spur to snap and come crashing to the ground, sending an electrical charge arcing into the grass.

It is the wind that picks up those first thin fingers of flame and transforms them into something extraordinary, propels them in long, expanding ellipses out into the grasslands, then into the pine and bluegum plantations to the south-east.

Bureau of Meteorology data suggests that the recorded wind reached speeds of up to 120 kilometres per hour. But a raging bushfire will generate its own tornadic winds, and they can be much more powerful.

Nic Gellie, who modelled the reconstruction of the Kilmore East fire for the Department of Sustainability and Environment, estimated that the wind around the fire was of cyclonic force, hitting speeds of between 150 and 200 kilometres per hour. (There were no weather stations located at the fire front, so these are estimates based upon the damage done at places such as St Andrews and Strathewen, where roofs were torn from houses and massive trees corkscrewed out of the ground.)

But what is wind? And why did it go berserk on Black Saturday?

Around the world, its names are legion and rich with local memory and lore: brickdusters and mistrals, cat's paws, diabolos, doctors, the Steppenwind. There is the bitter Pittarak that whistles off Greenland's fields of ice. The suicide-inducing foehns. The fire-driving Santa Anas. The Harmattan, the 'hot breath of the desert', the name given by Tuareg nomads to the sirocco and said to derive from the Arabic for 'an evil thing'.

Humans have struggled to make sense of wind since the dawn of consciousness. The ancient Indians saw it as the breath of life. To the Greeks Aeolus, the Keeper of the Winds, lived on a floating island, and is remembered for giving Odysseus the bag of winds that wreaked havoc on his journey. In Aztec theology, the god Ehecatl employed gentle zephyrs to awaken Mayahuel, the goddess of love, thereby endowing humanity with the gift of love. The Book of Genesis goes even further: when the spirit of God moves over the waters, it appears in the form of wind.

As humanity moved from myth to science, deeper thinkers sought more rational explanations. The Greek philosopher Anaximander suggested that wind was a current formed when mists were burned off by the sun. Meteorologists would say he wasn't that far from the truth. Our contemporary understanding of wind begins with the sun, and that instinct for balance that underlies the weather.

We think of air—well, we don't think about it at all as a rule, unless we're running out of it. But it's there all the time, it's the envelope of gases that girds our planet, and within which our respiratory systems have evolved.

You might not envisage air as having weight but it does, of course: that's what's pushing into your face when you step outside on a windy day. It is, in fact, surprisingly heavy—the air in a normal room weighs about fifty kilograms. If you had a 25-millimetre tube going from sea level to the top of the atmosphere, the air inside it would weigh about 6.7 kilograms. Each square metre of air bears down with a force equal to a ten-tonne weight, but because the pressure in liquid or gas acts uniformly in all directions and the downward force is countered by an equivalent upward force, we don't get squashed. When those particles of air develop a collective motion in a particular direction they become what we call wind.

It was the polymath Edmund Halley, he of the comet, who in 1686 first came up with a theory that approximates our contemporary understanding of how that motion works. Halley was struck by the correlation between information from two new sources: the data about air pressure provided by the recently invented barometer and the flow of the planetary winds reported by the mariners of the expanding British Empire. He deduced that the air along the equator was heated by the sun and lifted, to be replaced by cooler air drawn in from the temperate regions on either side of the equator— the trade winds, so crucial to the maritime industry.

Halley's observations were further refined in 1735 by amateur meteorologist George Hadley, who suggested, correctly, that the winds were affected by the Earth's rotation: the winds don't just ascend and run north or south: they tilt. Hadley also proposed that the thermal convection (warm air rising) at the equator is followed by subsidence at higher latitudes, a theory recognised today in the circulation pattern known as the Hadley Cell. Interestingly, Hadley's equatorial hot-air convection columns descend at around thirty degrees latitude north and south—thereby explaining the location of many of the world's deserts, from the Sahara to the Great Victorian, the Atacama to the Kalahari.

It was a cluster of those deserts, the ones that compose the vast mulga and spinifex plains of Central Australia, that would forge the terrible winds of Black Saturday.

In early February 2009, Australia was ringed—ringbarked, it almost seemed—by a triumvirate of high- and low-pressure systems. The procession of highs and lows that moves across our TV screens every night makes them seem like separate entities floating up there in the sky, but of course those diagrams represent patterns, not objects. Highs and lows are simply illustrations of the tendency of the molecules in the atmosphere to cluster together and move in a particular direction.

Like any other gas, air reacts when placed under pressure. Think of the air compressed inside a balloon; when given the chance, it automatically strives to achieve equilibrium by rushing to an area of lower pressure—the space outside. The greater the difference in pressure, the greater the rush; the steeper the gradient of decline, the stronger the wind.

The atmosphere is constantly swirling around, rearranging itself in response to the shifting centres of pressure created by solar radiation. These move in great cycles, their constituent air spiralling in towards the centre of low-pressure systems and outwards from highs. One of the outcomes of the Coriolis effect—the 'centrifugal force' generated by the Earth's rotation—is that the air cycling in and out of highs and lows flows in different directions in the different hemispheres. Here in the south, it flows clockwise into low-pressure systems and anti-clockwise around highs.

There were two significant lows affecting Australia in the days leading up to Black Saturday. The first was a monsoonal trough over northern Australia. This elongated centre of low pressure drew in vast amounts of moisture-laden air that whipped up deep convection clouds across the Gulf of Carpentaria and into Queensland (causing, ironically, widespread flooding). The ascending air associated with this cyclonic turbulence had to be compensated for by subsiding air elsewhere, and that subsidence was corralled to the south-east.

Then there was a second low over the Southern Ocean. This was drawing cold dense air northwards, pushing against the warmer subtropical air to the north like a giant bulldozer. Since the air in both of these systems was flowing clockwise, the resulting airflow was being compressed, heated, driven down over the parched Central Australian deserts.

But out over the warm waters of the Tasman Sea there was a third weather system, a blocking high so powerful that it would not be budged. This had the effect of locking the lows in place. It was the reason the heatwave lasted as long as it did.

High up in the atmosphere was yet another complicating ingredient in the mix: a subtropical jet stream ripping along at speeds of up to three hundred kilometres per hour. The air caught in the jetstream was subsiding on one side, giving the overall flow a

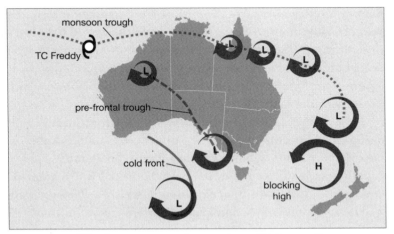

Weather systems on the morning of February 7

whirling, rotational momentum that was ultimately transferred into the surface winds tearing over and into the ground below.

These three weather systems—the monsoonal low with air flowing out from the upper reaches of its convection clouds; the southern low with its advancing wall of cold air; the blocking high—combined to squeeze the airflow of the subtropical jet stream downwards over south-eastern Australia. As the dry air descended it became hotter and faster: by the time it reached the surface, it was like the blast from a furnace.

As fire scientist Liam Fogarty, Assistant Fire Chief with the DSE, put it:

> The state was being squeezed tighter and tighter and the wind kept getting stronger. But the front over the Tasman was just sitting there, saying, 'You can keep coming all you like, but I'm not moving.' We in Victoria were caught in the pressure point between them.

The horrific twelve-year drought would have added to the heat as well, and was doubtless the reason why so many temperature records were broken. The ground was so parched and hard-baked that there was little evaporation to ameliorate the conditions. In wetter years, residual moisture in the soil and vegetation would have had a moderating effect, reducing the temperature. Now solar radiation heated the ground and was returned directly back into the atmosphere in the form of high-powered dry convective thermals, which further warmed and dried the air.

The confluence of these phenomena amounted to a massive blast of sun-dried, super-heated air being driven down to the south-east, into what fire historian Stephen Pyne calls the 'fire flume'.

A flume, in the common sense of the word, is a man-made structure: a deep, narrow defile through which a fluid—usually water—is channelled. A flume might be constructed to transport timber, to divert water from a dam or power a water wheel: a mill race is a flume. But in Pyne's elegant trope, it is not water that is channelled, it is wind.

The eastern ranges act like wings, shepherding heated air southwards, concentrating energy; the variable soil and precipitation produce vast amounts of fuel on the ground. Topography, botany and weather: these interwoven forces provide the dynamism that makes the great fire triangle of south-eastern Australia—its corners at Botany Bay, Port Phillip Bay and the Eyre Peninsula—the most fire-prone location on Earth.

CFA

In an observation tower at Kangaroo Ground, twenty kilometres south of Kinglake, a fire spotter named Colleen Keating watches in horror as fire comes rolling down from the north. She passes on the information to her Incident Control Centre, assuming it is being acted upon.

It isn't.

The CFA fire management policy is that a blaze remains the responsibility of the district in which it ignites until it is formally passed over to whatever region it enters. This fire, having commenced in Region 14, is initially the responsibility of the Kilmore Incident Control Centre. As it roars south-east, it crosses CFA boundaries and moves into the jurisdiction of the Region 13 Centre at Kangaroo Ground, the office responsible for the Kinglake Ranges.

But at Kilmore things are in a state of chaos. Communication systems—phones, computers, faxes—are completely swamped by incoming reports, many of them contradictory, as the managers struggle to cope with the unbelievable speed of the inferno. Fire-prediction maps are drawn up and ignored; warnings are not issued until the relevant communities are already destroyed. Most critically, due to the collapse of the communication system, responsibility for the fire is never formally handed over to Kangaroo Ground. There are staff at Kangaroo Ground who can see disaster looming, who beg for warnings to be issued to the towns in its path, but they are not heeded. The Incident Controller at Kangaroo Ground refuses to take action until the correct procedures have been followed and responsibility for the fire is formally handed over.

The control centre does issue warnings to SP Ausnet, the power company, that their power lines in Kinglake are in danger, but not to the people who live around those power lines. Warning notices are drafted but not released.

By 2.11 pm, smoke has been sighted at the foot of Mount Disappointment, just inside the boundaries of the Kinglake National Park. It crests this ridge about an hour later, sending out an incendiary barrage that begins raining down upon the rolling, heavily populated foothills at the base of the Kinglake Ranges.

Everywhere along its path, local brigades turn out to try and stop it. They hit it with all their resources: they water-bomb it, clear firebreaks, muster more than ninety appliances.

Everywhere they fail.

The fires of February 7 were a freak of nature, people concede that. They moved at a furious, unprecedented speed and spotted over record distances. But few who were in the Kinglake Ranges that day are ready to forgive the failure of the authorities to warn anybody in the path of the fire—even those responsible for community safety, the local emergency services personnel, the fire captains and coppers—that it was coming. A year later, many of those who were affected by the fire still struggle to contain their anger.

'We know those people,' says Kinglake West firefighter and Deputy Group Officer Chris Lloyd. 'We talk to them every day. A simple phone call could have made all the difference.'

Mike Nicholls, the captain of Panton Hill CFA, is even more cutting. 'I still feel angry when I think about it. There were a lot of things we could have done if we'd had a warning. I'm sure it would have saved some lives.'

Nicholls is one of those extraordinary characters who make your local CFA brigade the eclectic body it is. Originally trained as a plumber, he went off to university and has remained in academia. In 2009 he was a professor in the Psychology Department at Melbourne

University. He manages to combine the tradie's practical skills and blunt speaking with the analytical powers of the academic.

The way the disaster unfolded confirmed many of his doubts about the organisational structure of the CFA. His criticism is in no way aimed at the local volunteers, who were out there risking their lives to fight the fire with minimal information; it is the upper echelons about whom he is most scathing.

'Some of them are not the sharpest tools in the shed,' he says. 'They employ at the bottom and then promote them. I'd like to think I know a bit about these things. You can train someone all you like—at the end of the day you're not going to change their personality or intelligence. Those in charge of the ICCs didn't have the sense—or the balls—to make decisions on their own.'

*

The Victorian Country Fire Authority is an organisation that epitomises something unique, almost elemental, in the nation: it is volunteer-based, locally focused, practical, down to earth. It is, at brigade level at least, a bullshit-free zone: you either do the job or you don't. 'If you don't like it,' one member politely explains, 'you can pack up and piss off; nobody forces you to be here.'

There have been improvised fire-fighting groups since the beginning of European settlement, but the Victorian CFA arose as a result of recommendations by the Royal Commission into the Black Friday fires of 1939. The outbreak of the Second World War delayed its creation, and it formally commenced operations in April 1945.

Perhaps because many of those who made up the first units shared a military background, it adopted a structure not unlike the armed forces: each brigade has a captain, who is supported by a number of lieutenants. Where it parts company with the military is in the fact that its officers are elected by their fellow members.

One of its strengths is the autonomy of its individual brigades: they know their communities and are authorised to make decisions about their safety. They know the hot spots and the death traps, the bog holes and the back roads; they know where to find water when they need it, they know which old people are living on their own, which women are home from hospital with newborn babies.

There are over 1200 separate brigades spread across the state. Between them, they can muster some 58,000 volunteers. Whenever there is a threat or tragedy in rural Victoria—a fire, a flood, a traffic accident, a lost child, a fallen power line—you can be sure that somewhere nearby, a group of men and woman will be running from their workplaces and homes, scrambling onto their 'Berts'—big, expensive red trucks—and rushing to the scene.

There's generally a vehicle out the front door within five minutes of the call coming in. On a blow-up day like Black Saturday, the minutes become seconds. Most brigades have people geared up and waiting by the trucks.

The CFA brigades in the ranges are nothing if not diverse. Their volunteers range in age from sixteen to...too polite to ask. Their occupations show a similar diversity—there are tradies and businessmen, lawyers and nurses, office and hospitality workers— and they have a wide variety of reasons for joining. Some are there for the excitement, some are there for the friendship or from a love of working with heavy equipment. All are there because they think it's a worthwhile thing to do for the community. No one is there for the money.

There is an element of friction between the paid and the volunteer firefighters, with the latter sometimes mocked as a kind of dad's army. But in practice the experience and diversity in the local brigade is a strength. The truck that comes roaring up your road in the event of a crisis could be crewed by a group of your neighbours whose life skills include metal work or electrical engineering, first aid, plumbing, meteorology, land management, vet science, business.

Some might seem irrelevant: what use is a human resources manager in an emergency, for instance? But if you observe the response to a critical incident up close, you will be struck by what a complex operation it is, how crucial is the ability to coordinate people and resources, to think logically, make snap decisions.

The CFA is also an equal opportunity employer (albeit an honorary one): many of the firefighters out there driving trucks and operating chainsaws on Black Saturday were women, as were many of the crew leaders and captains. At one of the most critical moments of Black Saturday, when fire was directly impacting the National Park Hotel and the hundreds of people sheltering beside it, the firefighter standing alone out in the darkness with a spluttering 38 millimetre hose in hand was a seventeen-year-old schoolgirl who had just received a pager message that her own home—with the rest of her family in it—was under attack.

Each CFA firefighter completes, as a minimum, a six-month training course in wildfire management. One of the first things new members learn is how to save their own lives in a burnover, when the vehicle is overwhelmed by fire. Firefighters, almost by definition, often find themselves in the most dangerous part of the inferno, and you can't save anybody else if you can't save yourself. The routine is to jettison anything explosive—jerrycans, chainsaws—crouch down and cover up as best you can, spray a fountain of water over the truck, often with a hand-held hose, and pray that the water outlasts the fire. For a firie this is the most terrifying experience of all: they all know the names of locations—Upper Beaconsfield, Linton—where entire crews have perished in recent years. But burnover is, in fact, a rare occurrence. There's many a firefighter who's been on the job for twenty, thirty years and never experienced one.

There are two fire brigades on the mountain—at Kinglake and Kinglake West—with four trucks between them. In the next few hours, all four vehicles will be burnt over.

MAYDAY

Earlier in the day at Kinglake West: Captain John Grover is muttering a quiet prayer of gratitude for the new 225,000 litre tank they had installed just a few weeks ago. He still has concerns: the council hasn't slashed the overgrown roadside reserves to his satisfaction; his superiors have yet to pay adequate attention to his plans for a staging area for strike teams near their shed.

The experts have always warned him to expect a fire from the north, but his real worry is the fire that comes running up the escarpment with a southerly buster whipping it along. Fire accelerates as it travels uphill, doubling in speed for every ten degrees of elevation. The combination of steep slopes and heavy fuel load would mean devastation for the people—his people—at the top of the rise.

But Grover has an experienced, capable crew and is confident that, if it comes down to it, they'll be able to provide at least a level of protection for the crowds he knows will come in to CFA headquarters seeking refuge.

Many of his members have checked in early. The atmosphere in the stations is relaxed—on the surface. There's a lot of chiacking, some sorting of crews and rosters, much consumption of cigarettes and coffee. A last check of the equipment, though they've done it a dozen times already.

Similar scenes are being enacted at brigades all over the state.

Over at Kinglake they stretch out on deck chairs, keep a vague eye on a television. Di MacLeod cuts up a watermelon and passes it around. Underneath, they're on edge. Even those who've stayed at home until they're called keep an anxious eye on the sky, an ear on the scanner. They run thumbs over the pagers on their belts, reread old messages, wait for the call-outs. There's an iron-hard sense of foreboding in the shed. Most days, they manage to get most fires under control before they run wild. But on a day like this, who can tell what will happen? A blaze could be off and running in seconds. And when they get started they tend to keep going until nature intervenes.

Most of the Kinglake firefighters see the smoke plume in the north-west before they pick up it on the radio. The sky grows luminous, the sun a creepy scarlet. They move a little closer to the radio, ears pricked. They hear Region 14 crews being despatched, frantic messages ringing forth from the speaker: pleas for backup and support.

Then they pick up the first Pan calls—'PAN! PAN! PAN!'—'possible assistance needed'. A crew somewhere is getting caught in a desperate situation. More than one, by the sound of it. They stare northwards. What the hell's happening up there?

Later comes the most disturbing call of all: 'Mayday! Mayday!'

Not just once, but several times. Distressing: their colleagues on the fire front are being overwhelmed.

'Hearing those distress calls,' says Mike Nicholls, 'it was spine-chilling.' Particularly for his brigade, Panton Hill, which had lost an entire crew on Ash Wednesday in 1983. He and his members go past the community's memorial to their lost comrades just about every day. 'No crew leader would call a mayday unless the situation was life or death. You wouldn't want your mates to risk their own lives by coming to your aid.'

The Kinglake volunteers sit glued to the radio. It's excruciating to listen to, but the action is happening out of their area; nothing they can do about it until they are paged.

But their hearts pound a little harder, the adrenaline flows a little faster. Those who smoke, and a lot of them do, are into the fags like they were Minties. The more experienced among them kick at the gravel in front of their brigades, feel that god-awful wind whipping into their faces, think about the lie of the land between themselves and Kilmore and feel the small, hard kernel of fear growing inside them.

*

They make what preparations they can. At Kinglake West, First Lieutenant Karyn Norbury and her colleagues set up an extra pump, called a Godiva, on the new tank. Karyn is an experienced country-woman; she and her partner Dave operate a stud farm on the fringes of the town. She's accustomed to working with both hand and mind.

At Kinglake Paul Lowe and Aaron Robinson take the brigade car up to a vantage point at the top of Bald Spur Road, study the billow-ing column, make use of a kestrel wind monitor to get a heads-up on what the fire is doing.

They try the CFA website and the local ABC radio station, both of which prove useless. There is virtually no helpful information being given out by the official sources. Hours later, when the town is burning, the website will still blandly advise that there is a 'grass and scrub fire' at Kilmore, thirty kilometres away. Bizarrely, the website seems to tell you where the fire has started, but fails to give you the more pertinent information about where it's heading. There are people on the mountain whose last contact with the outside world will be a computer screen telling them the fire that's about to kill them is thirty kilometres away.

The fire crews find that the best means of following the unfold-ing drama is on their CFA radio network. Kilmore is on a different frequency, so they only catch the odd scrap of information, but what they hear sounds chilling. Unlike the CFA website, which is designed to convey general information to the public, their own radio network allows them to eavesdrop directly on their colleagues on the fire ground. They also have a police scanner, and listen in as the coppers around Kilmore shout warnings and rush around trying to get people to safety.

Aaron Westworth, one of their members who works in a pine plantation in Wandong, has been called in to work because of the emergency. He makes a couple of frantic phone calls back to the brigade around 2 pm, gives a running commentary as the fire storms the plantation, one block at a time:

'Block One's gone! It's into Block Two now!' A final, despairing: 'Ah shit, we can't stop it!' And he signs off, more pressing matters to deal with.

'I had a gut feeling we were going to wear a nasty fire,' says Chris Lloyd. He was at Macedon on Ash Wednesday, he's seen how bad a blaze can be. Based on what little information he can gather from his contacts—the intensity, the speed, the fire's behaviour in leaping across multilaned highways—he fears it will hit them later that night. Possibly on the Sunday.

Lloyd and his colleagues will be fighting for their lives in less than three hours.

ARSON

It is still early afternoon when Roger Wood drives back up The Windies to Kinglake with an eye on the smoke to the north-west and an ear on the radio. The fire sounds bad, but it's still miles away. No mention of Kinglake. He'd like to keep in closer contact with the CFA but, due to some inscrutable decision made in the upper echelons of the bureaucracy, the CFA and police radio networks are incompatible. He does put in calls to the CFA captains on his mobile, but at this stage they're doing the same as he is: watching and waiting.

He thinks back to the fire that threatened Kinglake in January 2006, on Australia Day. It had dawdled around for days before fizzling out, getting everybody all stirred up about nothing. Could have been a lot more than nothing though; the fire had started a run on Kinglake before it was suppressed by a heavy downpour. They were lucky then. Maybe they've used up all their luck. Perhaps that escape has lulled residents into a false sense of security.

Around 3 pm he receives a call from Trevor Connell, the police sergeant at Yea. They've just got word of a fire at the Murrindindi Mill over on the north-eastern edge of the Kinglake region, about forty kilometres away.

This is the first outbreak on Roger's patch. There's a chance he'll have to close the Melba Highway. He dashes out to the car, flicks on the flashing lights.

As he's racing north-east up the Healesville–Kinglake Road, he spots the plume of smoke in the direction he's heading. He knows straight away they've got no chance of stopping that. It's only been

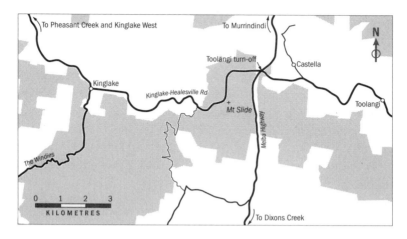

going for a few minutes but already it's massive, a storm of angry black smoke churning the atmosphere. The colour is a worry: black means the fire is running fast and furious, moving too quickly to consume the fuel, transforming half-burnt material into the carbon that colours the clouds.

Looks like it's heading to the south-east, away from Kinglake. But there's a cool change forecast this evening. What'll happen when the wind swings around is anybody's guess. Weird things happen when weather systems collide, he knows that much. Embers can go anywhere, fires can sneak around, stab you in the back.

Is there any chance it could link up with the Kilmore blaze, turn into a megafire? They're in trouble if it does.

He spots Trevor Connell on a siding near the mill and pulls over. When he opens the door the wind nearly tears it out of his hand: it's picked up something awful, and is blowing a ferocious gale now. He has to shout to be heard.

The two coppers stand there for a few minutes, discuss the situation at high volume, come up with a plan. Wood's going to head down the Melba Highway to the Slide—Mount Slide, where the road runs down to Dixons Creek. He'll prop himself at the Toolangi turn-off, keeping an ear on the radio. If the fire looks like coming their way he'll block the highway to stop all northbound traffic. Trevor's heading north and will halt any vehicles southbound.

Between them, they'll keep people out of the danger zone. Try to minimise the number of potential victims. There'll be tourists, day trippers, locals heading off to the beach or the mall. The rubber-neckers are the worst, stupid bastards. It's the most dangerous place you can be, out in your car when the fire's coming, but they always appear.

Wood jumps into the Pajero and heads back down the Melba to the Toolangi turn-off.

*

As they suspected early on, the Murrundindi fire will turn out to be the work of an arsonist. So were fires elsewhere in the state, at Churchill and Bendigo. Between them, these conflagrations will kill around fifty people.

There are around 54,000 bushfires in the nation each year. Experts now believe 20–30,000 of these are deliberately lit. This is a figure that ought to send a shiver down any Australian's spine. You live in the most fire-prone region on Earth, and 20–30,000 times a year one of your fellow citizens sneaks out and puts a match to the scrub. And he (for most of them are male) tends to do it in places where his handiwork will wreak the maximum amount of havoc.

One study has shown that deliberately lit fires account for 80 percent of the area burnt in the Port Phillip region, around Melbourne, but only 6 percent of that in the thinly populated north-east of the state. In other words, the fires that break out in remote locations, where they will do minimal harm to humans, tend to be due to natural causes. Where there is a sizeable human population nearby, it's a different story. Another study showed that 36 percent of deliberately lit fires occurred within two hundred metres of human habitations. On total fire ban days that distance will increase as the arsonist recognises that the extreme weather has amplified his firepower.

ARSON

Arson is the simplest of crimes, especially when considered in relation to the amount of damage it inflicts: it needs little more than a box of matches, a lonely road and a twisted mind. But it is one of the costliest crimes in Australia, both in purely financial terms and in the immeasurably greater domain of human suffering. Arson in all forms costs the community an average of 1.6 billion dollars a year. It has enormous environmental impact: the 2003 fires, for instance, increased this country's carbon emissions by a third. It can also have a devastating effect upon our major cities' water supplies: a big fire can decrease catchment yield by 20 to 30 percent for thirty to fifty years.

And yet despite the threat it presents, arson remains something of a black hole in the public discourse. This psychosis that is causing havoc in our midst has very little place in our cultural imagination. There are no TV series or feature films about arson, no best-selling novels or famous trials. On this single day, February 7, arsonists will kill fifty men, women and children going about their ordinary business, and the public will hear little more about it.

Researchers working in the field are dismayed at the level of ignorance about the crime, which stretches from the person in the street right through their own under-funded ranks to the upper echelons of government. As one delegate to a Monash University conference pointed out, if a fraction of the resources that were available after Black Saturday had been available before the tragedy, its magnitude could well have been reduced.

But we do know a few things. We know the myth that arsonists join the CFA is exactly that: a myth. Whenever a firebug who happens to be a member is convicted it tends to hit the headlines; and doubtless a few slip through the net. But a specifically targeted investigation into deliberately lit fires in New South Wales found eleven firefighters involved—a tiny fraction of a total membership of 70,000.

In more general terms, we know there is a strong correlation between arson and the usual predictors of anti-social behaviour: high unemployment, low income, dysfunctional families—phenomena that could be said to characterise the communities springing up on lyrically named estates on the peri-urban interface.

Studies of individuals convicted of bushfire arson reveal another familiar picture: young, single males with a range of intellectual and psychological problems. Many have prior convictions, not necessarily for arson. Around half of the females are victims of sexual abuse, as are many of the males. Psychologists have identified a range of motivations, including the venting of anger at society, the cry for help, the hunger for recognition (one arsonist saw the admiration afforded to the firefighters of September 11 and wanted a little of that for himself), the desire for stimulation (an arson squad detective recounts the story of a firebug who could only achieve orgasm when watching fire). If there is a common emotion among known perpetrators, it is a sense of powerlessness.

There are some seriously weird people out there: hard-core pyromaniacs, victims of an impulse-control disorder whose gratification at watching flames erupt far outweighs any empathy they might feel for their fellow humans. They will light fire after fire until they are caught, and they are perhaps the most difficult of all criminals to catch: they work alone, in remote areas, leave minimal evidence behind and have usually fled the scene before the crime becomes apparent.

This suggests another problem with the knowledge base. What information we have is based upon interviews with the convicted, but the vast majority of arsonists are never even caught, let alone convicted. There are convictions for a mere 1 to 2 percent of all deliberate ignitions and we have little idea about the motives or mind-set behind the others. The fact that arsonists who are caught have low intelligence, for example, may just be telling us why they were caught. Maybe the smart ones get away.

CAR ALARM

It is probably about 4 pm. Roger Wood is speeding down the Melba Highway to the Toolangi turn-off when he notices a change in the pitch of the voices from the radio. A greater sense of urgency at Kilmore. Will they need support? Will he be called up there? He can hear voices cutting across one another, his colleagues pleading for information, their bosses issuing orders:

'What's it doing now?' 'Alert everyone!' 'Where's it going? This side of Wandong?' 'Tell people to activate their fire plans!'

Activate their fire plan? Shit, it's a bit late for that.

The adrenaline is beginning to kick in. Wood's pulse quickens, his mouth feels dry, his chest is tight. He takes a swig of water, pops a stick of gum. He's got Murrindindi burning on one side, Kilmore on the other. His immediate concern is the Murrindindi blaze. Which way is it likely to go? Back towards Kinglake? Healesville? Marysville? Wherever it goes, there'll be thousands of people in its path. A glimpse out the passenger side window: Jesus, it's going ape out there now, the cloud billowing kilometres into the air.

He reaches the turn-off, gets out of the car and watches the pillars of smoke, miles high, rolling and folding into one another. He feels restless. He should be doing more than this, just standing around waiting. People need to be warned. Granted, if they've got any sense they'll be listening to their radios, watching the sky. Maybe.

Where to start? The Toolangi Tavern is the obvious choice. It'll be directly in the fire's path, and it's a place where people congregate. A meeting place for the locals, a watering hole for any travellers foolish enough to be out bush on a day like this.

It's only a few minutes down the road; he could keep an eye on the smoke, be back here in no time. He turns east, races down through an avenue of manna gums. Planes of light are filtered through the flickering green leaves.

The houses are deeply nestled in lush bush; the trees tower over them, the scrub creeps up to their back verandas, sometimes seems to be coming out their windows. If the fire does come through, anybody in these dwellings is in deep shit, but there's no time to warn them all. He can only hope they're watching events unfold and they've got their wits about them: that they'll be long gone before the fires come.

He pulls into the tavern—a beautiful weatherboard building that wouldn't last minutes in a fire. Like a lot of other buildings in the area, the tavern is a replacement for a building that burned down years ago. Toolangi's main claim to fame is as the home of the Australian poet C. J. Dennis—whose house burned as well. This is a region as much defined by its absences as by its presences, and a lot of those absences seem to be due to fire.

There are a dozen or so people congregated there, standing outside, anxiously staring at the hot red northern sky. Michelle Marshall, the owner, looks around when he drives up. 'What do you know, Roger?'

'Not good, Michelle. Coming this way, and it's a monster. Wouldn't be hanging round if I were you.'

Others in the crowd throw questions at him. He answers as best he can, but they're all stunned into silence when a car comes belting out of the nearby Murrindindi Forest. An old Holden, lights flashing, horn blaring: *Blarp! Blarp! Blarp!* A couple inside the car, the woman screaming herself blue over the din of the horn.

'Fire!' she yells as the vehicle slams to a noisy halt. 'The forest's all on fire! Get out of here!' *BLARP! BLARP!* 'It's coming. We nearly got burnt.'

The man driving catches Roger staring at him and figures, rightly, that the copper is puzzled by the unholy racket emerging from the car. 'Alcohol interlocking alarm,' he gasps. 'Had to short-circuit her to get it going.' He doesn't look well: he's covered in sweat and trembling, a gaping gold-fish mouth. Knuckles white.

Wood starts to speak but the bloke interrupts, shouting to be heard, 'We woulda died if I hadn't driven—it was hell in there.' He glances back at the bush. 'Fire all over the road.'

Wood follows the fellow's anxious eyes. 'How far back?'

'Dunno. Coupla miles?' He waves vaguely around him, indicating the raucous vehicle, and yells, 'Magistrate'll know I been driving. Can I have you as a witness? We had to get out of there.'

'No worries.' Roger bangs on the roof. 'Go on, off you go now. Get back down to wherever you're going.'

As the Holden speeds away, still shrieking, Wood turns his gaze up into the forest from which it came, hoping to hell there isn't anybody else in there. Nobody'd go for a picnic on a day like this. Would they?

There is, in fact, a group of twenty campers—men, women and children—in the forest. They are being rescued at that moment by a team of forest firefighters from the Department of Sustainability and Environment who guide them into the river and shelter them under tarps and blankets as the fire storms over them.

Wood knows nothing of that and wouldn't have time to help if he did: the Holden is barely out of earshot when he receives another call. 'VKC Wangaratta to Kinglake-350. Do you read me? Over.'

He picks up the mike. 'Kinglake-350 reading you. Over.'

'Kinglake-350, yours is to Whittlesea–Kinglake Road, traffic management point. Over.'

Wood pauses, puzzled. That's in Kinglake West. The Kilmore blaze is fifty kilometres away. Is there a third bloody fire?

He shrugs, shouts a quick farewell to the crowd at Toolangi— giving them another reminder to be somewhere else as soon as they can—and hits the road running.

FIRST STRIKE

The Kinglake CFA brigade members spot the Murrindindi fire at about the same time as Wood and begin making their calculations. Is Kinglake going to be struck by two fires simultaneously?

The sky over the town assumes an ugly red and streaky yellow luminescence. Carole Wilson, a member for more than thirty years, stands looking at the distant pyrocumulus monsters. 'If those two meet,' she says to her friend Trish Hendrie, 'we're in trouble.'

Even if they don't meet, the residents of the town are still in trouble: there's now no safe way off the mountain.

The Kilmore fire seems to be following a trajectory that will take it south of Kinglake, but fire projection is an incredibly complex task at the best of times. A fire's trajectory can be affected by a multitude of factors: fuel type, elevation, slope and aspect, as well as variables such as changes in the weather. Unbeknown to the firefighters, Melbourne University scientist Kevin Tolhurst and his team have already developed maps predicting that Kinglake is in danger. But due to poor communications within the inaptly named Integrated Emergency Coordination Centre—there's little in the way of integration or coordination going right now—the information in those maps is never passed on to the communities at risk.

The CFA crew in Kinglake don't have long to worry about such things. Soon after the Murrindindi fire breaks out, their pagers start to shriek with the first call-out for the day: an 'undefined' fire down on the St Andrews road.

'Undefined' means somebody's spotted smoke.

The trucks are out of the shed almost before the beeping stops.

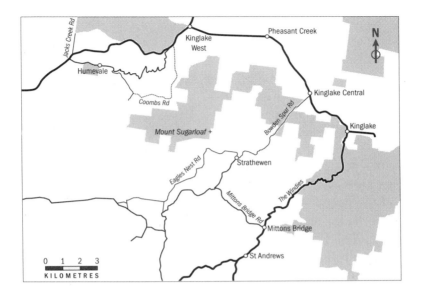

If there's a mantra to fighting fires in this part of the world, it's 'Hit it hard and fast'. The difference between a minor outbreak and an all-devouring inferno can be a matter of seconds.

All four appliances from Kinglake and Kinglake West tear off to the reported location, but it turns out to be a false alarm. Some anxious resident has misread the smoke drifting down from Kilmore, fears the fire is closer than it is.

They trail back to their stations, but the frantic exchanges screaming out of the short-wave do little to reassure them. They can hear crews being despatched hither and yon, then being recalled and sent elsewhere as the CFA's communication network, Vicfire, struggles to cope with fires breaking out all over the place and moving at what sound like impossible speeds.

Chris Lloyd receives a call from a friend near Wandong, who yells that they are under attack as he speaks.

'What?' Lloyd struggles to grasp the speed of the thing. 'It's there already? My god—it's already travelled twenty kilometres…?' The friend signs off. Soon afterwards he loses his home.

John Grover is on Kinglake West Tanker One when he hears a desperate plea from Ken Williamson, the captain at Whittlesea. 'More support! We need more support! If we don't round this up here we're going to lose it.' Then, shortly afterwards, the dismal follow-up: 'Vicfire, we've lost it.'

Grover and his driver, Karen Barrow, exchange a grim look. Whittlesea is their nearest neighbour. They'll be next cab off the rank.

The Kinglake West tankers are barely back at the station when they get another call-out: a fire in Jacks Creek Road, in the nearby town of Humevale. It's coming closer. They get going, but have barely hit the bitumen when they spot thin plumes of smoke snaking up from Coombs Road, a mere three or four kilometres away.

Their own region. The fire has arrived.

Spot fires, by the look of things, a scatter of wisps being tilted by the wind. Outbreaks ignited by burning debris ripped away from the main front. They have to be tackled at once, before they turn into something worse.

More plumes appear. Both Kinglake West tankers rush out to meet them, calling the outbreak in to Vicfire as they speed out over the asphalt and turn down the dusty tracks.

Frank Allan, on Tanker Two, sees at once they're going to need support. 'Make tankers five!' He radios in for five additional appliances, but no support will arrive until much later that night, long after the damage is done. They're on their own.

In Kinglake village, the call comes in at around the same time. Code One—lights and sirens—for Eagles Nest Road in Strathewen, a tiny community at the foot of Mount Sugarloaf.

Kinglake Tanker One is despatched, a team of five with Second Lieutenant Dave Hooper in command and Paul Lowe at the wheel. They debate briefly which road to take down to Strathewen: the dirt track along Bowden Spur is the direct route, but it's more dangerous. All that dust will reduce visibility, and the track descends sharply though thick scrub; a hell of a place to be caught in a fire.

They opt for the bitumen. Given the fire's subsequent movement, the decision probably saves their lives.

Kinglake captain Paul Hendrie is puzzled when he receives a request for the second tanker, this time for an outbreak in St Andrews. He assumes it's a mistake: protocol demands that one tanker always remains in its home district. He ignores the call, but then receives another. And another.

There's a major strike team being formed, and Vicfire clearly want his home-defence appliance to be part of it.

Hendrie and his remaining firefighters mull the question over. It sounds like something terrible is happening down there. The location is Mittons Bridge, on the northern outskirts of St Andrews. Almost in their area anyway. Chances are they're the closest brigade. He's loath to leave his town without defences, but, on the other hand, in fighting a fire at the foot of the mountain, they are in fact defending their own community. You fight the fire you've got. Hit it hard and hit it early. If they can stop it down there, it won't come up the mountain.

Hendrie makes the decision: he'll despatch Tanker Two, but on the proviso that it returns to Kinglake as soon as the rest of the strike team arrive. The vehicle sets out with Lieutenant Steve Bell as crew leader, Ben Hutchinson at the wheel.

The town of Kinglake is now without a fire appliance.

As Ben belts through the town, he's struck by the normality of it all. People are still going about their business, shopping, filling their cars at the service station, lounging out on the pub veranda. Kids are playing in front yards, drifting up and down on bikes in the way of country kids everywhere. The screaming, flashing tanker seems out of place, a rambunctious intruder in that rural idyll.

By the time they make it back to Kinglake, the town will be in ashes.

ROADBLOCK

As he races into Kinglake West at about 5 pm, Roger Wood wonders about the urgency of the call. His radio is going berserk, but it's still 'Kilmore, Wandong, Kilmore, Wandong'. That's thirty kilometres away. Surely it would take hours to cross that distance? The adrenaline is coursing through his veins.

He reaches the intersection, spots a red four-wheel-drive that has improvised a roadblock in the Whittlesea direction. A trio of yellow-clad firefighters are waving cars down. He wheels about to block off the road.

One of the group comes over. Wood recognises Chris Lloyd.

'Woody! Thank christ you're here. They're ignoring me, the stupid...'

'Who are?'

'People trying to run down the mountain.'

The police have the authority to stop traffic. The CFA don't. It was Lloyd who had requested the police support. He's just come in from Coombs Road, where the spot fires are breaking out. The Kinglake West tankers are still out there. He knows the main front won't be far behind. He's set up the roadblock on his own initiative, been there maybe twenty minutes, trying to keep people from driving down to Whittlesea. Dozens of cars have come racing through. Legally, he's acting without authority in blocking the road, but he figures he has a moral responsibility.

Lloyd is a fire engineer by profession, has been a CFA volunteer for more than thirty years: he knows what he's seeing. If the spots have come as far as Coombs Road, then the road to Whittlesea will

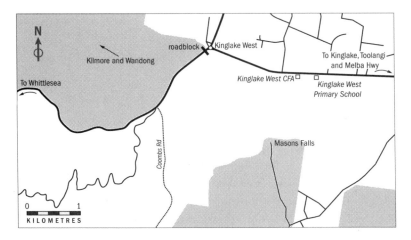

be a death trap; there's bound to be fire across it somewhere down the mountain.

Some of the drivers have taken his advice. Others haven't, have gone barrelling down the mountain. 'Some of them were very blunt, rude,' Lloyd explains later. 'Yelling we don't have to effin listen to you—people were in flat-spin panic mode.'

Wood recognises the urgency in the CFA man's voice. 'Okay, don't worry about that now, I'll take over. But is it that bad? Radio's still talking Kilmore.'

A station wagon loaded up with dogs and boxes comes skidding down a nearby drive. There's a woman at the wheel. Chris Butterworth, a local teacher, distraught, weeping. She and her husband John live in the middle of thirty-six hectares of dense bush overlooking Masons Falls. Picturesque, but suicidal in a bushfire. John is still back at the property, refusing to leave. The power has gone out, the only other car is locked inside the garage; he won't be able to get out even if he decides he wants to. She pleads for help.

'Okay, we'll go and get him,' says Lloyd, returning to his vehicle. He glances back at Wood. 'Please—just don't let anybody else down that road.'

Wood looks down towards Whittlesea. Trees are swinging wildly in the gale, smoke is whirling, thicker than it was before. But there's no fire that he can see.

If there's one thing he's learned in years of working in critical situations it's the need for a fallback position. He calls out to Lloyd: 'If it turns to shit, where'll you be?'

'Back at the CFA.'

'That's where I'll be too, then.'

The firefighters disappear into the Butterworth property.

Wood stands there, alone. That sky-tearing wind from the north is getting worse. It's a weird, freaky, threatening atmosphere. Debris from the forest whips past: shreds of leaf and bark, torn from the trees. He stretches out a hand: a fragment lands in it. An odd looking fragment: it's buckled, burnt. That doesn't necessarily mean much; given the ferocity of the wind, it could have come from anywhere.

Cars come scrambling from the Kinglake direction, their occupants anxious to head on down to Whittlesea. Word is getting around. He stops maybe twenty vehicles in ten minutes. Some argue the point, get a little irate.

'One woman was very shirty,' he says. 'In the car with her daughter. Wanted to get back to her house. Didn't let her through, of course.' He gives the encounter a moment's consideration. 'Good thing for her I didn't.'

He doesn't let anyone through. They turn around, head back to town. Some push on eastward towards the Melba Highway, others end up sheltering at the CFA.

There's a definite smell of fear in the air. The Murrindindi blaze is a vast pyrocumulus cloud roiling the eastern sky. No wonder people are getting rattled: fire on both sides of the mountain. What will happen when the change comes through? If the fires turn at the wrong moment, Kinglake will be caught in a pincer.

There's a rundown shack on the corner of this intersection. Wood and his crew often set up the booze bus to conduct random breath tests here on a Saturday night. Every night, without fail, a woman comes staggering out of the shack, feet bare, clothes bedraggled, wine bottle in hand, and yells at them to turn those fuckin lights out.

He's just sent another car on its way when he hears a cracked voice behind him. 'What's goin on?' She's standing there, holding the bottle, a glazed expression on her face.

'Bushfires about, Meg,' he replies. 'Somewhere down the mountain.' He glances at her shack: indefensible. Survival time seconds, not minutes. 'Wouldn't hang around here if I was you. Might be an idea for you to go somewhere safe.'

'We're staying put,' the woman growls.

'Dunno if that's…'

'Me husband says we're stayin, so we're stayin.'

That's it, he thinks. He gazes after her as she stomps back to the shack. If the fire does come through I'll never see her again.

Another car pulls up: locals, judging by the load. Dad at the wheel, kids in the back. Black dog, panting. Chook in a cage.

'But where are we supposed to go?' the driver pleads when Wood doesn't let them through. His options are limited: nowhere on the mountain is safe right now. Officially, he isn't allowed to tell them anything, but he's been letting all the drivers know what he plans to do: shelter at the CFA.

'Your best bet…'

He catches the look on the driver's face—the dropped jaw, the wide eyes—and spins around.

Jesus.

It's there. Exploding along the treetops, less than a hundred metres away. He's seen bushfires before but nothing like this, nothing this big, this close: massive whirls of naked flame, sixty, eighty metres over the trees.

The first wild bolt of fear shoots through his chest. The radio is still screaming: 'Kilmore, Wandong. Kilmore!' Still thirty kilometres away! What's this inferno doing here? How is that possible? There's been no warning, no mention of Kinglake at all.

There's been an almighty cock-up somewhere.

Roger Wood has a mental flash of what's about to happen: chaos is breaking loose. The rules have just flown out the window, and that means it's every man for himself. Except for him. He somehow has to be there for everybody else.

He thumps the roof of the car. 'Back into the CFA at Kinglake West! Safe as you're gonna get up here today. Go!'

As they disappear, Wood leaps into his own vehicle, grabs the radio. 'Kinglake-350 to VKC Wangaratta! Do you read me, over? It's here now. The fire's in Kinglake West.'

God help us.

He can't take his eyes off it.

The CFA vehicle comes back, its reluctant passenger on board. They had a hard time persuading John Butterworth to leave, had to chase him round the house. They finally convinced him to come with them by telling him how distressed his wife was. They beat the fire out by seconds.

Wood goes over and speaks to Lloyd. 'Chris, when do you want me to finish the roadblock?'

Lloyd nods at the fire. 'About now, wouldn't you think?'

Wood isn't arguing. This location has become suicidal, and his immediate duty—to stop people taking the road to Whittlesea—is done. Nobody in their right mind will be driving into that. He'll head on into Kinglake West, re-establish the roadblock, shepherd people into the CFA.

Kinglake West Tanker One comes rattling up, John Grover in command, Karen Barrow at the wheel. They're on their way in from Coombs Road. They've driven through a tunnel of fire to get out.

'What's happening in there?' asks Wood.

'Hell on Earth.'

'Where's the other tanker?' Kinglake West Tanker Two, under Frank Allan.

A flicker of anxiety. 'They're trapped in Coombs Road. We lost contact. Radio communication's hopeless.'

Lloyd nods his agreement. Like Wood, he's momentarily

mesmerised by the fire. 'People are going to die today,' he murmurs to nobody in particular. A straightforward enough comment, but there are thirty years' experience behind it, thirty years of studying the way fire runs, the ways in which weather, humanity and country interact.

There's been no official warning, but Lloyd has been around long enough to recognise a catastrophe when he sees one coming. He's spent weeks trying to warn people, alarmed at his fellow residents' lack of preparation. Coombs Road must be one of the most dangerous settled locations in the world—an overgrown ridge on top of a parched escarpment. He's been watching aghast as residents fiddled with garden hoses and cleaned out gutters, or stood around wondering what to do.

People are going to die today.

He doesn't know it at the time but he suspects it, and he's correct: some of the people who ignored him and went racing down the road before Wood arrived are already dead.

FIRE FRONT

Paul Lowe takes Kinglake Tanker One hurtling down the bitumen and turns right into Mittons Bridge Road, bouncing over the corrugations. Dust spools behind them, is whipped away by the wind. The crew's orders are to get to the fire at Strathewen, but they don't have to: the fire comes to them. They've just travelled the couple of kilometres to the Jacksons Road intersection when the fire comes rushing over the paddocks from the north-west.

'Jesus!' spits Dave Hooper.

'Where did that come from?' mutters Lowe. They are still fifteen kilometres from their destination.

'Grass fire attack!' Hooper yells to his crew, meaning that they are to drive at the fire, attempt to suppress it. But as Aaron Robinson and Steve Nash leap out to man the hoses, Hooper realises the fire is moving at a speed he's never seen before. It's about to engulf them. 'Back inside!' he calls. 'Crew protection!'

There are two types of truck on the fire front this day. On the older models, most of the crew are out on the back, exposed to the fury of the fire. The newer models have a twin-cab that seats the entire crew. The crew of Kinglake Tanker One have the good fortune to be in one of the modern tankers.

They've rehearsed this a hundred times, but can't help wondering whether the real thing will run as smoothly. They scramble inside, draw the curtains, hit the spray button, lie low, brace themselves.

'Here we go, boys,' says Lowe calmly. 'We're into it.'

The flames come roaring up and over them. Their world is transformed into a flaming red singularity.

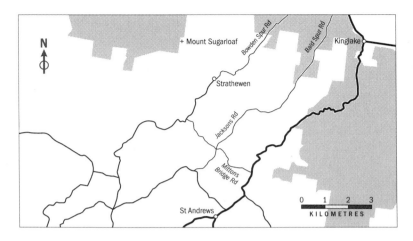

Lowe becomes concerned as the trees around them burst into flame: they're throwing out massive blasts of radiant heat, and he's worried that one of them could fall and entrap them. Mobility is one of your few defences in such a situation. He inches the truck through thick smoke, comes to an area that's more open. They spend an agonisingly slow few minutes sheltering in their vehicle as it rocks and shudders, belted by the wind and battered by falling and flying debris. The men inside are panting and sweating in the heat, clutching wheel or handrail, giving the jesus grip a thorough workout.

'Everybody okay?' grunts Hooper. A couple of nods.

Then the intensity diminishes. They creep a little further along the road. Decide they're going to survive.

Twenty-six years ago, in the Ash Wednesday fires, a dozen firefighters caught in a situation like this burned to death. The crew of Kinglake Tanker One won't be joining them. The system has worked. All the training, all the efforts to develop more sophisticated operational practices—crews often rehearse for entrapment, and always ensure they leave enough water to save themselves—have paid off.

They still have a job to do, 'putting the wet stuff on the red stuff' as Hooper expresses it, so they set about doing it.

A house on the hill opposite is surrounded by flames. Alerting

Vicfire as they jolt over the rough pasture, they race up to attack the flanks of the fire. The afternoon air rattles with the sounds of a fire fight: radio screaming chaos, pumps thumping, the jangle of metal, the hissing of water jets on flame, all in a haze of thick black smoke and mauling winds. And the strange distraction, as they crash around the paddock, of being followed by a mob of horses, who must have decided these yellow-helmeted aliens and their fat red truck are the closest thing to normal on this crazy day.

Other tankers arrive. Not a formal strike team, but local crews acting independently. The Kinglake crew work away until they run out of water, but now they hope the house is safe. As they go back to refill, they are joined by Kinglake Tanker Two, which has followed them down The Windies.

'The radio was going berko as we drove into St Andrews,' comments Ben Hutchinson. 'Fires breaking out all over the place.' There are tankers everywhere now, and a water truck belonging to local contractor Geoff Ninks is keeping them supplied. While Tanker One goes back to refill, Tanker Two patrols along Jacksons Road, its crew tackling whatever they can.

As is the case in any broad-scale conflict, the front-line fighters can only see what is happening in their little corner of the field, but they hear enough from the radio to know that things are going badly. And what they can see doesn't look much better: no sooner do they get one spot under control than another flares up. The foothills of north St Andrews are being bombarded with flaming debris arcing in from the ridges around Strathewen, fires are breaking out everywhere. Hundreds of them.

'Make tankers five,' they hear the fire ground controller calling. Then it's: 'Make tankers ten!' 'Make tankers fifteen!'

They'll take all the tankers they can get.

*

Fire spotter Colleen Keating is still in the observation tower at Kangaroo Ground, observing the battle as she has been from the beginning. Her own husband is on one of the trucks. At around 5.45 pm, those who are near a radio hear her calling:

'Red Flag Warning!'

RED FLAG

The Red Flag Warning system is a fire ground communications practice designed to alert firefighters to an imminent change in the weather. It was introduced after the Linton tragedy in 1998, when an entire CFA crew died after a sudden wind shift turned a tame flank into a raging killer.

Normally such a call would be issued by the Incident Control Centre at Kangaroo Ground, not by a fire spotter. But at that crucial moment the fighters on the fire ground were fortunate that a woman of Ms Keating's initiative was in a position to make the call.

The spotters are a remarkable group of people. They are all experienced firefighters; they understand fire behaviour, they know the topography of their regions like their own weathered hands. They can triangulate a puff of smoke rising from a thick stand of distant forest to within a hundred metres. The firefighters on the ground entrust their lives to these people.

Mike Nicholls tells the story, from an earlier blow-up day, of the spotter who noticed a string of outbreaks along a remote St Andrews road, immediately recognised the work of a firebug and was confident enough to radio Vicfire straight away: 'Make tankers ten!' A big call, and something that would not normally happen until the local tankers were on the scene. By that time it would have been too late, the fires out of control.

Communication systems were disintegrating in the chaos that was erupting all over the region, but Colleen Keating didn't need the bosses to tell her that the chilling wind she could feel ripping past her lonely stone tower would have disastrous consequences for those out at the front. She'd spent the day transmitting increasingly desperate observations of the fire's passage to the Kangaroo Ground ICC as the horror erupted before her startled eyes. She watched in disbelief at the size and speed of the thing as it came pouring over the slopes of Mount Sugarloaf and raced towards St Andrews: a mountain of smoke ten kilometres high, two wide.

All day the wind had been streaming down from the north-west. Suddenly, at around 5.45 pm, it swung around, roaring in from the south-west at ninety kilometres per hour, rattling her lookout something awful. She knew what that meant.

The southerly buster had arrived.

It had been forecast, but wasn't expected for another hour or two.

The experienced fire-ground controllers knew what would happen now. The northern flank of the fire would turn into the head and the inferno would go racing up the escarpment with an eruptive energy release anywhere between five and ten times that of the original blaze.

The wind change would prove to be a bullet dodged for the residents of Melbourne's outer suburbs, a close escape most still don't understand they had. At the time of the change, the firefighters on the front estimated the fire was two minutes from the town of St Andrews—the delaying operation carried out by the CFA crews on Mittons Bridge Road may well have saved the town. Given its speed, energy and direction, in another hour or two the inferno would have descended upon the tightly packed, overgrown suburbs of the northeast: Warrandyte, Hurstbridge, Diamond Creek, Greensborough, Eltham. If that had happened, the casualty figures would probably have been in the thousands, rather than the hundreds.

For Melbourne, it was a near miss. For the unwitting residents of the Kinglake Ranges, it was a catastrophe.

Colleen Keating, well aware of the implications, was aghast that this lethal change had arrived unannounced. 'We didn't get a pager to say there was a weather warning—weather coming early. We didn't get a phone call,' she would later tell the Royal Commission

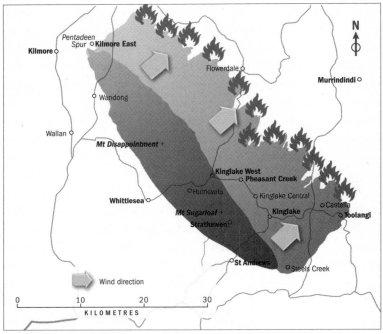

The Kilmore East fire after the wind changed

into the bushfires. '…It normally happens. Next thing, bang, here is this wind…I could hear people I know on the fire ground and I'm thinking, Oh my god. This is Armageddon.'

So she broke protocol and issued the warning directly to her colleagues.

*

Viewed from almost anywhere other than the fire front—from, say, the comfortable perspective of the suburbs—the southerly buster feels like an enormous relief: it's the long-awaited cool change. The temperature plummets, the sweat on your brow acts like air conditioning. Time to throw open the windows, let the refreshing breeze drift through the house.

But on the fire ground it's the horror moment, the slo-mo

sequence, the snake rearing in the grass. If you do think of it as a reptile, it may help to imagine it as one that is suddenly transformed from a single slithering serpent into a hydra-headed monster.

'The change is the killer,' comments senior meteorologist Tony Bannister. 'When the wind was from the north-west, we had these long, thin slivers of fast-moving fire. But with the change, the flank becomes the head...The whole thing goes ballistic.'

Instead of a five-kilometre front heading south-east, you've got an eighty-kilometre front, and it's rampaging all over the place. Historically, more than 80 percent of the destruction wrought by bushfires occurs after the cold front hits. Think of what your living-room fire does when you blow on it, then magnify that effect a trillion times over. A blast of cold air is driven into the heart of the storm; the fire turns upon itself—and comes across a massive source of untapped energy.

The very worst place, in time and space, is at the point of impact, when the weather systems collide. That's when things on the fire ground go nuts. The vast majority of the vehicle burnovers on Black Saturday happened around that time. The flames go dancing in every direction and individuals are battered by blasts of wind, whips of flame, flying debris.

Fire historian Stephen Pyne describes this moment as 'the deadly one-two punch, calculated to knock down by fire anything still standing after drought.'

That was how it had happened on the state's previous disaster days: Black Friday, Ash Wednesday, Black Thursday. The northerly wind kick-starts the fire, drives it south, then the southerly change comes sweeping in and whips it into a frenzy. It will generally move to the north-east, but in those first few moments it is swept up into a vortex that can send its missiles spinning in every direction. This is why so many of Black Saturday's victims reported that the fire came from directions they didn't expect, from every quarter of the compass.

'I felt like what we were fighting was a normal bushfire,' recalls one Strathewen resident. It was still horrific, it still managed to destroy his house. But he and his family survived. 'We were out of the house by then—watching it burn down. Everything around us was already burnt. Then the change came. I watched it change from a bushfire into a bomb. It swept up the slopes at a speed I couldn't believe. Those poor bastards up there, they never had a chance.'

All over the fire ground, firefighters find themselves caught up in a gothic vision, a world gone mad. Trees bend to breaking point. Branches fly through the air like burning arrows. Wheels and whirls of fire dance across yellow paddocks. The tea-tree on the south-east side of Jacksons Road goes up like a plantation of monster sparklers, sending red, blue and purple fireballs sixty metres into the air. Some describe horizontal vortices—burning black holes—rolling along the flanks of the fire.

'It was like a bloody tornado up there on Jacksons Road,' commented one of the firefighters, and that was no exaggeration. The winds wouldn't have seemed out of place in America's Tornado Alley, only here they were more dangerous because they were loaded with fire.

The fire vortex is a well-known phenomenon, described by US fire scientist Clive Countryman in an account written forty years ago that is still regarded as a classic:

> Moving air masses that differ in temperature, speed or direction do not mix readily. When they come into contact, a tearing or shearing action may be set up that can cause segments of the air in the boundary area to rotate and form eddies.

There are at least three wind types swirling around a bushfire: the dominant wind, which in this case is swinging from north-west to south-west, the convection column, and the air being sucked in to replace it. It's the interaction between these three that kicks off the whirlwind.

The vortices in a fire can be anything from tens to hundreds of metres in height. Sometimes they might come spinning out from the flanks of a fire. At other times a large portion of the convection column itself can develop a sudden rotational motion. The physics at work is explained thus by meteorologist William Kininmonth:

> It's all about the concentration of angular momentum. Imagine an ice skater spinning. The skater develops a certain angular momentum by pushing on the ice and as the arms are drawn to the body the angular momentum is concentrated further and the body naturally spins faster. The air has a natural angular momentum due to the Earth's rotation; if it is drawn into a small area by convection then the angular momentum is concentrated and the air tends to spin up.

Burning in whirls is five to six times more intense than burning in settled air and for those on the front line, it can be utterly terrifying.

Another extraordinary aspect of the fire at its most ferocious is that it can create its own weather.

CFA volunteer Andrew Brown commented: 'They told us about fires, how they can make their own weather. Bullshit, I thought. Pull the other one.' Then he watched, stunned, as the wind whipped up a maelstrom: the palls of smoke condensed into a fat pyrocumulus cloud that spat black rain into his face. There were crashes of purple lightning over the ranges, and a blast of wind blew him and his colleagues off their feet.

That a fire could create its own weather, that you could be lashed by black rain while in the middle of an inferno, might sound insane but it happens, and it is one of the factors that add to the chaos and confusion.

Again, it all comes down to convection. The same force that lifts heated air from the equator and regulates the Earth's climate is responsible for the micro-climate that forms around a bushfire. The convective updraft is of such strength that it will lift vast amounts of material—ash, embers—eight to ten kilometres into the atmosphere. Condensation starts to occur: any moisture in the vicinity, either in the elevated fuel or in the atmosphere itself, will accumulate around those microparticles of soot and ash. The air will become colder and heavier, lose its buoyancy. Eventually it gets so heavy that the column cannot hold it any longer, and it plummets back to Earth in the form of black rain. The lightning is a related phenomenon: the convection column is so unstable that it generates atmospheric friction and ultimately the cloud builds up more energy than it can carry, zaps it back to Earth in the form of electric bolts.

Sometimes this will be accompanied by terrible outdrafts of wind—hundreds of kilometres per hour—that come crashing out of the column and add to the chaos below.

Phillip Adams was crew leader on a Wattle Glen tanker. So powerful was the wind when the change came through, he could stay on his feet only by clasping the vehicle's bull-bar with both arms. The wind ripped his uniform open, sucked the lenses out of his goggles and sandblasted his spectacles so badly that he spent the rest of the day half-blinded.

That incredible suction effect is an indicator of yet another wild-fire phenomenon: the sharp drop in air pressure that occurs around the eye of the storm. One of the scientists interviewed for this book has heard of bushfire victims who've had their eyeballs sucked out by the force of the pressure differential.

COOMBS ROAD

The Kinglake West fire trucks are racing down Coombs Road, which runs along the top of the escarpment. The crew of Tanker Two encounter local resident Brian Naylor, the much loved Melbourne identity who read the nightly news for many years before his retirement.

He flags them down. 'The fire's in there,' he says, indicating a nearby property. 'I'll lead you to it.'

'What about your own place?' asks crew leader Frank Allan.

'We'll be right.' That familiar voice, an air of confidence and authority suffusing its every syllable. 'We're well prepared.' Naylor directs them to the threatened house, goes back to defend his own.

From all reports, it was exceptionally well prepared, equipped with the latest in sprinklers and fire pumps. But that will be the last time Brian Naylor is seen alive. His body and his wife Moiree's will be found in the bath.

Tanker Two swings into the property indicated. Embers are raining down, spot fires are breaking out around the house. The owner comes rushing out, says he's having trouble caring for his distressed elderly mother.

'You look after her,' says Frank. 'We'll look after the fire.'

There's a swimming pool. Good, he thinks, plenty of water. They set up the floater pump, run out three hoses, form a defensive line around the house. They tackle the spot fires, believe they're making good headway.

Then they detect a shift in the wind. Frank, as crew leader, is acutely aware of his responsibility to monitor threats. While the crew continue to attack the outbreaks, he walks to the rise in front of the house. Then stops, stunned.

The rise affords him a generous view of the valley and plains between Kinglake and Whittlesea. Before him is something he hasn't seen in twenty years of fighting fires, something he'd heard about and hoped never to see. A tsunami of roiling smoke and dancing flame, fireballs shooting off ahead of it, is surging over the foothills and up the escarpment upon which he stands. The flames are thick and fierce, fifty metres high, smoke pumping kilometres into the atmosphere.

The change has arrived and the fire is storming the escarpment. Frank knows its speed will be magnified many times over by the steepness of the incline. The roads along the top of the rise—Bowden Spur, Bald Spur, National Park, Pine Ridge—are about to be slammed, and Coombs, upon which he is standing, will bear the brunt.

He sees at once what every firefighter caught at the wrong end of that firestorm knows: they haven't a hope in hell of stopping or controlling it. A hundred tankers would make no difference, much less the single one he has at his command. Indeed, he and his crew will be lucky to survive.

It comes rushing at him, crowning through the treetops, moving up the slopes, jumping gullies, swarming around outcrops. 'It was incredible,' he says. 'A good seven or eight k's away, but it seemed to hit us in about two minutes.'

Frank wheels around, runs back to warn his crew it's coming.

*

Back down in St Andrews, Steve Bell and the crew of Kinglake Tanker Two see the invigorated blaze come screaming at them like a salvo of Katusha rockets. They've been fighting to protect a house in which nine people, including two police officers from Hurstbridge, have sought refuge. The policemen, Gary Tickell and Paul Kemezys, had been racing around ahead of the fire, trying to alert and rescue residents.

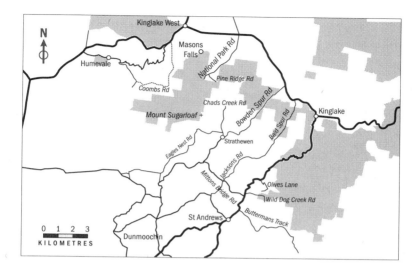

A battle the firies thought they'd won is suddenly teetering on the brink of disaster. They've been filling their tanks at the quick-fill pump, are coming back up the drive, when suddenly there's a wall of fire racing at them.

'It was like a jet engine blowing into your face,' comments driver Ben Hutchinson who, until this moment, thinks he's seen just about everything the Australian bushfire has to throw at him.

Andrew Brown is on the back of St Andrews Tanker Two. He and his fellow firefighters are on the hoses, blasting the verge of the road, when he looks down and is astonished to see that the dirt road itself is on fire: there are jets of flame as sharp as those from a Bunsen burner shooting out of the gravel. He hits it with the hose, but it flares up again. He repeats the action, with the same result. He taps his mate, Jeff Purchase, on the shoulder: 'Look at this.'

'Bugger that,' says Jeff. 'Look above you.'

Andrew raises his head, realises that the trees above and around them are blazing wildly. In the fury of the moment, he hadn't noticed. He looks down Jacksons Road, sees trucks caught in a tunnel of wild flame, crew members running every which way. Then he realises there are flames streaming out from under their own truck. The wind is so furious that the lid of the 'coffin'—the 120 centimetre long toolbox—is standing upright, the ocky straps taut.

The situation has suddenly become critical.

'We have to get out of here!' yells crew leader Kaz Gurney.

But they can't. They're boxed in, with trees, trucks and flame all around.

'Bolt cutters!' calls Kaz. She runs for the fence, shears it open, directs them into to a blackened paddock. Other tankers follow.

'God knows what would have happened if she hadn't had her wits about her,' comments Brown. 'We were in real strife there.'

The Kinglake crew are still back at the house. Working in tandem with a tanker from Wattle Glen, Ben Hutchinson and his colleagues begin a desperate battle to save the building and its occupants. They leap from the vehicle, rush out their hoses, form an arc around the northern perimeter of the building. Hutchinson, as driver, operates the pump while the crew hit the fire as best they can.

When the radiant heat gets too strong, they adjust the hose nozzles into the arcing fog spray that is meant to protect them, only to find it driving steam back into their faces.

The fire threatens to engulf the truck. Hutchinson, running out a third hose to protect it, does his best to extinguish a flock of goats that catches fire in an adjacent yard. A year later he shakes his head over it. 'Goats—catching fire! Never seen anything like it.'

A hose bursts; he struggles to replace it while dealing with goats, gauges and something hot and extremely unpleasant that lodges in his eye.

Now some of the occupants of the house are beginning to panic, trying to make a run for it. Crew leader Steve Bell, a solidly built bloke with a shaved head and a thick red beard, has to kick the door open and shove them back inside. The police officers struggle to free a woman who's become entangled in a barbed-wire fence.

For a desperate few minutes, as the front blows over them, they find themselves in the middle of a blazing hurricane. Engulfed in thick smoke, they can see little, hear nothing but the fire's roar. The rattle of the pump, the chug of the truck, the racket of the radio, they all disappear, overwhelmed by that deafening noise—the sound, as everyone says, of a thousand jet engines.

And then it dies down.

The firefighters regroup, surprised that they haven't lost anybody. Is it coming back? Is this apparent calm another sleight of nature's hand?

It seems not. The front has passed. They—and their charges—have survived. Ben Hutchinson is glad they were there: 'If we hadn't been that house would have gone up for sure.'

But there's no time to stand around and think about it. The change came from the south, the fire must be heading north.

'We need to get round that ridge, get after this bastard,' orders Steve Bell, and they wind up the hoses, scramble back onto their vehicle, refill at the water tank in the driveway.

The operation takes maybe ten minutes. They're about to head north up Jacksons Road to have another crack at what they assume will be the new front when their personal phones begin ringing. One of the firefighters, Katherine, gets a call from her partner, who's back in Kinglake with their two little boys.

The news leaves them all stunned. The fire that has just left them has hit their home town, some ten kilometres away. Ten minutes: it seems barely believable.

Their own homes and families are under attack, and their town is without a tanker to defend it.

SCRATCH CREW

Early evening, and CFA captain Paul Hendrie has been watching over Kinglake with a sinking heart and a rising concern. It's a regular country town, population about 1500, with all of the facilities and services you'd expect: a pub and a supermarket, surgeries and service station, a range of stores. Hundreds of houses. And it's virtually defenceless. He has not a tanker left, and only a skeleton staff.

Trish Hendrie and Carole Wilson are both long-time members, but not firefighters: Trish is communications officer, Carole in charge of catering. Kelly Johnson is a seventeen-year-old schoolgirl who has just finished her basic training. Di MacLeod has been rostered on to the brigade four-wheel-drive with Hendrie; she lost a close family member a few days ago, and requested not to be on the trucks this week, but she's come in when she sees how bad the situation is. Then there are Phil Petschel and Linda Craske. Phil is one of the older members, a retired electrician. Linda is a nurse who has just joined and is yet to commence her basic fire training.

A scratch crew, if ever there was one: none of them have come to fight. When the fire comes to them, they fight like hell.

By 6 pm the smoke from the Kilmore fire is beginning to roll more thickly over the town. Many locals are still going about their daily business, but more and more are coming in to the CFA, wanting to know what's going on, where to go.

Hendrie has little advice to give them. He's received not a word of warning or support from the Incident Control Centre at Kangaroo Ground or the Integrated Emergency Control Centre in the city. With fires reported down in St Andrews to the south and

Murrindindi to the east, there's nowhere safe he can advise residents to go.

And word is getting out: even though there's been no official warning, people have telephones. And eyes. The informal network is sparking up. They ring friends down the mountain, watch the columns of smoke building. They know something bad is happening down there; the more knowledgeable among them understand that it could be upon them soon.

Within half an hour of his last tanker leaving, Hendrie has maybe two hundred people gathering on the gravel area in front of his shed. Some are seeking shelter, others are wanting to make a run for it. Some call in for advice, don't like what they hear and head off, out to the Melba Highway or down The Windies.

Hendrie receives another pager message: there's a fire at Olives Lane, down on the St Andrews Road. That's getting awfully close. He calls for police to block the road but figures, correctly, that the only cops on the mountain just now probably have their hands full.

He thinks about the cars he's seen heading in that direction, decides he'd better investigate. He and Di MacLeod set off in the brigade vehicle.

They're approaching the reported location when suddenly—*bang*—the blaze is there in front of them, burning on both sides of the road. They see a house engulfed, fresh fires springing up all round. The change has arrived, the fire is running up the mountain and it's imperative that they get back to town before it does. The fire station will provide little enough support as it is; if there's nobody there to organise the defence, to operate pumps and generators, it will provide none.

Hendrie does a rapid turn-around. A ute bursts through the flames and Hendrie waves the fellow down. 'What's the situation down there?'

'I thought I was dead.' The driver is gasping and shaking at the wheel. No information to be had there.

'Get up the mountain!' orders Hendrie.

They sprint up the road, overtaking anybody in their way, just about running off the road.

'Not so fast,' pleads Di. 'We can't do our job if we're dead.'

They come across others trying to come down, and their response to every encounter is the same: a frantic wave and an order to the occupants to move their arses up to Kinglake.

'Go! Go! *Go!*' they yell to anybody close enough to hear them. They see fires breaking out around them as they make the ascent. The fire is hot upon their tail, at times they fear it's overtaking them. Embers go shooting overhead. There's a burning log on the tray of the ute ahead; not much they can do about that. Just hope the driver notices before the vehicle explodes.

They come across a trio of cars that has had a minor collision, the occupants standing on the side of the road, scratching their heads. There's little visible damage, so they yell, 'Follow us! Fire's just behind,' and keep going. They reach the top of the rise, are horrified to see fires already beginning to break out in the surrounding scrub. Where there are spots the main front won't be far behind.

Di rings through to Carole, tells her to get the quick-fill pump set up at the station and send a set of bollards down to the intersection: they need to stop people heading down into that twisting death trap.

They wheel their car sideways at the roundabout to block off the road. While Hendrie jogs off on foot to do what he can for the town's defences, Di remains at the intersection, stopping cars. She estimates that at least thirty vehicles, most of them full of people, pull up, their drivers desperate to get down the mountain. None go through. She can't tell them where to go—she can only say where not to go, and the St Andrews road is suicide right now.

Most of them join the crowd gathering on the gravel driveway in front of the CFA brigade.

Di spots her husband, Jim, cruising into the petrol station to fill up. He comes over, and as he does so they notice small fires beginning to break out in the town itself; the most threatening is between the service station and the pizza place.

'The front'll be here any minute,' she yells to him.

'Jesus.' He races back to their home down the Glenburn Road, hoping to pick up their pets and a few treasured objects.

The captain's daughter, Sally, arrives with the bollards. They fling them across the road and Di breathes as deep a sigh of relief as she can in the circumstances. Nobody in their right mind will be heading down there now; she's done all she can. She has to get back to the multitude of other tasks she knows will be screaming for attention.

Back at the CFA, Di is relieved to see Phil Petschel setting up the pumps. It's going to be all hands on deck for the foreseeable future, and there aren't many more capable hands than Petschel's. A stalwart of the brigade for many years, he's handy with a wide range of equipment, a smooth operator with a cool head that will stand them in good stead over the next few hours.

Phil's home is down the Bald Spur; he'd been intending to go down and attempt to defend it, but ran out of time while setting up the pumps. A good thing, he realises later when they take to calling him Lucky Phil: if he had made it back to the house he would probably have died. Most of his neighbours did.

All afternoon the smoke has been billowing in the western sky, miles high. But now it changes elevation and direction, comes churning out of the trees, through houses and power poles, into the eyes and mouths of the dismayed observers.

Hendrie is horrified to see people crowding into the pub: it's an old weatherboard building, put up to replace one that burned down years before. It's a death trap. Some idiot even wants to hide in the cool room. He rushes through the building, yelling, 'Get across to the CFA! This is no place to shelter!'

He looks out over the main street: people everywhere, frightened, confused, clustering together. Many of them already in the shed, hundreds more outside. Cars blunder about, lights glaring, occupants unsure of what to do, where to go.

Chaos.

The spot fires around the town are growing in intensity. The wind rips: the flag on the pole in front of the station is going crazy. The sun is a blood-red disc. From the south comes a pipe of thick, black, lowering smoke that tells Hendrie the main fury of the fire is about to fall upon them.

Di MacLeod, frantic with hoses and pumps, sees it as well and thinks, My god, it rushed up the mountain at unbelievable speed. Di is relieved when Jim arrives back: one less thing to worry about. He's rushed home, collected their animals, has had a nightmare return journey. The road was completely engulfed, he barely made it through.

Trish and Carole, friends and brigade members for more than thirty years, look at that column of churning smoke; know what it means. They say goodbye to each other.

Linda Craske rings her husband, begs him to tell the children she loves them.

Kelly Johnson feels the hose shaking in her hands. 'I don't want to die,' she says to her captain, and he takes her by the shoulders.

'I promise I won't let anything happen to you.'

Visibility is diminishing rapidly. Soon, Hendrie knows, he won't be able to see his hands in front of his face. He takes command, as much as anybody could in a situation like this: he has only minutes left. He issues orders, allocates jobs. He'll need people inside and out. Those inside the shed will need to keep order and deal with the casualties, those outside will have to fight for all of their lives.

Hendrie bellows into the crowd, 'We're going to need help here! Can anybody give us a hand?'

Two men respond: Wayne McDonald-Price and his stepson, Luke Gaskett. They've come in from Kinglake West, where their house has already burned down. They clamber into yellow protective gear and join Di MacLeod, who has taken up a position on the east side of the shed with a 38-millimetre hose in hand. On the other side of the building are Phil Petschel and young Kelly Johnson.

These five people remain outside, through blinding smoke, impenetrable darkness and blistering heat, for the duration of the fire's passage. One team is working from a rickety old pump behind the hotel, the other from a pump and tank behind the shed.

Trish Hendrie steps outside. A surreal vista appears before her. Figures loom in the half-dark, their faces fraught with anxiety, smoke reflected in their eyes. A fireball shoots overhead, a tumult of flame thrashing the trees behind it. She jumps back in, slams the door and calls to those inside:

'Brace yourselves! It's going to hit us now.'

GODSPEED TO YOU ALL

To the members of the public who stare at that fire coming in, it seems that the gates of hell have opened. But what does it look like to the professionals?

There is at least one experienced, qualified, professional fire manager who's positioned himself directly in the path of the inferno: Acting Ranger in Charge of the Kinglake National Park, Tony Fitzgerald. And even for him, a man who's been working with fire for more than twenty years, it's a frightful experience, one that comes close to claiming his own life.

Around 5.30 pm he's standing on Mount Sugarloaf with one of his team, Aaron Redmond, staring out over the hills and valleys below. Wondering how long they have left. Aaron is nineteen; he's only recently joined the DSE, but has been a member of the CFA since he was twelve. He knows fire. The two men have gone up there to get an idea of what it is doing, are horrified at the situation unfolding before their eyes.

They are looking directly down upon the destruction of Strathewen. They see the inferno rolling over the town, the spot fires and fingers of flame heading in their direction. They hear the local CFA captain, Dave McGahy, as he sends his crews into action.

'Godspeed to you all.'

'Godspeed? Not the sort of language I've ever heard on the radio,' Fitzgerald comments later. 'It sounded like something you'd say to someone when you feared you were never going to see them again.'

'Doomsday language,' adds Aaron.

Appropriately so, as it turns out: of the 120 houses in Strathewen, only sixteen will survive. One of the twenty-seven victims in the town is a member of McGahy's crew.

There are experienced emergency services personnel in Kinglake West who cannot speak highly enough of the DSE's work on Black Saturday. Fitzgerald was the first to warn them of what he feared was coming, and he and his crew risked their lives to defend their section of the community. Frank Allan from Kinglake West CFA rang the Kangaroo Ground Incident Control Centre around 2 pm to get more information on the plume of smoke he was watching from the driveway of his brigade, and was stunned that nobody there seemed to be aware of it. He assumes they were so busy looking at screens they hadn't even stepped outside to look at the sky.

Tony Fitzgerald wasn't relying upon computers or other equipment but on his own awareness—a knowledge of the way fire works, of the topography, the fuel loads, even his reading of the winds to predict the timing of the change.

It was an awareness based on more than twenty years of making fire his business. He understands fire at a theoretical level, with a degree in ecology, majoring in botany and geography from Melbourne University. But more importantly, he's been working at the coal—or fire—face since 1983. He was recruited to Kinglake primarily to work as a fire manager, and in the fifteen years he's been there has managed controlled burns on thousands of hectares, as well as holding command roles in some of Victoria's biggest bushfires.

It isn't until Fitzgerald comes into the Kinglake West station and tells them that according to his gut instinct the fire is going to hit them in about two hours—which it does—that the CFA has the first inkling of what they are in for. They make good use of the warning, ringing around various contacts in the community to alert them.

Fitzgerald makes an arrangement with the CFA: he'll look after the section of land along the National Park Road. He has a crew of eight firefighters in two 'slip-on' utes. After leaving the CFA, they race down National Park Road, knocking on doors, stopping cars, warning as many residents as they can contact. Then they take up a defensive position along the crest of the gorge near Masons Falls. Fitzgerald gathers his crew together, explains that they're about to undertake the most dangerous operation a fire crew can perform and gives them the option of leaving, returning to their homes. None do.

Whatever steps he and his crew take will be dwarfed by the magnitude of the blaze, he knows that. But they have to do something. At best, his hope is that they will be able to make some sort of attack on the fire as it crests the escarpment, take the sting out of it. There are some hundred houses behind them: if he can reduce the fire's intensity, it will increase the occupants' chances of survival.

Fitzgerald has earlier received a call from Steve Grant, his boss in Broadford, warning him that the incident control centres are barely functioning and that he and his crew are on their own.

Fitzgerald and Redmond have gone up to Sugarloaf to get a better view. They are there when the wind change comes through. Burning debris begins to bombard the slopes directly below them.

A piece of burnt bracken lands at their feet. Aaron stomps on it almost casually, then thinks, Hell, if the embers are coming this way...

Fitzgerald has the same thought. The clifftop lookout is no place to be; the fire will be on them in minutes. They hurry back and join their colleagues.

Fitzgerald has already discussed the options with his 2IC, Sean Hunter. The first is to beat a retreat; the crest of the escarpment will be where the fire is at its most lethal. The other, infinitely more dangerous, option is to attempt a backburn.

The creation of a backburn in the face of a firestorm is about as delicate and dangerous a task as a firefighter can attempt. The theory is that you burn a line just before the main front, timing it so that your fire will catch the convective wind and be drawn into the advancing flames. As the main fire hits the burnt area, it should lose

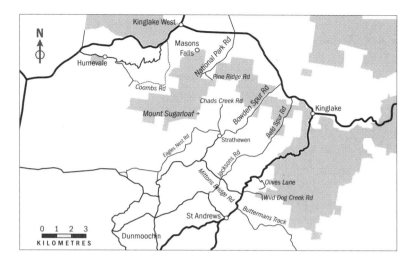

some of its intensity. The timing is critical: too early and your own fire could come back at you, too late and the inferno will overrun you.

Fitzgerald knows that the operation has only a slight chance of success, but feels he has to do it. If it works, it could reduce the impact of the fire upon the houses on National Park Road, saving lives and property.

He positions his team in a line of maybe seventy metres, waits for the slim window of opportunity. The tension is electric: a tiny crew with not more than a couple of utes for protection strung out across a ridgeline waiting for an inferno to fall upon them.

Aaron is struck by the smell in the air: a pungent mixture of smoke and eucalyptus vapour. There is a period of stillness. The fire is approaching, sucking the air in with such force that it cancels out the ambient wind.

Fitzgerald studies the bush intently, searching for the signs, and suddenly sees what he's been hoping for. A stirring of leaves on the ground, a tug of wind from behind their line. It gathers strength, as he'd hoped it would: the speed of the convective wind increases with its proximity to the fire.

The crew members glance at each other, anxious, waiting for the signal. 'Wouldn't say I felt afraid,' says Aaron. 'Just focused. We had a lot of faith in Tony.'

He is amazed to realise that he is standing in two different layers of wind simultaneously. The air around his upper body is perfectly still, but the debris on the ground is being sucked towards the unseen fire, leaves and embers tumbling in the opposite direction to the way they were blowing shortly before. The leaves accelerate; the fire is coming closer. Still invisible, but the signs are there.

Fitzgerald knows the moment has arrived. He gives the order, and his crew apply their drip torches. A line of fire springs up. An anxious moment—which way will it go?—then Fitzgerald is relieved to see the burn take off and begin to move towards the ridge. The gamble is working.

Sean Hunter, closer to the edge, starts waving frantically, and Fitzgerald sees a sixty-metre burst of flame roar out of the gorge directly in front of them. Almost simultaneously one of the houses behind their line erupts into flame with a suddenness that shocks him. In seconds, there are some thirty spot fires flaring around them.

Their position has suddenly become a death trap: the fire is vaulting right over them. Fitzgerald orders the crew to retreat to a pre-planned anchor point, a safety position. The flames are leaping over their heads. Aaron is aghast to see blue flame run straight up into the crowns.

They sprint for the cars. One crew don't even have time to roll up the hose; they clamber aboard and race away with a thirty-metre length of hose snaking wildly behind them. A possum, partly burnt and panicking, has the misfortune to pop up onto a rock and is flattened by the swinging hose.

They regroup some two hundred metres back at the corner of National Park and Pine Ridge roads, shelter there for a few minutes and wait for what they take to be the main front to pass. Fitzgerald instructs the crew to do what they can to tackle the spot fires igniting around them, while he and fellow ranger Natalie Brida drive back into the smoke to reconnoitre the area they've just evacuated and see if there's anything in there they can save.

He drives in slowly, carefully, nerves taut. To his relief and surprise, the half-dozen buildings are still standing, albeit under severe ember attack. Has the strategy worked?

The sky turns a sudden, luminous orange.

'Oh shit!' This fire is behaving like nothing he's ever encountered. What he took to be the main front was only the preemptive strike. The worst is about to come. Any second.

They have to get out of there fast. He slams the car into a U-turn, has just managed to complete it when the full fury of the fire's radiant energy blasts into them. The fire is crowning directly overhead. 'It was an absolute furnace,' he commented later.

The world is plunged into darkness. A branch flies out of nowhere and smashes the headlights. He feels the radiant glow burning the side of his face. He can barely see a thing, but he knows this patch of road intimately; his house is just up the road, and he's walked it nearly every day for the past ten years.

If I don't get us out of here, he tells himself—and he's one person who knows what he's talking about—we're dead.

He aims at where he hopes the gates are and revs the guts out of the motor. Nothing much happens. The blast of heat has apparently knocked out the electrics. 'Come on, baby,' he whispers to the Toyota.

The ute takes off, but slowly, walking pace; they go crawling, grinding and shuddering down the road. The fireside tyres are burnt, and he's driving on the rims. The tonneau cover catches fire. Fitzgerald is relying on adrenaline and memory, heading for where he figures the gates are.

Aaron, back with the rest of the crew and frantically fighting the fires breaking out around them, hears Natalie on the radio saying their lights are blown out.

Why don't you just replace the fuse? he thinks, and is stunned to see the boss's car come crawling out of the darkness, limping and flaming, one side completely black. He's struck by the look of desperate determination on Fitzgerald's face. Not even pausing to grab their bags, the occupants leap from the burning vehicle as it is overwhelmed, scramble aboard the slip-ons.

The rendezvous is outside Fitzgerald's own home. He's dismayed to see it's already on fire. He stares at it, momentarily stunned. Finds time to be grateful that his wife, Kerry, and their two primary-school-aged children left that morning—the first time they'd ever evacuated. 'If I'd been on my own, I probably would have had a go at saving the place, ' he says later.

But when he makes a move Sean shakes his head. 'It's gone, mate.'

From there, the crew fight a running battle down National Park Road—helping wherever they can, warning people to get out, assisting others to defend their homes. Fitzgerald sends Natalie out to the intersection to stop people coming into the road; some take her advice, some don't. Some of those she speaks to will die soon afterwards on the road to Kinglake.

Aaron Redmond, also in the roadblock team, is amazed at the chaos that suddenly erupts. Most people are scrambling to flee the area, but some are trying to get back in, either to protect their homes or do the most ludicrous things: somebody wants to retrieve papers he'd left on the kitchen bench, another wants to get his tablets. Aaron recalls thinking, 'You won't be needing your tablets if you go back in there.'

The Community Emergency Response Team—a local volunteer ambulance crew in a small Subaru—turn up, responding to a 000 emergency call from back in National Park Road. The DSE crew try to escort them back in, but the track is completely engulfed, impassable.

Of the hundred or so houses along that road, very few survive. In that intense kilometre closest to the Gorge, only one does.

As the main front overtakes them, the crews retreat to the relative safety of a ploughed carrot field, watch helplessly as the fire roars around them into the community. As soon as it passes, they move out to see what they can do to pick up the pieces.

Fitzgerald knows he'll be driving into a human tragedy. But it will hit closer to home than they expect; one member of the team is to lose two sisters in the disaster.

THE BOSS

Tony Fitzgerald learned his craft from an old forester named Fred Whiting, and he reminisces fondly about the apprenticeship. 'Here I was, just a fresh-faced kid, working on a fire crew in Gippsland. They were tough men, wouldn't give you any second chances, especially if you were from university. They'd been working with fire for generations. Fred was nearing retirement then, and he took me under his wing. He wanted to teach, I wanted to learn.'

Fred Whiting had a telling nickname for a bushfire: he called it the Boss. '"What's the Boss doing?" he'd ask. "Where's he think he's going?" And it is like a boss—it can crush you any time it wants. That's the first thing I learned: the fire's always in control. You have to respect it. You can bomb it or bulldoze it all you like, but it can turn on you any time. Sometimes you can play round with the boss, swing him round to your way of thinking. If he's in a good mood, maybe he'll go along with you. But when he's on the rampage—look out! Get the hell out of there!'

Tony Fitzgerald sees a lot of things in a fire, but one of them is a challenge, a mystery you have to call upon all your experience and guile to unravel. He thinks about fire the way you imagine a race-horse trainer thinks about a recalcitrant thoroughbred that shows a glimmer of promise.

'When you're looking at a fire,' he explains, 'you're thinking, Can I bring it round to my way of thinking? Can I use more fire to coerce it? Maybe put in a fuel break, guide it towards a natural obstacle, a creek or a gully.'

Fred Whiting has been dead for many years now, but Fitzgerald still speaks with great respect for the old master burner's way of working. One aspect of Fred's modus operandi that he has come to appreciate more with the passing of the years was his deliberation. From Fitzgerald's description, he almost sounds like Roger Federer lining up a backhand passing shot: there's an awful lot going on real fast, but to the onlooker, he's got all the time in the world.

The Gippsland team might have been on a routine job when there'd be a sudden outbreak, a fire whirl or a flare-up from a larger conflagration.

'I'd be doing a song and dance,' says Fitzgerald, 'wanting to do something. And Fred would just get out the tobacco and roll a smoke. Always. Probably take a good two minutes. He'd be doing more than lighting a smoke, of course; what he was doing was watching—he knew there was no point doing anything until he'd done an assessment. You don't do that, you're liable to make a mistake. Maybe a fatal one.'

Fitzgerald doesn't smoke, but he has absorbed the lesson: the need to stand back, study the situation, use your experience to work out what's about to happen. That's what he was doing on top of Mount Sugarloaf, and it's a lesson he's attempted to pass on to the generation coming up behind him.

Much of what he's looking at involves the wind.

Of course there are a lot of other things you need to know—the topography, the vegetation, the fire history—but when the crunch comes, wind is the vital component. Not just the ambient wind, but the wind created by the fire itself, the convection wind.

'The fire sends up a convection column,' he explains. 'The hot air rises. The effect is like a bicycle pump, sucking from above; air is pulled in from all around.'

This was the reason for that eerie stillness so many felt just before the fire struck. The convection column was so powerful that it was dragging in the north-westerly gale that was driving the fire, negating its momentum.

'We were in the lee of this huge plume of convection, north-west of where we were, and it was sucking in the dominant wind,' says Tony Fitzgerald. 'Convective wind is the fire manager's stock in trade. That's what Fred was looking at. It's the fire's way of talking to you. You have to understand it and use it to your advantage.'

That wind blowing around Aaron Redmond's feet was the convective wind in action, air being sucked into the inferno to replace the air that was rising in the column.

Wind, of course, is just one of the things the fire manager is studying. 'You watch the way the smoke moves, the way the flames are being fanned. Is it running up the trees? Racing through the crown? Is it shearing?'

Sometimes, like the Vedic Indians or the ancient Slavs, Fitzgerald talks about fire in almost anthropomorphic terms. 'You get two convection columns hitting each other—maybe from two different ridges—and at some stage they're going to fight it out. They'll push, pull, twist each other, and you'll get this interaction between the two. That's when you get whirlwinds, roofs lifted, trees sheared, corkscrewed out of the ground.'

While Tony Fitzgerald and his crew were fighting for their lives on the edge of the escarpment their colleague, Ranger Cam Beardsell, was at Dunmoochin down below, watching it run up at them.

'Cam said it was like a wave that rippled up the ranges: flame sheeting above the tops of the trees in a continuous pulsing motion. It would move, stop, roll forward, pause again'—presumably it was pausing to devour the fuel within reach—'then it would go skipping over the tops of the crowns.'

Liam Fogarty, the DSE's Assistant Fire Chief, is another who has made fire his life's work. Like Fitzgerald, he worked on fire crews in his youth, learning from the old hands before he went to university. Fogarty has worked as a senior scientist in places as diverse as Indonesia and New Zealand. Expanding upon the intensity of the convection process, he comments that one of the most fascinating aspects of convection in a megafire is the size of its footprint.

'The fire might be burning across a five-kilometre front,' Fogarty explains,

> but because of the drought, the humidity and the three desiccating days the week before, fuel from a much broader area—five to six times that distance—was contributing its energy to the blaze. In parts of the affected area, the fuel load would have reached thirty to forty tonnes per hectare. The first rush of the fire would have incinerated the fine fuel—twigs of less than six millimetres, leaves, dry grass. Then the heavy fuel—logs, branches and so on—would ignite, and keep burning for another twenty minutes to half an hour.

All of this contributes to an eruption of gaseous hot air that could blast as much as a kilometre out from the fire. The heat wave is a result of both convection and radiation, and it is composed of burnt and unburnt products of the combustion, including gases—known as pyrolysates—from the thermal degradation of cellulose and hemi-cellulose. That's the technical aspect.

The un-technical aspect is that it can kill you. Convection means that the column's natural direction would be upwards. But because of the ferocity of the wind on Black Saturday, it was forced down, lashing out like a chameleon zapping insects.

This also explains one of the things that puzzled firefighters in the aftermath: why many of the victims did not appear to be burnt, why one poor soul, for example, died untouched in the middle of the Strathewen football oval. It is because a fire like this will not merely burn its victims, it will often asphyxiate them, sometimes from great distances—up to five or six hundred metres.

The St Andrews firefighters were struck by the number of people who died immediately after the wind change. 'It was like a vast wave of heat had swept up Jacksons Road in seconds,' commented one member. 'If you were indoors you were okay, if you were out in the open you were dead.'

As the fire gathers intensity, it throws out embers and burning brands—initially, maybe three or four kilometres ahead, then further as it grows. These will ignite new fires, which will in turn feed their energy back into the main blaze—sending out more incendiaries. And so it storms forward, gathering strength, a self-sustaining cycle of destruction.

'There isn't enough oxygen in the fire,' explains Fogarty:

> The fire is sucking air in, trying to burn all this fuel, but it can't—so all these gases start to accumulate. The vaporised eucalyptus oil will be captured there. Finally when enough oxygen comes in, it will suddenly flash and flare and burst up above the fire.

What Fogarty is describing are the 'fireballs' that filled so many witnesses of the inferno with dread: they aren't so much 'balls' as massive bursts of igniting gas that can shoot hundreds of metres into the air—or snake out horizontally, torching houses that would otherwise have been untouched.

All of this amounts to an extraordinary amount of energy being released every second of the fire's existence.

A fire is regarded as unstoppable, even with the help of aerial bombardment, when it generates 3500–4000 kilowatts per metre. Firefighters know not to get in front of it; at best, they can attack its flanks, attempt to pinch it off, angle it in a particular direction.

The Black Saturday fires generated something in the vicinity of 80,000 kilowatts per metre. In the forest, where the DSE crew established their defence lines, that would have translated into temperatures anywhere between 1200 and 1500 degrees.

TANKER TWO

Kinglake West Tanker Two is still at the property on Coombs Road. There's no chance of escape—the road is overgrown and the fire would only overtake them. They're better off here, where there is water; not to mention that they have a responsibility to protect the residents sheltering in the house.

They stand and fight for as long as possible, extinguishing what they can, batting away the rain of sticks and burning debris that hammers them. 'Horizontal hail' is Frank Allan's description. The air is wind-whipped and thick with smoke, shot through with iridescence.

'At one stage, I had the hose on full bore—and it was coming straight back at me.' There's one bush he swears he's put out at least five times, but it keeps springing back to life. He's bowled over by a branch so heavy that the crew have to drag it off him. He staggers to his feet, does a quick check: nothing damaged. Gets back into it as the inferno rolls over them.

Nowhere on Black Saturday is the fire any more brutal than here, at the crest of the escarpment, just after the wind change. In the houses and on the rocky roads nearby is where the heaviest loss of life occurs: in Bald Spur Road, twenty-eight people stay to fight the fire and twenty-one of them die. Pine Ridge Road tells a similar story: there are around twenty deaths, nine of them in one house. Ten die right here in Coombs Road.

While there's water, Frank feels confident that they have a chance. They've already been fighting for half an hour, and normally that would be enough. But not today. As the intensity of the storm increases and day turns to night, the floater pump in the swimming pool begins to splutter.

Frank looks at it in despair. It's running out of fuel. Any second now they'll be out of water and at the mercy of the fire. He has spare fuel on the truck; he dashes back and grabs it. He's about to refill when he realises that standing in the middle of a fire with buckshot embers blasting about him and a jerrycan of petrol in his hands is not such a good idea.

He started out thinking they could save the property. Now the sheds are already gone and he's beginning to wonder if they'll be able to save themselves. First priority is shelter. 'Back to the house!' he yells at his team, then throws both jerrycan and pump into the pool and sets off running.

They are sheltering behind what they assume is a window when it flies open and the owner of the house appears, urging them in. They don't hang around for a second invitation. Those solid walls offer some protection from the radiant heat. It's pitch black inside the building. There's supposedly an elderly woman in here some-where—the owner's mother—and a German shepherd, but they don't see either of them the whole time they're there.

They make fleeting sorties outside in pairs—to extinguish what they can and to keep an eye on things. They manage to save one of the cars, but come close to losing their own appliance; would have lost it if Frank hadn't raced out and moved it to a safer location. They watch their hoses burn, their water run out, their defences disappear. Frank considers putting out a mayday, decides not to: he doesn't want any of his mates driving into this inferno to try and rescue him.

Eventually the storm dies down sufficiently for them to make a longer trip outside. They look around, warily: has the worst of it passed? Looks like it. They manage to rig up a hose capable of spray-ing a bit of water as long as one of the weightier members stands on it. They black out the area around the house to a stage where they feel it's safe to leave it in the hands of the owner, then drive back out onto Coombs Road.

What they see there stuns them. 'Like a lunar landscape,' comments Frank. 'Hardly recognisable from the place we'd driven into not long before.'

The blaze has swept over them and roared on towards Kinglake West, but everything is still on fire—every house, every tree, every blade of grass, even the roots of the grass. There isn't much they can do about it in their present condition; they have to get back to the station, change their hoses.

They are able to respond to an emergency call from Vicfire: a critically injured resident in a dam nearby. They locate the property and find that the Whittlesea captain, Ken Williamson, has already responded in his four-wheel-drive. The victim, Jason Lynn, is in a terrible condition: badly burnt, convulsing, vomiting mud. Williamson is desperately trying to get an ambulance. No success; he and his colleague decide to take the victim out themselves.

Frank sees they're doing all the right things, knows he has to get back to his own base asap. They leave, clearing the track for the four-wheel-drive behind them as best they can.

The fire truck is only a two-wheel-drive, and isn't equipped with a chainsaw, so the journey back is rough: every few metres they pull a tree off the road, drive round some obstacle, push their way through another. Often they are forced to cut down fences and go cross-country. Everything is still burning savagely, and with the truck the way it is, a simple stump-hole would leave them in deep trouble.

They come across scattered individuals and groups, and each meeting deepens their concern about the calamity that has hit their community. Survivors are staggering out of burnt buildings, stunned, confused. The firefighters help wherever they can. They encounter a mud-covered couple who were hiding in a dam while their house burned down; all they want is drinking water, which the firies are happy to provide. Others want lifts back to the CFA station, so they make room, bring them aboard. Soon they have a crowd.

They come across a farmer who's stroppy about them cutting his fence to get through, says he's worried about his stock escaping.

They realise the fellow is in shock, disorientated, having just seen his house burn down. His stock are all dead. But they do their best to accommodate him. They cut just a small section of the fence down one end, and replace it carefully behind them. Push on into the blazing landscape.

HOME FIRES

At the roadblock on the Whittlesea Road, before the cool change hits, Roger Wood gets into the Pajero to follow the CFA crew back to Kinglake West and help defend the station. As he throws the car into gear his phone rings. He glances at the number: home.

'Roger!' Jo, his wife. Screaming. 'Roger, the fire's here!'

In *St Andrews*?

'Can't be—it's here. Must be smoke drifting in from…'

'I can see flames in front of the house!'

He almost drops the phone. 'What…'

'It's coming right at us.'

In the background he can hear his children screaming. He struggles to collect his thoughts, to control the panic spearing his chest. 'You know what to do, Jo. Fight the spots for as long as you can, then get inside. Put the kids under wet blankets! Don't…'

The line goes dead. He stares at the screen, aghast, and frantically dials the number. No answer. Tries again. Nothing.

Christ. What the hell is going on? St Andrews is twenty kilometres to the south. What's the fire doing down there? How can it be up here on the mountain and down there in the foothills at the same time? Just how big is this bloody monster? And how is it that he, the police officer responsible for the region, has still been given absolutely no warning that the inferno is anywhere other than miles away?

If the flames there are anything like the ones in front of him, his family are doomed.

He hits the road. His natural inclination is to get back home, post haste. The thought of his wife and kids facing this inferno without him hits harder than any Saturday night brawler ever has. He'll try, but judging from the red angry flashes he can glimpse racing along the slope to his right, getting down the mountain is going to be impossible in the foreseeable future. The serpentine road to St Andrews will be cut off for sure.

And he has a job to do, a job which, he suddenly intuits, is going to be the worst he's had in twenty-five years.

He curses himself for leaving his family in that position. Everybody knew it was going to be a hell of a day. Why didn't he tell them to get out when they could?

He's racing back along the Kinglake road, furiously punching redial, his mouth dry, his heart jumping with each attempt. The phone goes unanswered, the ringtone tolling like a funeral bell. Horrible visions roll through his head: the house in flames, his children huddling...

He thumps the wheel. Puts his foot down.

The fire station at Kinglake West is a scene of furious activity by the time he arrives. The captain, John Grover, is a worried man. Still no word from Frank Allan and the crew of Tanker Two. They've clearly been trapped, burnt over, but have they survived? He's been trying desperately to reach them on the radio, but there's been not a word. No mayday, which is good. Unless they didn't have time to make one.

But Grover can do nothing about that right now. Hundreds of lives will depend on his decisions over the next few minutes. He's always feared that the station would be the last resort of many in the community. It wasn't designed as a refuge at all; it is, in reality, just an overgrown shed.

Strangely enough there are no fire refuges, in Kinglake or any other part of the state, in this most fire-threatened corner of the world. Country towns had them until a few years ago, but the policy has been abandoned as authorities shy away from both the direct expense and the complications of a disaster in our increasingly litigious society. The policy now is to shift the responsibility onto the individual—a dubious development, given that so few individuals seem willing or equipped to carry it.

Fire refuge or not, the locals are pouring in. No sign of panic yet, but Grover knows if he's to keep it at bay he and his brigade will have to lead by example. The fire could be there in minutes: the last thing he wants is people cracking up, doing stupid things. Making a run for it.

He gives the orders, and his members don't need to be told twice. They position Tanker One in front of the station and hook it up to water, lay 38- and 64-millimetre hoses around the grounds and out onto the adjoining oval. They start up the pumps and generator, and begin hosing things down.

As they work, they keep an anxious eye on the fire: from their reading of the smoke it seems to be running along behind the station, travelling in a south-easterly direction. Will it miss them? Perhaps, but Grover knows there's a southerly change due. When it arrives the inferno will turn about, come driving up at them.

It adds to the stress of his members that their pagers are constantly shrieking at them, and message after message is the same: members of the public, often their own friends or family, trapped in houses and fighting for their lives. One message says there are forty to fifty people in a single building.

There's not a thing they can do about any of that. The truck has to stay where it is, protecting the growing crowd. Some firefighters are so stressed by their inability to get to these jobs that they turn their pagers off.

Roger Wood assists where he can, stopping traffic from heading into the fire, doing his best to reassure the public. It's a drop in the ocean. People are seriously afraid. Many, like Wood himself, are separated from their loved ones. He's relieved when his colleague Senior Constable Cameron Caine appears, driving his old ute.

Cameron is as Kinglake as they come, a burly, goatee-bearded bloke who was a champion local footballer, still remembered for his role in the forward line in Kinglake's 1994 premiership. Nowadays he's president of the footy club, and, at thirty-five, still pulls on the boots, ligaments permitting. He's come in to work early, has already been down to the station, started up the generator.

They begin to discuss the situation but the conversation is cut short by a call from D24: a four-car collision on Deviation Road, further east, towards Kinglake. Reports of multiple casualties: people trapped in cars, fire closing in.

It sounds like chaos out there.

Caine is staggered. He's just driven down that road, seen sign of neither accident nor fire. He immediately thinks of his own wife and two children. While driving in, he'd spotted the first flames below the escarpment and rung Laura, told her to take the kids and get out. He assumes she'll be heading in to Kinglake. If so she'll be using that same road, the one that's now apparently slashed by fire and fatal accidents.

Wood runs to the Pajero, sets off in the direction of the crash while Caine follows in his ute. It's still light enough for Wood to see where he's going, so he revs it to the max, lights flashing, siren screaming when anybody gets in his way. He hits 120, covers five kilometres in maybe three minutes. No collision yet, but the smoke is growing thicker.

He sweeps round a bend and—christ, he's plunging into a wall of flame! He slams on the anchors, but it's too late. He has driven into an inferno: there are flames all over the road (a fallen tree, he later realises) and the scrub on either side is ablaze.

Darkness descends, a thick black mass of smoke envelops him: he can't see a metre in front, and then it's behind. Trees are crashing, brands flying about, the roar of the fire enormous. My god, he thinks, I'm about to die.

He grabs the mike. 'Kinglake-350 to VKC Wangaratta. *Urgent!*'

The radio is ringing with frantic exchanges as cops all over the state speak to each other—there are six hundred fires that day, all of them involving police in one way or another—but silence descends upon the network when they hear that word.

Urgent. There isn't an officer listening who doesn't understand the gravity.

'VKC to Kinglake-350. That you, Woody?'

A familiar voice. The operator is John Dunnell, a mate of Roger's. They worked together at Greensborough years ago.

'JD, I'm in trouble here.' He glances away to his right: through the blackness, a terrible red glow. 'Flames all round the car!'

'Get out of there, Woody! Get to safety!'

A pause. The glow gets brighter. 'Trying to, mate.'

He has no choice. To sit and do nothing is to die. To move could be death as well—he has visions of running off the road, tyres melting, immobilised. Fleeing vehicles slamming into his rear, ending up like the pile-up he was heading for.

But least he'll be doing something, and anything is better than sitting paralysed by this smothering darkness.

He cranes his neck, looks back. Blackness. He reverses a couple of feet. Hopeless—can't see a thing. The heat is growing, but the inside of the vehicle is relatively smoke free: he thanks the lord and Mr Mitsubishi for the tight seals. But how long will that last? How long before the rubber melts, the windows? It's the smoke that gets you first, the poisonous fumes. He's seen burnt-out cars before, incinerated bodies. Doesn't want to end up like that.

He clenches the wheel, takes a deep breath. Moves at what feels like a snail's pace into a ten-point turn, worried that if he goes too far off the bitumen he'll get snagged in the burning debris or melt his tyres. He completes the manoeuvre. Facing what he hopes is the direction from which he entered this hell hole, he inches forward. Smooth surface under wheels. The road?

Further forward. Yes; he sighs. The road.

He accelerates, ever so gently. Moves up to walking pace. Still unable to see past the bull-bar, but more hopeful now that he's facing the right direction. Further forward.

At last, a streak of light through the swirling smoke. Is he coming out of it? More light. He is. A stretch of time impossible to judge: seconds? minutes? Time is going every which way, but the light is brightening. He breathes again—no flame. Still smoky, but he's out of it.

He opens the throttle. Races back in the direction of Kinglake West with a battery of emotions storming though his brain. *Think, you idiot!* There's a disaster hitting the community. He's received no official information, but if the storm has come this far, what has it already destroyed? What kind of fury is falling upon the farms and bush blocks? On the heavily populated town behind him?

But what can he do? Not much. He has responsibilities in a situation like this, but he feels a terrible, unaccustomed helplessness. He has no information, little idea of what's going on. What's he meant to do—run around and knock on every door? God knows, he'll do what he can, but there are people all over the ranges, thousands of them. He can only pray that most of them have taken precautions and have either got off the mountain or know how to defend themselves.

And always pumping away beneath his immediate worries is, for Roger Wood, the darkest question of all: what's happening to his family?

A vehicle comes towards him, driving into the fire. He flashes his lights, slows, winds his window down. 'Follow me!' he roars, waving.

The car turns. Others join it. Soon he's leading a small convoy.

One of the vehicles is a four-wheel-drive towing a horse float, driven by a woman named Lisa Waddell, the owner of a nearby Horseland store. She's just hitched up the float, grabbed her four-week-old son Charlie and fled the family farm, but everything is burning and she has no idea what to do or where to go. Then she sees that reassuring vehicle.

Lisa recognises Roger later when he comes in to buy some gear and thanks him. 'Always be grateful to Roger and Cameron for that day,' she comments. 'If it wasn't for them, a lot more of us wouldn't be here today.'

As Wood drives, signs of calamity mount up: cars dashing everywhere, an inferno in the rear-view mirror, flashes of flame glimpsed on the surrounding hills. Fire all over the mountain. Spot fires, presumably, swept from the main front by the wind. Soon they'll coalesce, become a front themselves.

He comes racing up to the Pheasant Creek supermarket, then hits the brakes, groans out loud. 'Oh god, no…What are you doing *here*?'

There are dozens of cars parked around the store. People are milling about, huddled in little groups. More vehicles appear, passengers piling out, waving arms and pointing, clutching each other. Some are standing there with stubbies of beer in hand, like they're watching the New Year bloody fireworks.

He wonders, as he has before, at the primal instinct that drives people together when there's a crisis. All very well back when the crisis was a sabre-toothed tiger, perhaps; but not when it's a megafire that could swallow them all and spit out the bones. He thinks about some of the famous photos from Black Friday in 1939, taken not so far from here, back when Kinglake was a timber town. All the bodies—experienced bushmen, timber workers and farmers, their families—clumped together like cords of wood.

He's pleased to see Cameron running towards him. Time like this, there is nobody he'd rather have next to him.

The rest of the crowd are standing round, some in singlets and thongs. Drifting smoke restricts their vision: they don't know where to go, what to do. They have no idea of what's coming. The very fact that they're hanging around when the air is thick with smoke suggests they've broken the first rule of survival in a fire zone: stay or go, but if you do go, leave early.

They've left late.

They could hardly have chosen a worse spot to congregate. No shelter and a pine plantation across the road. Pine doesn't burn for long, but it goes up fast and furious. Behind them is the Pheasant Creek store: petrol bowsers, gas bottles, a horde of cars full of petrol. And a fire bearing down on them. A catastrophe about to unfold before his eyes.

No. Not if he has anything to say about it.

SURVIVAL ARC

How do humans respond to disaster? Why is it that some people rise to the challenge of a crisis, taking on roles of leadership, while others either panic or retreat into their shells?

One of the first modern scholars to think seriously about these matters was an Anglican priest by the name of Samuel Prince. Prince happened to be in the town of Halifax, Nova Scotia, on the morning of December 6, 1917 when a French munitions freighter called the *Mont Blanc* caught fire and exploded. Such was the power of the blast that a fragment of the anchor was thrown more than six kilometres; a gun barrel landed in a lake five and a half kilometres away.

In the minutes that followed, the town was subjected to a battery of traumas almost biblical in their scope: the explosion flattened the town, blinding some one thousand people in an instant—many of the town's residents had been at their office windows, staring with fascination at the ship burning in the harbour.

A tidal wave followed the explosion, then a fire swept through the town. That night the devastated community was hit by a blizzard that finished off many of the injured who were still out in the open. By the time the catastrophe was over, 1963 people lay dead.

Samuel Prince had been eating breakfast at a restaurant near the port when the blast occurred. He rushed to the scene, rendered what assistance he could. But he was more than a cleric: he was a thoughtful observer of human behaviour and a scholar. Certain things he saw that day stayed with him, left him wondering about humanity and how it reacted to calamity.

Why was it, he asked himself, that the first relief station was established by a troupe of travelling actors? How did patients endure emergency operations in the street without apparent pain? How was it that a soldier could spend the day working to assist victims when one of his own eyes had been knocked out?

In 1920 Prince published *Catastrophe and Social Change*, the first scholarly study of human behaviour in times of crisis. His main concern was that we should learn from disasters. The book begins with an epigram from St Augustine: 'This awful catastrophe is not the end but the beginning. History does not end so. It is the way its chapters open.'

In the last ninety years psychologists, physiologists, planners and other professionals have taken up Samuel Prince's baton, and we now know a considerable amount about the normal human response to the abnormal occurrence of disaster.

Not all of it is self-evident. You might expect widespread panic, for example, but disaster studies show that the victims are often calm, orderly, considerate of their fellow victims. Think of those long queues of people patiently making their way down the stairs at the World Trade Center, pausing to let colleagues from lower storeys enter the line, rendering aid to the injured. (One man, a quadriplegic in a wheelchair, was carried by ten of his colleagues down sixty-eight floors.) That is, in fact, a more typical response than panic.

There was evidence of such behaviour whenever people gathered in groups on Black Saturday. John Grover, the CFA captain at Kinglake West, was struck by the manner in which members of the public sheltering at the station helped each other out, assumed positions of leadership, assisted the old and the young. In Kinglake itself, a number of nurses emerged from the crowd and began spontaneously rendering aid to the injured.

But accompanying this willingness to help their fellow victims are other, more complex reactions. Psychologists who have studied the human response to disaster have identified what they term 'the survival arc'.

The stages on this arc are:

1) Denial
2) Deliberation
3) The decisive moment

Most people who have the misfortune to be caught in a crisis will move through this arc, but they will do it at different tempos, the rate of response governed by their personalities, life experiences and training. Every stage of the arc, it can be argued, is based upon sound evolutionary logic: denial, for example, can help calm you down, give you the mental capacity to move into deliberation mode; deliberating before you act will decrease the chances of your making a fatal mistake.

People in the denial stage of the arc tend to display what psychologists call a 'normalcy bias': they can't believe what's happening. Things have always worked out okay before, why shouldn't they now? I've never been killed before, why should I be now? Sure, we've all got to go some day, but today is never going to be the day.

These folk are seduced by the Lake Wobegon Effect—the town where everyone is above average. This is why 90 percent of drivers believe they are safer than most others, or why three out of four baby boomers imagine they look younger than their peers. Most of us think we are less likely than our neighbours to suffer a divorce, a dismissal or a heart attack.

Initially, at least, we tell ourselves there is no crisis, that everything will be okay. For this reason we tend to be slow to react and reluctant to leave the scene, even when staying increases the danger. During the September 11 attacks, for example, the occupants of the towers waited an average of six minutes before attempting to evacuate. At least a thousand took the time to shut down their computers, 40 percent of them gathered up their belongings. Seventy percent discussed the situation with colleagues before leaving. Many phoned friends and family, sent emails, stood around wondering what they were meant to do now.

Sometimes the response can seem almost like lethargy. In the

1977 Beverley Hills Supper Club fire, for example, people remained passive, waiting for somebody to take control. They were paying customers, after all, and this was a classy joint. The performers kept performing, the diners continued to eat and watch the show as smoke crept in from the kitchen. Whether or not an individual survived was largely a matter of initiative, but not necessarily their own. Sixty percent of the club's employees tried to help their fellow victims, but only 17 percent of the guests did. One dining room had the good fortune to have an eighteen-year-old busboy with his wits about him who promptly led them all to safety. Others didn't: many of the 165 dead were found—a bizarre image—still seated at their tables.

All of these phenomena were witnessed on Black Saturday.

'Normalcy bias', for example, is one of the reasons people fail to prepare their properties or leave early: they think of wildfire as some sort of distant, abstract threat. Or denial: one of the survivors interviewed for this book described the terrible moment when the fires came thundering over the hill. Her first reaction? This can't be happening. I've been dreading it for years, preparing for weeks, raking and pruning all day, but it can't be happening.

This denial can add to the indecision. Stay and defend the house, or make yourself scarce? The trouble with a bushfire, of course, is that indecision can be fatal. If you are grappling with the question of whether to stay or go when the fire—or even the smoke—is in sight, you've left it too late. The St Andrews firefighters still shake their heads in amazement at the fellow they came across blithely standing on a ridge completely unprotected as the fire bore down upon them all. 'What do you think I should do now?' he asked them.

'I'd suggest you get the fuck out of here,' somebody yelled from the back of the truck. 'We are!'

The knowledge that people will act this way is one of the dilemmas the emergency authorities must face. For years they've been attempting to hammer home the message: it is your choice whether you stay or go, they say, but if you are going to stay, make sure you are fully prepared. If you are going to leave, leave early. But emergency planners know that many people will attempt a lethal combination of the two: they'll plan to stay, then make a run for it when they see what a real fire looks like.

What's going on in our brains to make us act this way? What happens when we experience fear? Like a lot of other aspects of our behaviour, our responses to imminent danger are governed largely by the most primitive of instincts.

One's hair, for example, might stand on end. Not a particularly useful reaction these days, but it is probably a genetic remnant of the trait that makes threatened birds flash their feathers, fish their fins. A warning: watch out, I'm bigger than I look.

At the first sign of danger, your neurons transmit a message to the amygdala, an ancient, almond-shaped mass of neurons in the temporal lobe of the brain. This in turn triggers a range of automatic responses throughout the body. The blood vessels will constrict, so that you bleed less. The blood pressure and heart rate shoot up. A slew of hormones—cortisol and adrenaline in the main—surge through the bloodstream, giving the gross-motor muscles a sort of bionic boost (which is why people in fear can be capable of great feats of strength—and also why they sometimes experience an odd chemical taste in the mouth). The muscles become taut, tensed, primed. The body creates its own chemical painkillers. We are ready for action: to flee, fight or defend ourselves.

All of this sounds positive. They all seem like reactions—hardwired into us by evolution—that will help in a crisis. But these primitive responses can also lead to inappropriate outcomes.

Sometimes, for example, the body will simply shut down. There's more to this than a calculated decision to play dead. A survivor of the Virginia Tech massacre, the only member of his class to come out of the atrocity unharmed, reports that his body was literally numb, frozen with fear. He had no control whatsoever over his normal bodily functions.

To military psychologists, this is a well-documented reaction:

in moments of extreme danger, they know, there will always be a certain percentage of soldiers who simply curl up and do nothing. Because of its security implications, physiologists have made extensive studies of this phenomenon: they know that the heart rate and temperature drop, the respiration goes up, the eyes close or gaze ahead, the pupils dilate.

For an individual in this situation, the thinking brain has been bypassed. This is why those closest to a disaster often have little memory of it other than a string of random images. The part of the brain they use for solving everyday problems, even for storing memories, is cut out of the loop. (It is also why some of the stories in this book may seem sketchy or episodic. Virtually everybody interviewed remembers events through an adrenaline-soaked haze: isolated images and incidents predominate; time is distorted.)

Paralysis must have had its evolutionary benefits. For example a predator on the plains of Africa, having learned the dangers of eating rotten prey, would be more likely to leave the unmoving victim alone. You can see this in your own backyard: a bird will instinctively attack and seize a fleeing mouse but ignore a dead one. If you were a small hominid and your attacker had the speed of a leopard and the strength of a tiger, it could be your only option.

But in situations where technology has outstripped evolution, it can increase the danger. Kent Härstedt, a survivor of the sinking of the ferry MS *Estonia*—the worst sea disaster of modern times— describes seeing large numbers of people standing on the deck doing absolutely nothing as the waves rolled towards them. Others made it to the lifeboats, but then just sat there, clutching the sides, making no attempt to launch the boat as the *Estonia* slid under the waves. Those passengers were immobilised, frozen with fear. The paralysis reaction may have had its uses in our evolutionary past, but in the case of a sinking ship, it led to death.

'What we may be witnessing is a situation in which a previously adaptive response has now become maladaptive as a consequence of technological change,' says Gordon Gallup, an expert on paralysis in animals. 'Our brains search, under extreme stress, for an appropriate survival response and choose the wrong one, like divers who rip their respirators out of their mouths deep underwater. Or like deer who freeze in the headlights of a car.'

If there is one crisis in which an active response is essential, it is the bushfire. Report after report has emphasised the fact that your best chance of survival is to stay alert, patrol your property, fight for as long as you can stand. The firefighter's axiom—hit it hard and fast—is as valid on the micro scale as it is on the macro. The crack in the window that lets in the fatal spark may be easily defendable, but you won't notice it if you're hiding in the bath—as 27 percent of Black Saturday's victims were doing when they died. (The bathroom is possibly the most dangerous room in the house: it may have water but it usually has no escape route. Its reputation as a safe haven presumably comes from American tornado culture. Too much *Wizard of Oz*.)

Another potential consequence of stress is tunnel vision. Individuals can become so fixated upon a particular aspect of their situation that they will ignore others, potentially more fatal. In her excellent book on disasters, Amanda Ripley illustrates this with the story of an air crew coming in to land in Miami. They became so obsessed with the failure of their landing-gear green light to come on that they didn't notice that they were losing altitude. The resulting crash killed 101 people.

There were many examples of tunnel vision in the stories that emerged from Black Saturday: the resident so worried about embers zapping through a crack in the front window that he didn't realise the back of the house was engulfed, the firefighter so absorbed by a burning tree in front of him that he didn't notice the flames roaring up behind.

As cortisol and adrenaline flood the body, they can interfere with that part of the brain responsible for complex thinking so that even the basic ability to reason deteriorates. The most mundane tasks—opening a door, turning on a tap, flicking a switch to start a pump—can become confusing. Emotion overwhelms the brain, often at the expense of reason, sometimes at the expense of other bodily functions—digestion, salivation and bladder control—which the amygdala recognises as less important to immediate survival. A Kinglake firefighter remembers a mother scrambling up onto the truck with her kids, then apologising because they had wet their pants. 'They're not the only ones,' he replied, glancing at his crewmates.

None of these reactions, it should be remembered, are signs of moral failing: of cowardice, incompetence or irresponsibility. They are genetically programmed automatic responses to an abnormal situation that need to be understood if we are to improve our responses in the future.

Nevertheless it is true that while some people curl up and die, others automatically swing into action. Why? Genetics has a lot to do with it. Research into animal behaviour has found that the tendency to paralysis, for example, is passed on to offspring.

But in our own species the most effective response is based upon a solid foundation of preparation, training and experience. The more familiar the situation, the less chance of the brain shutting down or succumbing to the more extreme manifestations of stress. That is why firefighters practise such basic skills as bowling out hoses and operating pumps until their arms ache; they need those procedures to become ingrained, automatic. That is why every family in the bushfire zones should practise fire drills until the kids are screaming with boredom.

Police officers like Roger Wood and Cameron Caine had the kind of training and experience that made them less likely to go into panic mode or develop tunnel vision. One of the firefighters who encountered Wood at a critical moment later that night was struck by the way in which he seemed to be able simultaneously to maintain a conversation, issue instructions, make decisions and monitor the wellbeing of the people around him.

Obviously the better the training, the more effective it will be, but it need not be formal or organised. A ten-year-old English school-girl named Tilly Smith was on a beach in Thailand in 2004 when suddenly the tide ran out and the water began to bubble strangely. The beach was full of tourists standing around staring at the phenomenon, but Tilly's class had seen a video about tsunamis two weeks before and she recognised the signs. She alerted her parents, who organised a frantic evacuation of the beach minutes before the wave struck. It turned out to be one of the few in the area on which nobody was killed.

Another important element is leadership, particularly when those affected by the disaster have clustered, as they tend to do. Coming together for mutual support is a natural instinct. On September 11, 70 percent of the survivors discussed the situation with the people around them before taking any action. After the 2005 London transit bombings some victims refused to leave the Undergound, so reluctant were they to abandon the groups they'd formed.

Again, Black Saturday has its parallels. One survivor said that she was terrified to leave the truck that had rescued her, so desperate was she to remain with the group.

'What you actually look for in these circumstances is someone who can tell you what to do,' said Ian, a victim of the London tube bombings. 'Even if it's just a basic "Stay here" or "Move there", you just need guidance, because you are a bit all over the place, as you can imagine.' For Ian, badly injured, the most comforting thing he heard was the voice of the driver telling him to make his way out of the tunnel.

If individuals or groups demonstrate any of the negative responses outlined above—paralysis, tunnel vision, indecision—their best hope is that somebody will stand up and take control. They need people with training and experience, who have been taught to assess risks, to judge the best course of action, encourage others to follow. Massad Ayob, a veteran police officer and trainer commented: 'The single strongest weapon is a mental plan of what you'll do in a certain crisis. And an absolute commitment to do it, by god, if the crisis comes to pass.'

*

Leadership. Experience. Judgment. A commitment to a plan. When the two police officers came together at Pheasant Creek, the crowd had a pair of leaders who ticked those boxes.

Months after the fire their senior officer, Acting Senior Sergeant Jon Ellks, was to comment: 'Those two, they're smart and they're sensible, both of them. Good coppers. If it hadn't been for them, a lot more people would have died that day...They had a plan. Even if they didn't know it, even if it was formulated in a moment, on the run. Even if they had to bend the rules. They knew their community backwards, they knew the options. All that knowledge and experience came together. They had a plan.'

PHEASANT CREEK

Roger Wood is happy to see Cameron Caine coming towards him. When he gets close enough for speech, though, Cam's beside himself.

'Woody, I can't find Laura and the boys.' He's been trying to call his wife, without success. Have they tried to get through, been overwhelmed on the road? Have they even left home? Are they trapped back there?

One of Cameron's neighbours rolls up: she only just made it out, drove through a wall of flames. No, she hasn't seen Laura.

Wood puts a hand on his colleague's shoulder. 'Mate, we can't do anything about that right now. The fire's about to hit. We have to get these people out of here.'

Just at that moment the Caine family car comes racing out of the smoke, the shaken family on board. Cameron rushes over to embrace them, relief telegraphed in his every gesture.

The two officers reconvene to canvass their options. People gather round, hoping for answers. If anybody has any idea of what's going on, surely it will be them.

If only, Wood breathes to himself. He feels the burden of responsibility pressing down across his shoulders.

The distant roar gives an added urgency to the exchange. The fire is closing fast. The crowd is growing thicker by the second, the tension mounting. They can't stay here.

As police officers, they have no authority to evacuate members of the public, but this is not a day for following regulations. It's a day for a good copper to follow his instincts and take the initiative.

But where the hell can they go?

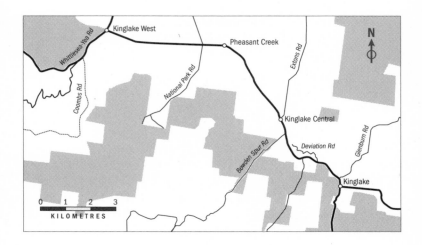

The CFA at Kinglake West was the best option half an hour ago, but is it still safe now? Fires are breaking out everywhere, as far as they can see.

The roar of the fire is a heavy bass thud now, rattling the windows. Embers fall around them. That terrible darkness is descending again. They have no choice.

'CFA's our only option,' says Wood. 'I'll go on ahead, check the coast is clear. Give you a call.' That makes sense: he has the car. 'If I can't get through, I'll come back.'

Cameron will stay behind, shepherd the crowd out when Wood confirms it's safe.

Wood drives off. Cameron stands in the gravel, fear building in the back of his mind. Time passes; the roar grows louder. Visibility diminishes. Darkness. The fire is almost on them. Where the hell is Woody? The first flashes of orange begin to crackle among the pine trees.

The phone rings. His hands trembles as he answers it.

'Cam.'

Woody. Thank christ.

'Send 'em down. Fast. Road's clear; won't be for long.'

Caine doesn't need any more prompting. He runs through the crowd, waving his arms and screaming: 'Get on down to the CFA! Kinglake West!'

His own family move out. Others join them. The trickle becomes a flood, but he shakes his head in frustration at how slow it is. Don't they have any idea what's coming? People are dying out there; he can sense it. He doesn't want to join them. He doesn't want any of the crowd from Pheasant Creek—this haphazard mob who've suddenly come under his care—to join them, either. There are mothers and babies in those cars, old people, little kids, their eyes up against the window staring at him as they roll past. Some of them are neighbours and friends.

A bloke in a twin-cab towing a trailer is facing the wrong way, takes an eternity to turn around and join the convoy, blocking other people off in the meantime.

'You!' Cam roars. 'You're holding everybody up!'

The driver doesn't hear, or doesn't want to.

The smoke pouring out of the pine plantation is growing thicker by the second. The roar is tremendous. He's having trouble breathing now, smoke filling his lungs, biting at his eyes. Visibility is going.

The twin-cab finally completes its snail-paced turn, rattles off down the road. Others follow. He runs among them, slapping roofs and tailgates, yelling, 'Go, go! Move!'

Still it takes forever. Does time stand still in a crisis? He can feel the radiant heat now. He spots flames flickering through the treetops. He shelters behind a bus stop, keeps yelling, trying to kick a bit of urgency into the stragglers. Christ, how many of them are there? Why is it all taking so long? Is he going to burn to death here at Pheasant bloody Creek? More cars come drifting in through the smoke. He waves them on.

At last, there's only one vehicle left. A white van. He runs across to catch a ride, stares at the occupant. The driver is one of Kinglake's recalcitrants—'known' to the police. They arrested him only last week.

'Give us a lift out of here, mate?'

The door flies open. 'Jump in.'

As they bolt out of Pheasant Creek, a terrifying sight looms in the rear window: the bus shelter he was standing in seconds ago is engulfed in flames. A vast wave of fire roars out of the pine plantation, swallowing the store. The explosions begin, the first of hundreds he is to hear this night: bottles and cans burst through the windows. The gas tank out the back goes up in a sheet of blue flame. He's made it out by the skin of his teeth, by the hairs on the back of his hand.

Maybe. The inferno is throwing out jets of flame, igniting the bush alongside the road, and Caine has the eerie feeling this damned fire is seeking him out, hunting him down. He and his driver find themselves white-knuckle racing through a tunnel of fire. And finally coming out of it.

At last the Kinglake West CFA appears through the windscreen, and Cameron is relieved to spot the familiar figure of Roger Wood out on the road, directing the cars out onto the adjoining oval, making sure nobody panics and heads down the deadly Whittlesea track. He gets out to lend a hand.

The fire can't be far behind. The CFA brigade members are working furiously, hosing the building down, spreading foam, doing their best to make it safe.

A later count showed that there were more than two hundred people sheltering at the CFA at Kinglake West. Vehicles of every description, trailers and trail bikes, horse floats, a horde of four-wheel-drives and panel vans, a mini-bus.

The atmosphere is quiet but tense. People are crying, passing round bottles of water. Some are punching frantic thumbs at mobile phones, mostly without success. Telecommunication is random at best, hopelessly choked, deteriorating progressively as the transmission towers fall.

There are people in the crowd who already know they've lost their homes. Many are rigid with fear for family and friends they've left behind. Kids are fretting about pets, although there is a menagerie of them here: cats and dogs, birds, horses, goats. The smoke is growing thicker by the minute. People are spluttering and gasping, passing round smoke masks, pulling shirts over heads. Some are in shock, dazed, their faces blank.

The two policemen assist stragglers, deal with the odd desperate individual wanting to make a run for it. One old man in a ute nearly mows Cameron down in his determination to get away. Cam has little choice but to leap to one side and watch the bloke go rattling off into the smoke.

Wood makes another attempt to reach his own family, again without success. He feels a quiet despair biting at his heart. Tells himself there's nothing to be gained by thinking about it.

Wood and Cameron mainly stay outside, two tall men silhouetted against a horizon on fire. How can this be happening? Wood asks himself. Let me blink and rub my eyes, surely it will be a dream.

For miles around them, out over the valleys and the flatlands, across the glowing scrub, all they can see is monstrous clouds of fire-laced smoke. They've got—what?—a couple of hundred people sheltering here. They're relatively safe.

But there are so many more people out there across the ranges, thousands of them, in isolated farms and leafy towns, from Flowerdale to Pheasant Creek, from Strathewen to St Andrews.

What's happening to them?

SNAPSHOTS

Fire scientist Kevin Tolhurst would report to the Royal Commission into the Black Saturday fires that they unleashed energy equivalent to 1500 times that of the atomic bombs dropped on Hiroshima. They produced radiant heat capable of killing at a distance of four hundred metres. They generated jets and balls of explosive gas able to travel six hundred metres in thirty seconds.

All that energy, that vaporising radiation, those fiery jets and missiles, those gaseous clouds, are unleashed upon the scattered properties and leafy communities of the Kinglake Ranges as the policemen stand helplessly at the CFA in Kinglake West.

It comes first from the sky. Ember attack, it's called in the literature, but that's a feeble term for such lethal missiles. The fires race up the slopes, hit the ridgelines and send a barrage out over the hills and valleys ahead. There are spot fires, hundreds of them, breaking out simultaneously: in the bush, the farms, the roadside reserves, the town streets. Because of the spiral motion of the convection column at the fire front, they can come bursting out of the sky from any or every direction at once, spark fires that take off, coalesce. Nowhere on the mountain is safe.

Phil Petschel, a Kinglake CFA veteran and keen student of fire behaviour, explains what happened: 'Everywhere one of those fireballs landed there was an immediate big fire. There was no build-up, they just *phew!*'—he smacks his hands together—'they're there! When a fireball the size of a caravan crashes to the ground with that roaring wind behind it, it's off!'

Petschel is speaking in the back office of the CFA building, the room that was his home for several weeks after his house on Bald Spur Road burned down.

'That's what happened all over,' he continues. 'That's why we got caught out at our end. We were assuming it would come up the slope like a regular fire, but it didn't. There was a multitude of rapidly growing smaller fires starting everywhere and merging—they didn't have to travel up—they were just there. It was virtually all up the escarpment in one hit.'

That about sums it up.

While a few hundred refugees shelter behind the hoses of the CFA, hell is breaking loose all round them. Along the foothills and up the escarpment, on into the farmlands to the west, in the leafy streets of Kinglake, firebrands are crashing down, kick-starting fires that merge into a monstrous front. A thousand small battles to save lives and homes are being fought.

An appalling number of them are lost.

Snapshot 1:   The Zulu Moment

Drew Barr and Angie O'Connor live with their two children, Lucy and Grace, in Lorelei, a historic homestead they've lovingly renovated over the past twelve years. The weatherboard house was a memorable sight on the road to Kinglake: white-painted, with wide verandas and a fretwork balustrade, stained-glass windows, a flying fox that arced out of an old oak tree and had given hundreds of hours of joy to young and, occasionally, old.

Lorelei has stood on the site for some 130 years and survived many a bushfire. The family have built up a lush garden upon which Angie, a horticulturalist, has lavished her skills. The garden blossoms with exotic trees: pears, guava, a beautiful gingko they were given as a wedding present.

They're well prepared: they've installed a fire-fighting pump, hoses, spare tanks of water, sprinklers on the roof. The land around their home is mainly cleared farmland and they are situated in a valley. They take the threat of bushfire seriously and work furiously every summer to keep the immediate environs free of debris. Ange has even been up on the roof with a vacuum cleaner. There isn't a blade of grass, a scrap of vegetation against the walls.

They take the CFA warnings seriously too. On February 7 they've been on the go since 5.30 in the morning, cutting back a photinia hedge that runs along the front of the property, trimming branches, chainsawing a row of cypress trees they feared might have presented a threat. Their plan is to leave for the day, but they want to give the house as much chance as possible should the unthinkable occur. As they are felling one of the cypresses, a ring-tail possum darts out, and they find a trio of babies. Lucy makes a nest in the laundry, intending to restore them to their mother as soon as the clean-up is over.

They spot the smoke to the north at around noon. Drew checks the CFA website: a fire at Kilmore, forty kilometres away. Not likely to be any sort of a threat; the cool change should be here well before then. It is a spur, though, a reminder of what can happen; they speed up the work rate. They move combustibles away from the building, coax geese and ducks onto the veranda, don protective clothing. They spend the morning running round clearing decks, hosing walls and roof, flooding gutters. The kids join in; they begin to think of the day as a kind of extended fire drill.

By mid-afternoon they're wondering whether there's any point leaving. What Ange describes as 'indecision evacuation fatigue' sets in: they realise it would be wise to go, but leaving is such a drag. You have to sort out animals and valuables, drive in the heat, hang around the suburbs. They've already evacuated so many times this summer. The change can't be far off now, and the internet says the fire is still at Kilmore.

'And we were exhausted,' says Ange. 'Maybe we weren't thinking clearly by that stage.'

By 5.30 they assume they've seen the worst of it. Surely the change will be coming any minute now? They take a breather. Drew is sitting out on the veranda, cup of tea in hand, when a charred leaf lands at his feet. He stares at it, suddenly wary. He looks up: the sky is fraught with a screaming yellow intensity, the clouds are low and dark.

The wind dies down, and an eerie stillness descends upon the countryside. Strange. He steps out from the veranda for a better view, then spots the first flames sweeping up from St Andrews.

The change has arrived all right, but it's bringing the fire with it. Because the fire is to the south of their house, the change is no longer a welcome relief; it's now a deadly threat.

Ange is hosing down the back of the house when she hears Drew roar: 'We're on!'

Her initial reaction is a sense of disbelief. 'My god,' she remembers saying to herself. 'Surely it's not actually going to happen...'

She looks around, has what she describes as her 'Zulu Moment'— the scene in the film when the attackers suddenly crest the hill. An angry red tide appears on the top of the rise to the west. It's coming from two sides at once?

'We felt like ants,' she says later, still appalled at the sheer size and fury of the flames.

The air grows thick with embers: strips of swirling candlebark, sparks of grass and branches carried from god knows where whirl by. The couple run around frantically attacking the tiny fires that begin to break out.

They've always expected a fire would come as a front, but this one isn't following the rules: there are outbreaks to the west, the south. Darkness descends. The fires are coming from everywhere.

They don't realise it at the time, but they are smack in the middle of what fire scientist Kevin Tolhurst describes as an 'area of fire'. As we've seen, the main front, rather than acting like a wave that rolls over you, would send out embers and firebrands that ignite more fires, which are in turn sucked back into the conflagration. This prolongs the danger period. A normal front might last about fifteen minutes, but today any point in the zone could be blasted by lethal radiation and convection for up to an hour.

A bloke races past on a motorbike, disappears into the smoke, travelling north towards Kinglake. The bike returns, goes down towards St Andrews, vanishes again. Reappears, vanishes again; he's obviously struggling to find an escape route. Drew and Ange are so frantic and afraid themselves that they don't think of running out to intercept him as he goes racing back towards St Andrews.

A volley of incendiaries shoot overhead and the pine plantation on the hill behind goes up in a blaze of red and green and wild black smoke.

'We can't do this,' mutters Ange, shivering with fear. But they have no choice.

The youngsters retreat indoors, arm themselves with wet towels and mops. They leash the dogs, begin blocking entrances, do all the things they've been trained to do. Their parents stay outside until the front is maybe ten metres away. Drew shuts down the pump and brings the hose inside. They connect it to a gravity-fed tap in the laundry, dash around wetting down the interior.

In seconds the windows are glowing like a mad blacksmith's forge. Sparks and spikes begin shooting in through gaps, cracks in the walls they never knew existed.

Outside it's like the air itself has ignited.

'You've seen a fire when someone throws petrol on it?' asks Ange. 'That's what it was like. There'd be a pocket of unburnt gas; an ember would strike it, and boom! Up it went!'

They have always drilled into the kids that if they are ever caught in a fire, they have to fight it: they all understand that to shelter passively can be lethal. But in the chaos of those moments, they don't realise that twelve-year-old Lucy has remembered the lesson too well. She's taken the initiative to move around inside the house, checking doors, making sure that the rooms aren't engulfed. A courageous move that could have ended in disaster if any of the rooms had been in flames.

The sturdy little building does a magnificent job of keeping the conflagration at bay. But as they watch flames hammering at a section under one of the eaves, they realise that the heat is being trapped in there, that the weatherboards are about to ignite.

A sudden shout of alarm from Grace: 'Mummy, there's fire inside the house!'

A plume of particularly noxious black smoke puffs through, then bare flames are lacing across the ceiling. They blast it with the hose, but the inferno is making its own entry points now, poking and prodding their defences, threatening to overwhelm them.

'You promised we wouldn't be here!' sobs Grace, while Lucy gasps that she can't breathe.

Drew, 193 centimetres tall and up where the smoke is thickest, is having even more problems, sucking at thin wisps of air as if they were his last. Every breath tears at his lungs.

'When you're that terrified,' reflected Ange afterwards, 'it's like all your senses disappear. All that adrenaline and cortisol pumping through your body, you think you're going crazy. Even the noise of the fire disappears. You can only focus on one thing.'

For her, that one thing becomes the corner of the room where the flames are threatening to break through. Like many other people in the region right now, she sees the fire in anthropomorphic terms. She swears at it, screaming, leaping onto the table and blasting it with the hose.

Survival inside the building is rapidly becoming impossible. The room is thick with acrid smoke. The air rattles with a deafening chorus of shrieking smoke alarms, kids and dogs, venting gas bottles, exploding cars and cans of fuel. Above it all, the fire itself roars with a noise to wake the dead. Their eyes sting, their throats ache, their faces are racked and hollow with fear.

They're caught in the deadly game of chance being played by families all over the district. It's a balancing act: the killer outside against the killer within. The atmosphere out there is irradiated, but the roof is about to fall in on them. You have to judge the right moment. Make the wrong choice and you're dead.

In many a location across the ranges—particularly around the top of the escarpment, where the vegetation was thick and the incline vertiginous—you're dead anyway. The dice are loaded, there's a horseshoe in the glove: the moment never comes. Inside and out coalesce into an infinity of heat and light, darkness and smoke.

This family are fortunate to have that gravity-fed hose, something few in the region have; it gives them precious minutes. So many others are relying on electric pumps that give out when the power goes, or petrol pumps that cease operating when the fuel evaporates. But it can't keep the fire at bay forever. The smoke grows thicker, more bitter. They're groping around on their knees, still pouring on the water, swatting and smashing. They get the closest thing they've had all day to a stroke of luck—a tree smashes a large plastic pool near the back of the house and releases a stream of water. Most of it flows under the house.

Somewhere in the chaos, the thought shoots through Drew's head that this isn't going the way they said it would. We've done everything the experts told us, we were well prepared. It's supposed

Roger Wood | Photo from Victoria Police Image Library

The fire surges over Mt Sugarloaf | Photo by Anita Norris

Cameron Caine and Roger Wood | Photo from Victoria Police Image Library

Tony Fitzgerald's crew starts the backburn described on page 86

A minute or two later: the fire 'roars out of the gorge'

Seconds later: the view through the windscreen as the DSE crew escapes

Photos by Tom Chambers, Parks Victoria

Landscape with burnt trees: Bald Spur | Photo by Darrell James

to last for fifteen minutes. What the fuck's going on? When will we be able to get out?

He cracks the door three or four times, but each time the radiant heat drives him back. Death to go out into that. But they can't stay in here much longer either: they'll suffocate. Or be burnt to death. Or be crushed by the roof. He tries it one more time. Bearable?

Maybe. 'I'm going for the pump,' he yells, praying it will give them another weapon, buy them some time. He'll attack the fire from the outside.

'Daddy, don't go out there!' the girls are screaming. Ange has to drag them off him as he crashes out the door. She catches a glimpse of him through the window, a blurry figure racing through blinding light. She finds herself thinking, This is the way Drew dies. Goodbye, she thinks. Thank you.

They're no longer fighting for the house, they all know that. The building is doomed. 'And we are too,' Ange says to herself. 'We're dead.' She wonders if it will be quicker for the girls if she embraces them.

Drew comes staggering back, fire hose in hand. 'Out now!' he roars as the flames burst through the roof.

They unleash the dogs, grab a few beloved objects; Lucy clutches her teddy bear as they give themselves a last soak and rush out onto the patio. They jump to one side as a burning tree crashes onto it. The dogs bolt. Drew sprints back inside: if they do make it out alive, they'll need something to convince themselves that their lost world was not a dream.

The girls watch, horrified. Breathe sighs of relief when he re-emerges with a photo-album box in hand.

They reach the shelter of the massive oak tree that is yet to ignite.

A pause. But they can't stay here. It's too close to the shed, full of explosive items: cars, mowers, paint, fuel. They'll have to go through the front hedge. Drew soaks the photos—he's too exhausted to carry them—and they set off.

It's a nightmare trek. They're shocked, scared and soaking wet.

Grace burns her hand as they crawl through the red-hot wire of the fence. They scramble down onto the Kinglake road. Creep down-hill, fires raging on every side, trees crashing. They can't bear to look back at the house, the only home the kids have ever known.

They trudge over burnt ground, blistered asphalt, thank god they had the foresight to put on heavy footwear. They're having enough trouble just breathing without worrying about burnt feet.

They stagger down the road, shoes bubbling, the world in flames around them. They see cows up against the fences, dead or dying, gaping mouths, beseeching eyes. Every house is on fire. Are the neighbours all dead? They cannot envisage how anybody could have lived through that.

'Flatlining,' says Ange. 'That's what it was like, that walk— you're moving through this weird, weird world.' Interviewed in their living room months later, she is momentarily overwhelmed by the memory. 'It was so lonely... We thought we were the only people left alive.'

Through a gap in the smoke they spot red and blue lights spinning.

A tanker from Wattle Glen has run up the hill to attack the fire in Olives Lane. They crew have just survived a bad burnover, sent out a mayday, gone into crew-protection mode, found themselves trapped in a paddock.

Kerrie Redmond, a local St Andrews CFA member who'd come along as a guide, looks up in disbelief as the four ghostly figures wrapped in blankets, one of them carrying a teddy bear, come stum-bling through the smoke.

The family are ushered aboard, treated for burns and smoke inhalation. Angie speaks almost lovingly of the CFA team: 'There was one older fellow, Wombat they called him, he was so sweet and caring to the girls. He had first aid experience and he treated Gracie's burnt hand, washed out their eyes. He told them they'd be okay, said it was all right to feel afraid because he was too.'

They're stuck there for hours. When the crew eventually chain-saw their way back down to St Andrews, the truck loaded with victims of the fire, they have to shield the children from the sight of the motorbike rider's body, the one whose progress Drew had followed as the fire struck. At Mittons Bridge Road, they cross over the fire line, move into the unburnt, unreal world on the other side.

In body, at least, they do. The fires behind will haunt their dreams for a long time yet.

Snapshot 2:   A Martial Art

Tim Huggins is coming home from work in his 1970 HG Holden. He cruises through St Andrews at around 5.15, is troubled to see a police roadblock at Mittons Bridge.

He's been worried about the smoke drifting in from the north. The radio says there's a fire at Kilmore, but this looks a lot closer than that. He pulls over to speak to the sergeant in charge.

'What's the problem?'

'Fire up on Jacksons Road.'

That's, what? Four, maybe five kilometres to the north? 'What about Kinglake?'

'No, Kinglake's still okay.'

'I need to get back to my family.'

She waves him on, but his threat detector is ratcheted up a notch. His wife, Linda, and their two young children Aaron and Alexandra are at home. He narrows his eyes, accelerates away.

Huggins has spent a lifetime in situations that call for alertness of mind and awareness of risk. He's an Australian tae kwon do champion, has been for five years in succession. He specialises in sports fighting and once reached the final four of the US Open.

'Sport like that,' he explains, 'where you could get your head smashed in any moment, your nose broken, you develop a sense of danger.'

Seconds after leaving the roadblock, he sweeps round a blind corner at Wild Dog Creek Road and runs headlong into the fire.

'What the hell?' He reflexively plants his foot down and zooms through the flames. Being stuck behind an inferno with his family on the other side is something he will not allow to happen.

Interviewed over a cup of herbal tea in his office, where he edits *Mountain Monthly*, he expands. 'The secret of martial arts is to see the threat coming—and to not be there when it does.'

He'll have a hard time not being there when this one comes. He's going to need every scintilla of the Zen mindfulness he's developed over a lifetime's practice to bring his family through the next few hours.

Huggins floors it up the mountain, just about cooks the motor. He's worried when the temperature light comes on—visions of breaking down on the road swarm through his head. But the old HG holds true, as they tend to do. Twenty, maybe thirty cars pass him coming down the mountain. People are getting out of Kinglake, but do they know what they're heading for? He flashes his lights and waves, does his best to warn them, but he can't hang around.

Finally he swings up over the last ridge and flies through the town. He's struck by the eerie silence: at this stage the CFA shed is open, empty; presumably the trucks have gone down to the fire.

Huggins' home is a beautiful split-level mud-brick house he and Linda have been working away at for eight years. It's nestled in thick bush less than a kilometre from the town centre.

When he pulls into the drive, the kids come running out to greet him, Linda close behind. She's worried; there've been phone calls from the neighbours, troubling smoke clouds. The town is on edge. Nobody knows what's going on.

Huggins doesn't need to know what's going on, he can sense it. He knows a southerly change is due this evening, assumes that the flames he's just driven through might well be coming up with it. Every warning siren in his head is going off, but part of his strategy is not to alarm Aaron and Alexandra. If the fire does come, panic-stricken kids could kill them all.

He plays briefly with the youngsters, has a cup of tea and a quiet word with Linda. 'It's looking really bad,' he says. He tells her about running the gauntlet at St Andrews.

They listen to the radio, check the web: nothing about Kinglake. Then again, there's nothing about St Andrews either, and he's seen it burning down there. They discuss making a run for it, but are well aware of the danger of that; the open road is no place to be this late in the day. Their only option is to stay where they are.

They take a last sip of tea, put the cups down, get to work.

They swept the place clear this morning, but the gutters are already full of debris stirred up by the wind. They clean them out, plug them and fill them with water. They wet everything down, block up the house as best they can: wet towels on doors and windows, curtains drawn.

As they race around, Huggins keeps an eye on the plume gathering over Strathewen. He's alarmed but not surprised to notice a change in its angle: previously it was leaning to the south. Now it's vertical. By his reckoning, that means it's coming straight at them. They up the tempo of their preparations.

He's puzzled when the wind dies down. For maybe five minutes, there's silence.

They stand for a moment, stare to the south, ears pricked. Then they hear it. A distant rumble. They can almost feel it: the earth shakes, their bones tremble in sympathy. It comes in swiftly, the thousand-jet-engine roar everybody on the front line heard.

All sportspeople know about the zone. From that moment, Tim Huggins says, he was in it. 'If you focus hard enough,' he adds, 'you generate your own zone.'

He sees the first flames: a swirling red chaos rushing through the treetops. It's crowning, coming straight at them, fast and furious, twice the height of the trees—and the trees are forty metres tall.

Huggins calls upon all the instincts honed by a lifetime's commitment to his discipline. The essential components of his strategy are to minimise the expenditure of energy, to expect the unexpected—and to stay focused. In reality, he's been doing those things since he first drove into the fire at Wild Dog Creek. Everything he's done since, even the hugging of the kids, the cup of tea, has been part of the plan.

Linda and the children rush inside; Tim sprints around outside, getting out all the water he can, fighting the embers that are beginning to split the air, fizz against the walls.

The front is still seventy metres away when a ball of fire shoots out in his direction, its trajectory low and flat, like something Viv Richards might have belted off the bowling of Dennis Lillee. It carves a flaming parabola through the air, never more than ten metres from the ground. Smashes into the bush alongside the house. The whole patch—maybe a hundred square metres—instantaneously bursts into flame.

'I was stunned by that,' he says. 'It was like an incendiary bomb had landed.' Another fireball appears, arcs past the other side of the house.

Outside is clearly not a place to be, not in a barrage like this. The next one could take him out. He rushes around the back, tries to open the door. Can't. What...? He's locked out. A heave of the shoulders and it budges. Slightly. Jesus—Linda and Alex have jammed wet towels against it. 'Lemme in!' he screams and thumps, thanks god when the door is wrenched open, because suddenly the outside world explodes.

He and Linda form a team as fire starts to overwhelm their home. Linda, like Tim, is a black belt martial artist, blessed with the same cool head and smooth coordination. Despite their fears, the couple never stop thinking, moving, looking ahead. One decision they make is to tell the kids to get onto the concrete floor and stay there: a seemingly simple instruction, but there were families who died that day because the parents were trying to find their children in the chaos of smoke-filled houses.

The kids are huddled under wet towels in a central position, midway between three exits. Tim's plan is to fight what he calls 'a slow, staged retreat' as the house catches fire, always making sure to leave themselves an escape route. At one stage the children get up to go to the toilet.

'*Stay there!*' he yells. 'How can I keep you safe if I can't find you?'

Embers insinuate themselves through weak points in the upper level. A window breaks and in they shoot. Tim and Linda recognise this as their Achilles heel. They dash up there with mops and buckets, but carefully—the stairs, the water—this is no time for a broken leg. They have some success in extinguishing the flare-ups, but the smoke is so bad you can only stay up there for a minute or two. They take it in turns. Another window smashes: the wind, the heat and the pressure are cracking glass everywhere.

The alarms go off, scream through the house. So do the children. 'Stop screaming!' he yells at them. 'The only person who's allowed to scream is me!'

Months later, reflecting upon the comment, he shakes his head: 'Stupid man.'

'Mummy, are we going to be dead?' asks Aaron.

'No darling.' She cuddles him.

Not if I have anything to do with it, thinks Tim. But one of the upstairs windows is jammed open. More windows crack, give entrance to embers. The room turns from a smoky twilight to a pitch black, illuminated only by the flames licking against the windows, the sparks spitting through the cracks.

The noise—alarms, kids, the indescribable roar of a billion cells exploding in the bush outside—grows to a climax. The house is nestled into an area of the thickest bush: the fire is crowning around them, reaches the full 1400 degrees, subjects the building to a blistering radiation.

'You're not getting my family, you fuckin beast!' he roars out into the inferno, and a kind of madness descends upon him. 'I found myself attacking embers that were trying ignite a timber venetian blind and I was singing—a Wurundjeri song an elder had taught me: *Wandit Kundawa, Kundawa Wandit*. Figured they knew a thing or two about fire.'

Huggins finds time to reflect on the care he's put into ensuring that the house was relatively secure: the packing in the ridgecapping, the space-filler products used to close corrugation gaps under the flashing's edge. The house is built on a slab: nowhere for fire to get underneath. Cathedral ceilings, so no roof cavity for the flames to invade. All that effort is paying off, but will it be enough?

An anxious glance at the window: nothing out there but red angry flame thrashing in the dark. How much longer can it last? How much longer can they?

Then, magnificently, a glimpse of sunlight. It's been about an hour, by Tim's reckoning. Certainly not the ten minutes they'd imagined. He opens the door once or twice, but it's still painfully hot out there. He's desperate to see what's happening to the exterior. They catch sight of the neighbours' house engulfed. He waits a minute or two, then has another go at the door.

A sigh of relief: it's bearable.

He staggers outside. The roof is ablaze. He sprints around with the water backpack, extinguishing it. Looks around. Sheds, cars, fences and tanks: incinerated. The trees are fired up and crashing down.

He takes a deep breath. Splutters. He doubles over, sucks air. Then stretches himself upright, punches the sky and lets out a rebel yell: 'Whoo *hooo!*' They've survived. By christ, he hadn't thought they were going to.

His family creep outside. They huddle together in shock, comfort each other with their breath, their arms, their beating hearts.

The silence. A strange, unearthly hush, the likes of which they've never known. As if a giant vacuum cleaner has sucked all noise from the air. They gaze around, anxious. Is everybody else dead?

Tim tries the phone. Amazing—it works. He rings Kinglake CFA and gets Trish Hendrie. They're alive; can somebody come round and lend a hand? The bush around them is still raging.

'Nobody here just now,' replies Trish. She sounds under a lot of stress. 'We'll send somebody when we can.'

The family bunker down in the house, holding each other, grasping for the small things that assure them the world is still revolving. They look at each other in a new light. They seem reborn.

There's no power of course but Linda has had the foresight to prepare a thermos. She pours them all a brew.

'Oh, that cup of tea,' says Tim. 'Like liquid gold.'

They spend the night huddled together on the floor and patrolling the house, gazing in awe at the cascading embers and leaping flames. At 3 am Panton Hill Tanker One turns up, gives them some much needed water, blacks out the area around the home.

Dawn breaks and the nightmare deepens. The police turn up with the local CFA. Their neighbours, the O'Sheas—Graham and Debbie and their kids, Lyric and Trey—have been reported as missing. Tim is surprised. He'd always believed their plan was to leave in the event of fire. The two families are close; they're all involved with martial arts. He goes down to the house with the emergency service workers. He feels he owes it to the O'Sheas, as friends and neighbours.

They find four bodies in what's left of the kitchen.

Tim trails back home to his own family a different man. Wiser, he says, than the one who set out on that charcoal path.

*

Two families. Two snapshots of survival amid disaster. Sketches of the combination of luck, foresight, coolness, desperation—and luck again—that might save your life in that dreadful onslaught. All over the ranges the sequence is repeated: the blowtorch wind, the sudden chilling stillness, the rush and the roar, the bitter smoke, the devil's hammers battering, the evil tongues of fire snaking across the ceiling, the dash outside or the crash of steel and timber.

These families survive.

Many around them don't.

Pandemonium

So many people in the district have been going about their business, completely oblivious of what is coming at them. There are blokes in singlets lounging around the veranda of the pub, shoppers picking up a few last-minute items for a Saturday night barbeque, picnickers lazing by the creeks, girls out riding horses.

The lack of 'situational awareness' that firefighters speak of is about to come screaming back at them with a vengeance. Of the 173 Victorians to die in the several fires of Black Saturday, 120 of them perish in this one.

The tsunami pulses up the beetling slopes of the escarpment, whipping missiles in every direction. It rips great branches from the trees along the crest, transforms them into incendiaries that are sucked up into the whirlpool and fall to earth in places like the Yarra Valley, thirty kilometres away. Fire comes from all points of the compass.

For some, sitting in a darkened room with the TV and the air-con blasting, the first they know of the approaching conflagration is when the roof blows off or the veranda bursts into flame. At least one person that day learns for the first time that his house is on fire when he notices pink slurry dribbling down the wall—dropped by a helicopter trying to extinguish his burning roof.

Pandemonium breaks loose.

People make hideous, panic-struck mistakes. The CFA policy is to stay or go, but many attempt a fatal combination of the two. They stay for as long as they think they can, hoping to save the house, then bolt, suddenly deciding that an assemblage of steel and wood isn't worth dying for. Cars barrel blindly through the smoke, T-bone each other: sometimes the occupants are knocked unconscious, others wish they had been as the fire rolls in at them.

Some make a run for god knows where and die on the side of the road, in gutters and cuttings, in ditches and driveways. Some bury themselves in creeks and dams, then in mud as the water evaporates, then dirt as the mud dries.

Particularly poignant are the stories of some of the newer arrivals to this country and the dozen or so people of other nationalities who will die today. Kinglake is not a particularly multicultural community, but like any contemporary Australian farming area, it has its share of migrants who have chosen to make it their home. And whereas native-born Australians are at least raised with some awareness of bushfires, these people must have wondered what kind of hell they'd stumbled into.

An Italian-born immigrant watches helplessly as his wife and two children die. A Vietnamese family who've only been in the country for a few weeks huddle in a house, terrified, bewildered, as the inferno rages around them. The Indian family Wood visited that morning, the Singhs, run for the safety of a broccoli patch as their house burns down, lie watching in disbelief as the inferno storms past.

Cattle bellow and panic, crush fencelines and become entangled in wire, are roasted alive. Horses bolt through blackened paddocks with rolling eyes and tails ablaze. Birds ignite in the air and arc to earth like comets. Sheets of corrugated iron go swinging on the wind like butcher's knives. Gas bottles fall over: they absorb the heat, and when they eventually explode they shoot across the yard like torpedoes, take out the neighbours' living room. A woman watches as a blood-red rose of melting glass blossoms in her window.

Artists, much given to little mud-brick cottages in the lyrebird bush, find themselves in a landscape on the rampage. Environmentalists die in it. Lovers' hearts melt and flow into one another's. At least one St Andrews hippy stands on the edge of the forest, arms open, eyes closed. Says later he's seen God.

The fire is the great equaliser: rich and poor, old and young, famous and infamous, abled and not, greenies and rednecks: the distinctions disappear and they die in droves.

Luck always, always plays a part. Among the thousands of stories that emerge from the disaster, there are those of brilliantly prepared families who perish, of shambolic incompetents who ignore every rule in the book and walk away unscathed.

But the luck, like most luck, has its roots in knowledge. There are those who've always known about fire, who took it into consideration when building or buying their homes, who've carried out their preparations. But many more are newcomers, both to the region and the bush. They don't know what preparations are.

*

None of this is to blame individuals. When the level of unpreparedness is that high, it becomes a matter of culture. Ours is a society that has failed to come to terms with its environment, an environment that was always dangerous and is now becoming positively lethal, stretched to breaking point by the stresses of global warming.

Time and again, as the survivors came together in the ash-grey aftermath, you'd hear the phrase: 'I don't understand—I didn't imagine it would be like that.'

Professor John Handmer, a disaster management expert at RMIT, conducted a detailed study and found that only 20 percent of those who died were well prepared, even though the definition of 'well-prepared' used in the study was minimal: a water supply and buckets and mops. Forty-four percent of the victims were aged, disabled or under twelve. Thirty percent were taken completely by surprise, despite the CFA warnings all week and the massive smoke plumes lowering over the region all afternoon.

Residents stand there stunned with their pathetic little mops and buckets in hand as a mountain of fire falls onto them. It sucks the moisture from mouths, the sweat from forearms, it desiccates tongues and throats, it would drive them out of their mind if they weren't out of it already with fear.

Manna gums are screwed out of the ground, massive mountain ash snap and shatter. Candlebark fulfils its destiny. The Anglican and Catholic churches go to meet their maker, the Buddhist temple doesn't. Bursts of flame shoot hundreds of metres into the air. One resident describes a paddock in front of him, some distance from the fire front, suddenly bursting into flame as if it has been touched with a sorcerer's wand. He can only assume that a cloud of gas has descended upon the paddock and been ignited.

Some say the wind generated by the fire does as much damage as the fire itself: certainly the two work in terrifying tandem. The wind is whipping like a mad thing, up the gullies and over the ridgelines, through the trees. A shed roof turns up in an orchard a kilometre from its base.

Some residents have fire plans, but plans evaporate like puddles of water on this godforsaken day. They follow the official line: they fight outside for as long as they can stand it, pouncing on spot fires, pouring on the water, then gather up the family. Retreat indoors and wait for the radiant heat to die down. And wait. And wait.

They try the doors, whip away their fingers as the skin blisters and sticks to the handle. They watch in horror as the fiery tide probes their defences, finds little chinks and cracks in the armour— the rotting windowsill they've been meaning to repair, the crack in the joinery, the gap under the door—and sends the shock troops in: sparks and jets and tongues of light.

Some feel as if the fire is hunting them down, and in a sense they're right, although it's not so much them that the fire is searching for. It's oxygen, of which the inside of your house—or your body—is a convenient reservoir. The fire needs the oxygen to sustain itself and will take every atom it can get.

Terrified residents hear the jerrycans explode, the cars go up, the gas bottles vent with ear-piercing screams. Above it all is the roar, that blood-curdling, heart-stopping *whomp* of the fire itself.

'What the hell is that noise?' somebody screams. In part, it's the thrashing of wind-whipped branches and leaves, but it's mainly trillions of individual plant cells crackling as they explode.

Only somebody who has lived through that dread-filled noise can begin to imagine what it's like. It's still kilometres away, but the air shakes and the trees shiver—the ground begins to vibrate. Cockroaches and ants scuttle for cover, disappear into cracks in the ground. Then it rips into your ear drums, your brain, into the depths of your being.

Soon the rooms fill up with smoke, the alarms go nuts, the kids and the dogs go mad, the walls bubble, the ceilings glow, red ribbons run along the cross beams, burst into open flame. You creep, crab-like, to the door and by christ it's still too hot out there and you wonder when it will be safe to go outside.

The realisation falls on you like a cold hand, the one cold thing in this black hell: it never will be safe outside, not for you. Your life—the regrets, the joys, the unfinished business, the chances half taken, the words of love unspoken, the precious pitter-patter of irrelevance—cavalcades through your head.

Time storms and the blood stands still as you huddle under the blanket and gaze at each other in disbelief. You watch their faces twist, their eyelids grip, their foreheads' red reflected pain, you stroke their hair, you tell them it'll be all right. And it will be. You kiss their devastated lips and pray that it will be quick

FIRE: AN ILLUMINATED HISTORY

Unholy Trinity

There are cultures in recorded history—the Ainu of Japan, the Slavs of Central Europe—who thought of fire as if it were a living being. In the Trobriand Islands, fire is born of a woman. In the Arrernte dreaming there is a myth with an even stronger resonance of the link between fire and life: first fire emerges from the genitals of a butchered male kangaroo. In the Vedic period of ancient India, the fire in the hearth was regarded as a witness, an eternal eye gazing out upon the comings and goings of the household, a source of memory and oracle. For the people of those worlds, fire was life.

Science would tell us that they weren't far off the mark: if not actually living, fire is inextricably bound to life. The valence between the two is as critical as the gravity that holds the moon in place.

*

For its first billion years, Earth was a thin-skinned rocky body carving a lonely path through space, one of a number of satellites orbiting a minor star on an arm of a spiralling galaxy. There was no fire.

The planet was enveloped in a mixture of gases—nitrogen, oxygen, argon and others—whose proportions waxed and waned according to the convulsions of its molten interior. In the Carboniferous and Permian ages, the oxygen component climbed as high as 35 percent. It wasn't until 150 million years ago that it stabilised to its present 21 percent. The reason for this change was the appearance of another phenomenon unknown anywhere but here: life.

The plants came first. Around 3.5 billion years ago, photosynthesising prokaryotes—a type of blue-green algae—appeared. Not a particularly auspicious beginning: they were so primitive they didn't even have a cell nucleus. But it could be argued that they are still, at least in chronological terms, the most successful species. They hung around for a long time and evolved, eventually, into *Homo sapiens*.

The key to their influence was the fact that they absorbed carbon dioxide and pumped out oxygen. Initially they poured it into the surrounding ocean (creating, incidentally, the iron ore that drives today's economy) and then into the atmosphere.

Aerobic photosynthesis appeared 1.3 billion years ago, aerobic respiration some 700 million years later. It wasn't until as recently as 400 million years ago that the conditions which would allow sustained burning coalesced.

Like the Church, fire has its own holy trinity: in fire's case, the elements are oxygen, fuel and ignition. The latter had always been there, but only in fits and starts, flashes and flares—the odd spark from a tumbling rock or burst of lava, a crack of lightning. But with the emergence of life and its by-products—oxygen in the atmosphere, fuel in the form of combustible biomass—the triangle was complete. The chemical reaction that we call fire became possible.

For we now know that fire is not a living being; it is not even matter. It is a manifestation of matter changing form, a chemical reaction between atmospheric oxygen and a fuel that has reached ignition temperature. (The ignition point will vary according to the material. Wood, for example, ignites at around 300 to 500 degrees Celsius, hay at 260 degrees.)

The first stage of the process is known as pyrolysis, which is the thermochemical decomposition of a fuel by the application of heat. Look at a sheet of paper thrown onto a camp fire: that initial crumple and twist, that creeping discoloration, is pyrolysis. Paper is basically cellulose, and the vegetation at the heart of the bushfire is composed primarily of cellulose too. As heat is applied, the material undergoes a change in its chemistry. The bonds that hold the cellulose molecules together are torn apart and gases are released. At around 260 degrees Celsius these gases combine with the oxygen in the air and give off heat and light. So pyrolysis releases gas from the fuel, and it is the combustion of these gases, rather than of the fuel itself, that produces visible incandescence, the eruption of heat and light we call flame.

Very quickly, in geological terms, after fire became possible it became more than that. It became essential. Fire was an informing principle for the evolution of the terrestrial biota. Sparked by lightning, it ranged across the continents, seeking out fuel, synthesising ecologies of every description.

Organisms adapted to this new regime or they perished. Their adaptive techniques varied. Some developed protective traits: banksias had succulent leaves to protect their reproductive organs, grasses stored the bulk of their biomass underground. Others—spinifex for example—used fire almost as an instrument of war, purging rival species, colonising, conquering.

Fire enriched, quickened, transformed, recycled. But it was still a random event. The biosphere had no means of deliberate ignition, no means of controlling that essential first spark. Until the emergence of one more fire species.

Somewhere on the plains of southern Africa, maybe half a million years ago, a member of the Hominidae family, *Homo erectus,* figured out how to light a fire.

From that moment, the cycle was complete; the fire triangle became organic. The biosphere had achieved mastery of the process: it organised spark as it did oxygen and fuel.

*

Just as humans made whole the cycle of fire, so did fire transform humans. There is a cave at Swartkrans in South Africa that dramatically illustrates this. Among the layers of fossil evidence uncovered there, three are of particular significance. In the first, the bones are those of hominids, scattered and torn so as to suggest they were eaten by predators. Then there is a layer of charcoal. In the final stratum, the bones are those of antelopes and warthogs, and they are burnt: cooked by the hominids. The tables have turned. Somewhere in the intervening period, around the time of that second, charcoal, layer our ancestors learned to control fire, and it had a transformative effect upon their relationship with their environment. It gave us a primacy from which we have never retreated.

Fire formed the world of early humans. It was used for every aspect of daily and nightly life. The hunt was a fire activity, from the rousing and herding of prey to the cooking of the catch. Fire stimulated the plants for which the first people foraged. It provided warmth and light, protection from the jostling spirits of the night, shelter from mosquitoes and snakes. Fire was at the heart of every technology, from the sharpening of spears to the preparation of ochre and wax, from pottery to primitive metallurgy. As Prometheus exclaimed, in giving fire to humanity he had 'invented all the arts of man'.

The changed diet brought with it other effects, a feedback loop that enhanced humanity's position in a fiercely competitive world. Palaeontologists speculate that cooking, for example, made possible a change in dentition and released the skull from having to brace the enormous muscle required to chew uncooked foods, thus allowing the skull to swell and the brain along with it.

Fire was power. It unleashed the magic in a lump of wood, a tuft of grass. Inevitably, it entered the inchoate religious life: as myths from India to the Tanami attest, the golden chain that linked humankind to the gods was a fuse.

With this new firepower, humans spread across the world. Wherever they went, our ancestors brought fire, expanding upon the pyric patterns already inherent in the land.

In Stephen Pyne's words:

> Fire and humanity pushed and pulled each other around the globe. They advanced together—spreading like flaming fronts, spotting into favourable sites, probing into marches, flaring amid thickets, smouldering amid peat, crackling through scrub, all as the fuels of environmental opportunity and the climate of culture allowed.

Sometime in the Holocene period—50,000 or 60,000 years ago—that global migration reached the northern shores of the continent that would come to be called Australia. And if early humans were fire creatures, the continent they had come across was their spiritual home. There was nowhere on Earth more primed, dried and ready to burn than the Great Southern Land.

Flame Trees

Its beginnings were hardly auspicious.

Thirty million years ago, as the continent was rafting towards the equator, warming up and drying out, a scraggly, hard-leafed, sun-loving weed made its first appearance in a clearing on the edge of the rainforest.

French botanist Charles Louis L'Héritier de Brutelle would eventually give it the name 'eucalypt'. The word comes from the Greek—ευ (*eu*), meaning 'well', and καλυπτος (*kalyptos*), meaning 'covered', a reference to the plant's bud structure: there is initially a covering on the calyx that conceals the flower.

Ever the most opportunistic of colonisers, the eucalypt flourished in the changing environment. It was able to thrive just about anywhere—in the alps, the desert, on coastal strips or river margins, in rich and poor soil alike—and came to dominate the continent of its birth in a way that no genus does any other continent. At the time of Captain Cook's arrival in 1770, it accounted for some 70 percent of the Australian flora.

Its partner in that colonisation, the secret of its success, was fire. What water is to the rainforest, fire is to the sclerophyll. In the moist conditions of a rainforest, leaf litter and debris decompose. When the climate is dry and the soil poor, it is fire that carries out the essential task of recycling litter. The eucalypt captures nutrients released by fire and stores them for later use. It takes advantage of fire to purge hostile microbes from its vicinity, to encourage better percolation of ground water and to open up areas to sunlight, thus allowing its seedlings to choke out less sun-tolerant rivals. Fire mobilises vital nutrients such as molybdenum, evaporates leachates in the litter.

Eucalypts constantly shed material—leaves, bark, branchwood—that is both nutrient and fuel. The leaves are ready to burn at every stage of their existence. They burn when they are green because of their oil. They burn when they are brown and fallen because of their rich mineral content. You could even say they burn in the air: the distinctive blue haze that shimmers over the Australian bush on summer days is caused by vaporising eucalypt oil, and it is extremely volatile. Those who have the misfortune to witness a bushfire up close often describe the sky as being on fire, fraught with flares and fireballs, flaming whirlwinds. What they are describing is clouds of eucalypt vapour released by the heat, whipped by the wind, igniting.

In recent years there has been a significant decline in the health of the temperate eucalypt forest. Most observers automatically assumed that the drought was responsible, but a major study now suggests that a significant factor in that decline has been the reduction of burning.

The displacement of traditional burning has meant a thickening of the understorey vegetation—tea-tree, acacia, she-oak—which has brought about a revolution in the arrangement of the forest, with changes to light intensity, ground temperature, litter accumulation and soil processing. It also leads to an accumulation of nitrogen, the binding up of nutrients such as phosphorous and copper and a reduction in the mycorrhizal fungi essential for the uptake of water.

The nutrient and water stress means that the eucalypt becomes vulnerable to insect attack and disease. And when fire does come, it can be so intense that it will actually kill the genus it once nourished, or at least weaken it in favour of tea-tree and acacia. The high-intensity fire will also be much more devastating for the wildlife that makes its home in the eucalypt forest.

'There are hundreds of thousands of hectares of forest in decline throughout Australia because of the inappropriate use of fire,' comments botanist Neil Davidson.

In essence, without fire the eucalypt cannot thrive. Fire is not only useful to the genus among which we build our homes, it is essential to it.

There was a long period before the eucalypt came to dominate the continent during which it carried on a kind of protracted guerrilla warfare with the rainforest. As recently as 80,000 years ago, the scleromorphs and the ancient gymnosperms were evenly balanced. But the sclerophyll eventually won out, and its final victory came some 38,000 years ago—a date that roughly coincides with the arrival of humans. The two events were clearly connected.

A Salamander Race

When John Stokes, an English naval officer who was with Darwin on the *Beagle*, stepped ashore in Van Diemen's Land in 1841, his most memorable impression of the indigenous inhabitants was of their relationship with fire. He has left a vivid description of a hunting party in which he captures the shouts and the smoke, the beating with green boughs, the scuttling wallabies:

> The dexterity with which they manage so proverbially a dangerous agent as fire is indeed astonishing...The whole scene is a most animated one, and the eager savage, every muscle in action and every faculty called forth, then appears to the utmost advantage, and is indeed almost another being.

Australia had always burned, but with the arrival of its first humans, the burning intensified. Many historians of the Australian environment argue that Aboriginal people did more than just enter the new environment, they manufactured it. The question is hotly debated: did Aboriginal people actually transform the land with fire, or did their arrival simply coincide with climate changes that increased its volatility?

What is not in doubt is that the fire stick was the most important implement in the Aboriginal toolkit. With it they transformed the country: they opened forests, encouraged grasslands, cleared trails. Wherever they went those first inhabitants of the land carried fire sticks: they used them for hunting and cooking, for medicine, warmth and signalling, for working their weapons, repelling pests. Anthropologist Rhys Jones estimates that a single family grouping of perhaps thirty people would be responsible for some five thousand fires a year.

Fire hallowed every stage of the Aboriginal existence, from the ritual smoking of the newborn baby to the lighting of the funeral pyre from which the dead were propelled into the cycle of rebirth. Initiates ran a gauntlet of fire, and the association of flame with entry into the adult world would have remained with the boy for life. The dreamings were replete with images and tales of fire. The people sang of its origins as a gift from the ancestral beings and passed on to their youth admonitory tales about respecting its power and maintaining its vitality.

For tens of millennia, Aboriginal people behaved thus: refining, polishing, utilising the pyric patterns inherent in the land. The cornerstone of their firecraft was their alliance with the eucalypt, an alliance so powerful that it volatilised much of the country, exaggerating its flammability.

That most erudite of explorers, Ernest Giles, was to report: 'The natives were about, burning, burning, burning; one would think they were of the fabled salamander race, and lived on fire instead of water.'

Non-indigenous Australia knows something of this, but does not fully understand it. There is a perception that Aboriginal people burned just for the sake of it, that their torches were random and indiscriminate. It's a view that has profound implications for the present: 'The blackfellers burned that bush; we need to as well.'

But Aboriginal burning, whether to light a campfire or a landscape, was an extraordinarily complex procedure. It was far from indiscriminate and never random. The practice would have varied immensely, regulated by a web of dreamings that was a reflection of the accumulated knowledge for each locality. The burn was limited, persistent, a mosaic, and scrupulously planned.

Listen to an elder from Arnhem Land describing his people's preparations for a burn:

> ...there is one kind of burning which is men's business alone—and it is dangerous work. This is the fire drive mainly for macropods (the larger ridge-dwelling species like *kalkberd, djukerre, kandakidj, karndayh*) rather than the agile wallabies (*kornobolo*) which favour monsoon jungle and thicker forest.

> When the most senior landowner from the area where the fire drive (*kunj ken manwurrk*—fire for kangaroo) is to be held sees that the time is getting close, he will talk with his senior *djunkay*. They sit down and discuss how the *djunkay* will organise the drive—where it will be held, when it will be held (expressed by reference to floral seasonal indicators and moon phases) and who will be invited.

The decision to put spark to fuel was based upon an intricate knowledge of the country and its cycles, a knowledge acquired and refined over tens of thousands of years. They knew the intricacies of the weather, which plants needed fire, which didn't. The questions of when and where to burn, of who was to be involved and how the vegetation would respond, were matters of serious consideration. Those who transgressed—whose fires, for instance, roared into somebody else's country, or flared at the wrong time—were likely to be severely punished.

Rhys Jones comments on the practice of the Gidgingali people of the Northern Territory:

> People used their fires accurately, aiming them into a natural break such as an old fire scar or a swamp, timing the fire so that the predictable wind changes later in the day would blow them back onto their own track, or so that evening dew would dampen them down.

These people were, in the phrase coined by Jones, 'firestick farmers'. Their farming was locally based, firmly controlled, carefully crafted towards the requirements of the biota. Areas that supported food plants such as the yam daisy or the hyacinth orchid would have been burnt with precision, to encourage their growth, as would the grassy woodlands that attracted grazing animals with their sweet green blades.

Fire was viewed as an element of the natural world, one that was there to be lived with, accommodated, exploited.

The disastrous megafire was not unknown. A. P. Elkin describes a myth of the Ularaga people of Lake Eyre that features a figure named Yigaura, responsible for dangerous fires that can travel underground and spring up far ahead; it sounds very much like spot fires whipped by the wind to fall kilometres ahead of a crowning ridgetop fire.

But deliberate, broad-scale burning of the type we see now, the burning of thousands of hectares to protect settled communities, would not only have been unnecessary. It would have been unthinkable.

Burn Everything about Us

Around two hundred years ago a new coloniser arrived, one who preferred his landscapes tamed and his combustion in an industrialised form. The British found the vegetation monotonous, the topography impenetrable and the animals bizarre. The platypus was an essay in contradiction, the marsupials bounded about on two legs, the dogs didn't bark. And the fires had a ferocity that their own green land had never known.

The interlopers quickly learned its potency. In one early encounter, when Cook's *Endeavour* was beached for repairs, the gentleman naturalist Joseph Banks paused to admire the deftness and facility with which Aboriginal people worked their fire—and then found himself running for his life as the resulting inferno drove him and his men back to the boats.

But indigenous fire, for all its subtlety and tradition, stood no chance before the brute strength of European firepower. In the blink of an eye, it seemed, the newcomers were swarming all over the continent, softening it up for their animals and plants, hefting axes, pushing ploughs—and dropping matches. Banks' reaction to that first attack was a portent: the next time they made land, he determined, they would 'burn everything about us before we begin'.

Those who came after him took up that advice with an enthusiasm born, perhaps, of some primordial memory of the African plains. They didn't burn just to defend themselves, they burned to attack. In what they quickly recognised as a primed and volatile environment, fire became an offensive weapon not just against the original inhabitants, but against the land itself.

They burned freely, those first settlers: they burned to clear the land of its pestilential scrub and towering trees, to uncover its mineral wealth, to foster the succulent 'green pick' for which their cattle tongued. Sometimes they burned just to relieve the boredom. For many a lonely stockman or shepherd, the vision of all that wild energy emerging from his fingers to devour mountains must have been a welcome relief from the extraordinary monotony of existence. One can imagine a mob of rum-stoked wild colonial boys galloping about in their cabbage tree hats and laughing with wild delight as the fire flickered in their eyes.

The shifting frontier between black and white Australia was aglow with the blaze of innumerable fires, large and small, measured and wild. Fire scientist Phil Zylstra, looking at the evidence of burning in the Alpine area through dendrochronology—the science of examining rings on trees to study events in the tree's history—concludes: 'All fire regimes increase dramatically in frequency following European occupation.'

He suggests that fire frequency in the high country during the early European years was five to seven times greater than it had been during the period of Aboriginal management. Furthermore, he adds, 'European settlers missed entirely the subtlety of indigenous fire practices.' Seeing the native species as messy, ugly and obstructive, 'they interpreted indigenous fire management as nothing more than Aboriginal attempts to get rid of all the rubbish and make the landscape look the way it was supposed to.'

This attitude to the land manifested itself in two almost contradictory ways. When settlers first moved into an area, they burned hard and they burned often. The burn-off was their most significant technique for clearing land. As Robert Clode, a senior inspector with the Forest Commission, commented to the Royal Commission into the disastrous Victorian fires of 1939: 'We have inherited a point of view from our ancestors. They had to clear the land and they regarded every tree as an enemy. Unfortunately, we still have many people who feel that way.'

The pioneers fired whole mountains, river valleys, scrubby plains, vast tracts of what they regarded as wilderness. But then, as settlement developed and population grew more dense, they were forced to change tack: they now tried to eradicate fire, particularly in the places they valued most—close to homesteads, trails or towns, or on the prime pasture they wanted for their cattle.

Neither approach worked. Each brought disruptive new elements into an ecology of which fire was an informing principle. Each brought its own dangers. Stephen Pyne writes of the pastoralists:

> In some regimes they changed the timing of fire; in some they introduced fire where it had previously not existed; in others, by consuming the fine fuels, they denied routine fire. Everywhere, during their initial passage, they inadvertently promoted larger, more unpredictable bushfires.

Frequent and indiscriminate burning led to the rampant growth of volatile pyrogenic species—bracken, sedges—which made future fire more likely. An account by forester D. M. Thompson illustrates the conundrum soon faced by graziers in Victoria's Cann Valley:

> Only constant burning kept the fuel hazards sufficiently under check to allow settlement. But more fire only encouraged the flammable scrub that served as fuel, which demanded control by more fire…Their 'extensive use of fire'…was thus a double-edged sword. It made the valley habitable, yet it compelled still more fire, which stimulated flammable fuels, which made it more likely that, on some gusty day, a fire would inevitably escape.

One old timer put it more colloquially:

> Sixty, seventy years ago I shepherded a thousand sheep out there. I could let 'em all feed out and I could stand in one place and watch the whole flock. Only twenty years ago I could walk out there and shoot a kangaroo a hundred yards off, easy. Now if I walked in there twenty yards and didn't watch where I was going I'd bloody get lost.

So rampant pyromania ultimately increased the danger to the fledgling communities. But the attempt to banish fire altogether led to the build-up of fuel which, when the big one came—and come it must—would explode with devastating intensity.

The high-intensity fire will also have a horrific effect upon the native fauna. 'Frequent low-intensity burns create a mosaic that fosters heterogeneity and biodiversity—it could leave gullies for animals to hide in, or boundaries across which animals can forage,' says Neil Davidson. 'The wildfire, on the other hand, burns everything.'

Legends of Destruction

The pages of Australian history are so scorched with the legends of the fires that have roared through them that we are running out of days for which to name them: Black Thursday, Red Tuesday, Black Tuesday, Black Friday, Ash Wednesday.

The legend of Black Thursday—February 6, 1851—is encapsulated in a narrative painting of the same name by William Strutt, a massive work of art that has stopped in their tracks generations of visitors to the State Library of Victoria. The story it tells is one of panic and flight, of an immigrant people shocked by the savagery of their new country: the rolling eyes of man and beast, the babes in arms, the scattered bones, the circling birds.

A quarter of the Colony of Victoria (it had yet to become a state) was incinerated that day: five million hectares. Ships thirty-two kilometres out to sea were subject to ember attack, and even in faraway Tasmania the skies turned the colour of polished brass. Despite the widespread devastation, however, only twelve people are known to have died. But then, whites had only really arrived sixteen years earlier and settlement was thinly scattered. The gold rush kicked off a few months later and by 1860 Melbourne's population was twenty times larger. Had the fire come after that, the casualty figures would undoubtedly have been far higher.

Fire was a constant threat to the growing prosperity of rural Australia but by 1939 the country had settled into a kind of she'll-be-right apathy, its eyes more fixed on the storm clouds gathering over Europe than the pyrocumulus ones building in its own backyard. Australians were shaken out of that complacency by the sudden ferocity of Black Friday. That holocaust claimed seventy-one lives, burned close to two million hectares, destroyed timber mills, farms, entire towns.

Ash Wednesday—February 16, 1983—is remembered for the monstrous cloud of dust five hundred kilometres wide and a hundred deep that blanketed Melbourne the week before. As is always the case, it was the weather that built the stage upon which the tragedy was played out and that dust storm told the tale eloquently: years of drought, desert winds, minimal humidity.

That fire is still sufficiently close in memory for us to know that the bald statistics—75 deaths, 2400 homes destroyed, more than 350,000 hectares of forest and farmland burnt, 350,000 head of livestock killed—draw but a very thin veil over a deep trough of human misery. We know that a trauma of this dimension will inflict substantial levels of depression, grief and anxiety upon the affected communities. Substance abuse will run rampant, post-traumatic stress disorder (much of it among the emergency services personnel charged with fighting the fire) will affect more than one in ten. Young people are particularly vulnerable to long-term psychiatric difficulties. One study showed that a third of children affected by Ash Wednesday remained preoccupied with fire for years after the event.

Two other fires, Hobart in 1967 and Canberra in 2003, were ominous pointers to the future. They showed that the so-called 'bush' fire can rampage far beyond the bush. The Hobart fire was the first major bushfire to hit a capital city, roaring to within two kilometres of the CBD, incinerating entire suburbs and claiming sixty-two lives. Canberra, though less deadly, was even more significant: a fiery dagger aimed at the heart of the nation. The most significant single site destroyed was the Mount Stromlo Observatory, symbolic, perhaps, of a nation more ready to turn its gaze to the skies than to its immediate surrounds.

Fire scientist Phil Cheney, who studied both fires, noted a significant difference between them. Hobart was terrible, but it could have been worse. In 1962, the residents of Hobart favoured neat green lawns and exotic plants that tended to slow the fire down. By the time Canberra burned, landscape fashions had changed: the transplanted English garden had been replaced by the volatile native and the fire carried much further.

*

Despite this constant threat of attack, our collective memory is short and the atavistic lure of the bush strong. More and more of us are taking the gamble and moving out into the flame zone. Tree-changers are relocating onto the peri-urban fringe, investing their all in flammable dwellings on north-facing ridges or in green glades in the midst of towering forests. Even sea-changers often unwittingly find themselves in areas vulnerable to bushfire: on Ash Wednesday the communities along the Great Ocean Road were among the hard-est hit.

The demographics are startling. One study of three major Australian bushfires found that all houses within seven hundred metres of bushland were in danger and that the highest risk was for those within fifty metres. Four percent of the residents of our capital cities (excluding Darwin) live within that highest-risk area. Twenty percent are within seven hundred metres—that's more than 1.5 million households in the capital cities alone. If rural towns are taken into consideration, that amounts to some two million house-holds—around four million people—living within striking distance of what their great-grandparents called the Red Steer.

The predictive map drawn up by Kevin Tolhurst and his team on Black Saturday indicated, as we have seen, that the inferno was poised to descend upon the heavily populated outer suburbs: Greensborough, Eltham, Warrandyte.

Next time there may not be a wind change to save them.

THE SCHOOL

It is early evening when Roger Wood, Cameron Caine and the rest of the crowd gathered at Kinglake West CFA hear that fearful, thousand-engine roar. The wind grows wild, the trees swivel on their roots. A rain of embers begins to batter the building. Firebrands whirl through the air, set off spot fires. People inside the shed glance at each other, tension in their eyes. Mothers hold their children close, whisper and sing to them.

Outside the firefighters do their best to quell their own anxieties. They put on masks and pull up coat collars, clutch their hoses and wonder whether they'll have the strength to see this through.

One of their own tankers has disappeared into the inferno. For hours now, it's been ominously silent. Will those at the shed fare any better?

Members of the public take on leadership roles: helping old people, settling kids, swatting at embers.

The two policemen stare into that nightmare to the south-west the way men and women in authority have stared into out-of-control flame down the centuries. Somewhere inside them a thin voice insists, in the midst of all this chaos, that they have a function to carry out. It may achieve sweet FA, it might be pissing into the volcano—but it's the reason they're wearing the uniform.

They're astonished to see another police car appear out of the smoke: a Traffic Management Unit vehicle from Epping. To this day, Wood has no idea how they got there; he assumes they came in off the Melba Highway before the town was cut off. He's glad to see them. He feels his own sense of isolation diminish.

The four men shake hands.

'You the blokes from Kinglake?'

'Yep.'

'Everybody in Melbourne thinks you're dead.'

'Just about were, mate, both of us.'

The new arrivals, Alex Barron and John Liddell, are senior constables from Epping. They will work alongside Wood and Caine for much of the night.

From the vantage point of the CFA compound, they can see flames whipping along the hills and valleys around them. At least the men themselves feel relatively safe here, under the defensive perimeter flung up by the firefighters. Then John Grover comes over and shows them a pager message he's just received.

There are twenty people, including a large number of children, trapped in the recreation room at the Kinglake West Primary School.

'Where's that?' ask the Epping blokes warily.

Wood and Cam exchange a glance then nod at the school. Just two hundred metres away, but what a two hundred metres: the building is directly in the fire's path, across the oval. The fire has already got as far as the trees behind the school, is impacting on the buildings. Whoever is in there is in trouble.

Cameron's boys attend that school. Chances are he knows the kids inside.

'Let's go,' says Wood, and they set off running.

The four men find themselves charging through a barrage of flying debris and the deceptively named 'embers', battered by a fusillade of burning sticks and debris that intensifies as they come closer to its source. They're inhaling painful amounts of smoke, can feel the heat radiating from the blazing bush.

They sprint across the oval, clear the fence, come to the school. There's some sort of construction work going on and the front is sealed off by a cyclone-wire fence two and a half metres high, so they dash round the back. Closer to the fire, but there's no choice. They make it to the rear entrance. Cam knows where the rec room is; they find it empty.

They split up, make a frantic search of the grounds and buildings, boots crashing down empty corridors. Nobody there at all. Somebody's got their wires crossed. There are three schools between Kinglake and Kinglake West; must be one of the others. Which is a worry in itself.

Time to be somewhere else. They make to retrace their steps, but now the pine plantation alongside the school has ignited and is burning ferociously: they're trapped. They crouch in the shelter of the rec room, look around, desperate to be out of there. The fire spits and surges.

'Run for it!' yells Cam.

Roger Wood finds himself moving at a speed he hasn't managed for twenty years. His heart is going like a jackhammer. The adrenaline rush: it does weird things to your head. Time bends. Light spins. It sends a blast of energy into your brain, gives you powers you never knew you had.

Speaking months later, he still can't work out how he did it and doubts he could do it again, but he finds himself flying over that two-metre fence in a single leap and crash-landing on his back.

The coppers pick themselves up out of the hot red dirt and sprint for the CFA shed, the wind from the fire driving them, missiles crashing into their backs.

They make it to the shed but there's no time to rest: the grass had been igniting as they dashed across the oval, spreading under the cars crammed together there. If one goes up, others will follow. They alert the CFA people, who tackle the fire while the policemen organise another impromptu vehicle evacuation.

They find out later the pager message they'd received was wrong, and that the school in question was Middle Kinglake, seven kilometres down the road.

*

In the Kinglake West CFA shed the atmosphere grows more and more stressful. Those sheltered inside gaze anxiously at the ceiling, worried that any one of the embers they can hear crashing into the building could take hold. The shed is brutally buffeted by the wind.

The CFA volunteers remain outside. They're very aware that whatever concern they show will be magnified in the eyes of those under their protection, and that could spark alarm. As the fire approaches they lay down A-class foam, pounce on the spot fires and brace themselves for the onslaught.

They don't have long to wait.

'The wind generated by the fire buffeting the building is what shook us most,' says Karyn Norbury. 'I was on a hose out back. Propped myself between the tank and the building—leaned against the shed and thought, I'll be okay here. But the fire was so strong it blew me over, actually knocked me off my feet.'

Norbury watches in alarm as it storms down the Whittlesea–Kinglake Road, the heavily vegetated roadside reserve 'acting like a wick'.

But John Grover has made the correct decision in keeping the crowd there: an orchard and paddock below the station split the fire front, diminish its ferocity. A house across the road catches fire. This is something the firefighters hate to see: asset protection is an important part of their responsibility. But protecting lives is their *raison d'être*, and they can't leave the hundreds of refugees in the shed to fend for themselves. They watch the house burn.

Norbury's fears intensify when the fire sweeps around them and carries on into the heart of Kinglake West. Her husband Dave and their two daughters are there at the family stud farm. Nothing she can do about them right now: she has other responsibilities, and can only pray that their resourcefulness and the defences they've installed—pumps, a generator, their own water tanker—will see her family through.

As the roar of the first wave dies down, there's a slight easing of the tension. But only slight: they're all worried about unaccounted-for family and friends. Often, as the final casualty figures were to attest, families were split up as the women and kids made a run for it while the men stayed behind to defend the family home.

There is some contact with the outside world, but telecommunication is hit and miss. Roger Wood still can't get through to his own family. Others do succeed, but much of what they hear is bad. Rumours fly through the room like sparks through volatile gas: eighteen kilometres down the road, Kinglake is gone: the town centre wiped out, the hotel, shops and public buildings all destroyed.

Local musician Ross Buchanan takes a call, and the policemen notice Cam's wife, Laura, suddenly move to embrace him. The call was from his wife, Bec, and the horror of the message stuns them all: two of Ross's children, Neeve and Mackenzie—Macca—are dead. They were at their grandparents' house, only three hundred metres from the town centre. Ross sent them there because it was safer, while he stayed behind to defend the family home in the far more dangerous location of National Park Road.

Cameron, a good friend, can only hug him. There'll be a time for tears and consolation, but for the police officers, it isn't now.

People are dying in the middle of Kinglake?

The radio and phones are jammed with pleas for help but there's precious little information. From what they can gather, the main front has passed. Now, as coppers, they need to get out into the community, assess the damage, coordinate the response.

They make an initial sortie after a call comes in from Extons Road, closer towards Kinglake, where a family is trapped, fighting for their lives, their house ablaze. They move out onto the main road and are stunned by the devastation that greets them. Night has fallen and the mountain is ablaze.

Everywhere they look—east, west, farmland, bush, houses and stores, the distant hills—they see destruction. Nothing, it seems, has been spared.

Progress is hopeless for two police vehicles without water or chainsaws: there are trees burning all over the road, power lines snaking out from fallen poles, frantic animals on the loose, others burnt and bloated in the paddocks. Incinerated vehicles of every description. Chaos.

They need help. They turn around, make their way back to the fire station.

As they enter the building the captain comes over and hands them the satellite phone.

'Roger. It's Carole.' Carole Wilson, from the CFA in Kinglake.

'Carole. Glad to hear you're still alive. What's it like in there?'

'It's a disaster. Most of the town's gone.'

'Gone?'

'Destroyed.' Wood takes a sharp breath. It sounds worse than he'd feared.

'We need help,' says Carole. 'We've got hundreds of people here—some burnt, critically injured. There's nobody here, Roger—no emergency services, no ambulances, doctors. Nothing. Our trucks are all stuck down the mountain.'

Wood glances around him. The scene Carole has described sounds like the one in front of him, but worse. At least they have no critically injured at Kinglake West—not yet, anyway. What's going on in the surrounding community is too awful to imagine.

'I've been onto Whittlesea,' says Carole. 'We're begging for help, but they're refusing to let anybody up the mountain. There's teams down there, ready to go, but they're not allowed up. Too dangerous. Roads blocked. Trees still coming down.'

Wood looks around the room and catches Cameron's eye.

'We'll get to you, Carole,' he says. 'Not quite sure how but we will. Me and Cam. Just hold on, do the best you can.'

'There's people gonna die here, Rodge.'

He replaces the phone, turns to John Grover. 'We need to organise a strike team.'

*

Kinglake West Tanker Two finally limps back into its home station from the ordeal in Coombs Road some time after 8 pm, more than four hours after they set out. Frank Allan and his crew are exhausted, thirsty, badly smoke affected, worried about their own homes and families. At least one member of the crew, Phil Betteley, finds out that his family home is gone. They wouldn't mind a break. Given the scenes of chaos and despair that greet them, they don't reckon they'll get one any time soon.

They're right.

John Grover goes over to the truck. He knows Frank is handy with a chainsaw. There's a group being formed to cut its way through to Kinglake, he says: he asks Frank to go along and do the grunt work.

FIREFIGHT IN KINGLAKE

While those at the CFA station in Kinglake West are undergoing their trial by fire, those in Kinglake itself are enduring a situation that is, if anything, worse.

When the fire front comes close, Carole Wilson slams the door and calls out a warning to the people inside. The crowd outside huddle under their blankets or in their cars, stare at the sky, clutch their children. The more active among them swat at the spot fires with whatever comes to hand: blankets, coats, bottles of water.

Everything goes completely black. Some begin to panic. More and more of them seek refuge in the shed; Carole estimates there are around three hundred in there at the fire's height.

They can trace the fire's approach by the chain of explosions advancing towards them: gas bottles, cars, buildings, one after another, dozens, hundreds of them. The windows rattle, the wind goes mad, the rain of embers hammering through the air grows thick and fires begin to break out round the shed. Wherever they spring up, one of the CFA scratch teams rushes to extinguish them. So dark and chaotic is the atmosphere, neither team knows of the other's existence until they swap stories weeks later.

'I kept seeing people walking in out of the smoke,' says Di MacLeod. 'They were injured. In shock. It was like a war movie.'

Her husband Jim is on duty at the side door, letting people scamper inside then slamming it shut: the less smoke in there, the better their chances.

A large eucalyptus ten feet behind the station catches fire; Di, a short woman, is grateful for Wayne McDonald-Price's longer reach: they hit it with the full force of the hose and extinguish it, but keep an eye on it all night. If the tree goes up, it could well take the shed and its occupants with it.

The service station across the road erupts with an explosion that rattles walls and eardrums, unleashes two mighty jets of flame twenty metres into the air. A car in the main street blows up. The pizza parlour cooks. There's a four-wheel-drive parked in front of the police station with a trailer load of trail bikes attached. The whole lot ignites.

Di didn't know either of her companions before this moment, but she's full of praise for their courage in sticking to the dangerous task. She hears Luke Gaskett roaring at the shed as he dashes from one outbreak to the next: 'You will not go up! My family's in there!'

When it is totally black and a hot wind is streaming off the fire directly into their faces, he taps her on the shoulder and yells, 'At what point do we go inside?'

She gives a wry smile. 'We don't.'

They see the block of shops across the drive catch fire, and Di is caught in a dilemma. She can't leave her charges in the shed unprotected, but nor does she want to see these businesses—which include the doctor's surgery—go up. If nothing else, the radiant heat they give off will threaten the people in the shed.

She makes a snap decision: they run out a line, manage to extinguish the fire. As they scuttle back to the shed, a kangaroo comes plodding by, looks up at her forlornly. She finds time to give it a quick, cooling shower. 'Good luck, feller,' she whispers. Looks around. 'To all of us.'

Another house starts to go up nearby. The owner comes running over. 'Me house is on fire. Can you help?'

It is a horrible feeling, but Di is forced to say no. The building is a just a little too far away; she's worried about running out of water and abandoning those under their care even for a few minutes.

She manages to put a quick call for help through to one of the Kinglake tankers and asks when they'll be back.

'Sorry darling,' comes the reply, 'we're entrapped ourselves right now.'

Entrapped? She realises even down in St Andrews they're fighting for their own survival, and feels a moment of despair. Is the whole world on fire?

The team on the other side of the shed are having problems of their own. There's just the two of them: Phil Petschel and Kelly Johnson, the veteran and the novice. Kelly's day takes a sharp turn for the worse when she looks at one of the pager messages—a house under direct attack—and realises it's her family home. With the rest of her family in it.

Phil has to talk her out of trying to get back and help them, convince her it's death out on the roads right now, even if they didn't have hundreds of people in their care. On that subject, Phil's main worry is the pub. If that goes up, it'll cause a conflagration that could spread to the crowd in front of it; if the fire got in among the cars, the chain of fires could be devastating.

Phil and Kelly spend their time scuttling between the two buildings dragging a sixty-metre length of canvas hose. Their immediate worry is whether the fire will spread to the CFA shed, with all those people inside, but they're alarmed when the motel units behind the pub catch fire. Members of the crowd do their best with buckets of water from the pub's water supply, a shaky enterprise at best.

The hose will always be their main weapon, but it's pump-fed: Phil's worst moment comes when he realises the fire-fighting pump needs fuel. This is bad. The pump is the only thing between them and catastrophe. Operating a hose in those conditions is normally a job for two experienced firefighters, but he has no choice other than to leave his young offsider behind, grit his teeth and feel his way back along the hose.

For Phil, this is the hairiest moment of the whole day. He's been in plenty of dangerous situations during his twenty-four years in the CFA, but he now finds himself groping his way through pitch darkness guided only by the hose in his hands, fire burning all round, the air rocked by fearsome explosions. Eventually he locates the pump, finds the petrol. Now he has to get it into the tank.

Phil Petschel is a quietly spoken, thoughtful man, self-effacing in the extreme; loath to think of himself as any sort of hero. But his actions during that incident seem to crystallise the courage shown by so many on Black Saturday.

'It was Kelly's first fire,' he explains, 'so I didn't dare turn the pump off, for her sake.' For a firefighter, there are few experiences more dangerous than suddenly running out of water at the fire front; water isn't just your weapon of attack, it's also your main defence. 'Plus there was a chance if I did turn it off, it wouldn't restart. When I got to the pump there was just the faint red glow of the muffler— because it was an ancient thing it was rattling and shaking—petrol splashing everywhere—hissing and popping on the red-hot metal. I poured the petrol, got most of it in, but there was a pretty good chance the whole lot'd go up.'

Phil is about as no-nonsense a fellow as you could imagine, and he isn't exaggerating. That night there are several people in the district whose last moments are spent struggling with their pumps.

Once the main front has passed, Kelly comes in to help the people inside the shed.

Phil stays outside for several more hours, dragging the hose around, keeping the spots under control. It's a job that normally involves two people. When Trish and Carole see Phil later, they're staggered by how exhausted he looks, a grimace etched onto his mouth, ash and sweat everywhere, tongue between the teeth.

'But he and Kelly saved the hotel,' comments Carole. 'Saved a lot of people too.'

KINGLAKE: INSIDE THE SHED

While a handful of people are fighting a small war for their own lives and everybody else's outside the Kinglake CFA, those inside the building are caught up in a struggle of a different kind. They know the crews outside are working hard, but have no way of knowing whether the battle is being won or lost.

For the most part they sit or lie there in silence, sipping from water bottles, staring at loved ones. Many of them are in shock.

They can't see much anyway—the doors are shut to keep the smoke and embers out. But they can hear, and what they hear is terrifying: the roar of the fire, the chain of explosions, the debris enfilading walls, crashing into the roof, echoing through the room. A groan ripples through the crowd when the service station goes up: an ear-shattering roar, the likes of which few of them have ever heard. The gas bottles stored in the back of the service station begin to explode and shoot into the air like rockets: there are more than forty of them, and most of them end up scattered around a nearby paddock. 'Thank god they were stored around the back,' commented the young man who'd been working at the store. 'Anywhere else, the debris could have landed in the crowd.'

There are some three hundred sweaty bodies in the shed and the atmosphere is tense; the temperature is in the fifties, the room is filled with biting blue smoke and animal noises. People have brought in their pets: not just dogs and cats, but lizards, snakes and birds, all confused and terrified. One fellow carries a bird on his shoulder all night.

Trish and Carole struggle to keep people calm, dealing with phones, radios and pagers that are going berserk. They take call after call from locals trapped by the fire, people in cars and houses, sheltering in dams and culverts as the world burns around them. The women do their best to reassure them that they'll get rescuers to them as soon as possible.

'The phone was going absolutely wild,' says Carole. 'You couldn't say, "I'm sorry I can't help you, because we haven't got a truck on the hill." You just say keep safe, do this, do that. You do what you can.' Fearing all the while—and the fears are later proved to be well-founded—that for many this call is the last they'll ever make.

They are particularly distressed by a string of calls from Wendy Duncan, one of their CFA colleagues and a good friend, who lives down on Bald Spur Road. She'd been about to board a fire truck herself when she heard that fire was threatening her house and asked her captain's permission to go back and defend it.

Wendy gives them a blow-by-blow account: the fire's onslaught, the flames engulfing her home, the windows blowing out, the roof caving in. She makes the last call lying on the side of the road, badly injured and struggling for breath, her lungs burnt. Assuming that she's dying, Wendy is using the last of her energies to warn them that the fire is worse than any of them could have imagined.

They promise they'll get help to her when they can, but are wrenched by the knowledge that they've no idea when that will be.

Inside the shed the CFA crew do what they can for the refugees: settle them down, find chairs and stools, attempt to get in touch with missing friends and family. They hand out water and smoke masks; when they run out of masks, they improvise with toilet paper. Trish and Carole neglect to keep masks for themselves, soon find their eyes and throats are giving them hell.

There are no windows in the main body of the shed, which is probably a good thing, since the ones in the office dance with an incandescent glow that gives those who look at them the feeling that they are being cooked. 'It was like the windows were painted red,' says Trish. 'I looked at everybody out there and thought, We're all going to die together.'

There is little or no hysteria, everybody attests to that. People in general remain calm. But there's an awful lot of anxiety. Nobody has any idea what's happening outside, many are wondering whether these desperate hours huddled in a tin shed on a blazing mountain are to be their last. In the bitter smoke, the heat and the tension, the very act of breathing becomes difficult. Several young girls faint. Older people are having trouble with heart palpitations and fretting about missing medication.

Linda Craske has only just joined the CFA, is yet to commence her training, but she is a nurse with seventeen years of experience, a qualification that is going to be of more use to the traumatised residents of Kinglake than anything else on this appalling night.

Initially, though, as people come to her with their problems, she feels panic rising in her own chest. I can't do this, she says to herself. It's been years since she worked in Emergency, she has little experience with burns, she hasn't done the CFA first aid course. She doesn't know where to start.

Hit by her own mini crisis, she doesn't want the crowd to see. There's only one place to be alone in this environment right now: the toilet. She goes in there for a moment or two, tries to breathe deeply. I can't cope with this. *What the hell am I going to do?*

Then she does something. She walks out into the main room and shouts: 'If there's anyone with first aid skills, I need your help!'

The initial response is far from encouraging: somebody who's done a St John's first aid course, a nurse who hasn't practised for years. But the word goes through the crowd, and soon there are some four or five nurses or first-aiders working to assist the growing number of casualties. Months later, nobody seems to quite know who they all were: a single mum from Watsons Road, a woman named Kylie who'd already lost her house. One turns out, most helpfully, to be a nurse from the burns unit at the Alfred Hospital. Another is an off-duty policewoman, Senior Constable Samantha Spencer. In this frantic setting, identities and introductions are unimportant: what is important is that they bring their individual skills to the catastrophe, instinctively melding into a team.

They clear out the back room, transform it into a sick bay. Initially the injuries are minor: cuts and burns, smoke inhalation, sore eyes, people who've fainted from the heat and stress. They do their best with what is at hand, dispensing band-aids and reassurance as the roar outside peaks and that evil incandescence lashes the windows.

None of them knows how long it lasts. 'Maybe an hour' seems to be the best guess anyone can make. They measure the fire's progress by how close the explosions sound. But at some stage it feels as if they grow more distant, the glow at the windows fades and the roar of the fire subsides. The sky grows lighter, the smoke thinner.

Is it over?

They decide it's safe enough to open the doors to give people some relief from the intense, smoke-filled atmosphere. They walk outside. They are staggered by what they see. The town is ablaze about them. Houses, shops, a kindergarten, the petrol station, the pizza shop, the SES compound, the animal hospital, the surrounding bush and paddocks: all burning. One of the cars that's exploded was full of caged birds; it makes a horrible sight.

Carole and Trish look at other, the relief seeping from every pore in their skin. They've survived, the worst of it is over. They hope.

And then the serious casualties begin to arrive.

IN EXILE

While their home station is under attack, the Kinglake firefighters are still kilometres away down the hill in St Andrews.

In Jacksons Road the crew of Kinglake Tanker One, under the command of Dave Hooper, have just refilled their water tanks from the supply brought in by Geoff Ninks when the southerly buster comes sweeping in and the fire explodes away to the north. In an instant the number of fires to be fought multiplies many times over; the entire region between St Andrews and Kinglake is ablaze.

St Andrews captain Helen Kenney is desperately calling for all the trucks she can get. The Kinglake crew respond, and she gives them one of the dozens of jobs screaming for attention: a house is on fire near Mullers Road, four kilometres to the north, two children reportedly inside.

Mullers Road is impassable due to fallen trees, but there are several houses burning in the vicinity. The first two are totally engulfed, beyond salvation. Whoever was in them is long gone—literally, they hope. They find an elderly man still fighting a hopeless battle to save his home while his wife shelters in the car. He's blistered, badly dehydrated, in shock. And it's too late to save the house. They persuade the woman to take him back to St Andrews and press on, going to the assistance of viticulturalist David Lance.

David and his wife Cathy have owned the Diamond Valley Vineyards for over thirty years, but David was on his own when the fire struck. Cathy, affected by a chest condition, had followed CFA advice and left early. David was in the winery tackling spot fires among the equipment when the main front passed over. Then:

'There was a huge gust from the south,' he says, 'and it swung around, incredibly strong and full of embers. It was like a blow torch, a horizontal blast of carbonised grass.'

Now his home is under attack and he has been frantic, spraying everything down as the outbreaks he extinguishes keep coming back. Redgum sleepers, veranda posts, they're all bursting into flame. The garage and the car go up. The house walls and doors are battered by embers; sooner or later one of them will take hold and destroy everything. He sees neighbouring houses completely consumed.

He tries dialling emergency 000; wastes precious minutes waiting for a response that never comes, the line engaged. He pauses to watch his neighbours flee and sags for a moment, overwhelmed. The house is gone.

Then he looks up in surprise as a series of loud horn blasts resound over the fire's roar and a big red truck comes charging through the smoke. Kinglake Tanker One has arrived.

They swing into action as the vehicle slams to a halt: the crew run out their hoses, begin hitting the fire with a hundred times the volume of water David had at his disposal. The fire in the winery office is emitting a foul black brew, thick smoke laced with toxins from burning plastic. Paul Lowe and Rod Elwers scramble into their breathing apparatus to get in close enough to extinguish it.

Then Paul takes a look around the building. 'What about the house?' The smoke inside is so thick they have to keep the breathing equipment on. There's fire inside the roof, between the plaster and the corrugated iron. They rush outside, attempt to hit it with their hoses but it's too far away, and their own water is getting low by now. Paul grabs a knapsack from the truck and scrambles up into the roof on his knees.

Even that's looking borderline, but then another tanker rattles up the drive. A Hurstbridge crew. A quick conference and the two crews rip the iron from the roof and give it a blast that brings the fire under control. Col Evans, a mate of David's, arrives from Hurstbridge with his own trailer tanker and takes over the night watch.

David is exhausted and seriously dehydrated; in the fury of the battle, he's forgotten to drink. Cathy has left six litres of water in milk cartons by the door, ready to put on the seedlings. David swallows all six of them in one go and lies down, finished.

The sheer exhaustion of fighting a fire is something that often goes unremarked, but those who've done it shake their heads in disbelief when they look back on it. The eyes throb, the throat burns, the muscles reach the point of near collapse. Heads ache and backs spasm, bodies are a mess of burns and blisters, of splinters and wounds. The adrenaline surges crazily: a lot more firefighters die from heart attack than fire.

Surprisingly, the one thing many don't feel is the heat. They're out there working furiously in heavy suits and boots, fifty degrees Celsius or more. One firefighter reported his boot soles melted and anchored him to the truck so that he had to unlace the boots and step out of them to free himself. But the adrenaline rush means the heat is barely noticed.

'You feel it afterwards, though,' commented another firefighter. 'I feel crap for ages after a big fire. All that smoke and fumes,' he adds warily. 'Can't do you much good in the long run, can it?'

The crew of Kinglake Tanker One draw together to discuss their situation. They've been at the winery for an hour, been scrambling so hard all afternoon they've only picked up snatches of news from home. But what they hear is deeply disturbing.

'They were distraught, just about in tears, the Kinglake guys,' commented a firefighter from one of the other trucks. 'They started to get calls from their families, telling them the town was on fire, and they were stuck down here, cut off.'

'What are we going to do?' Dave Hooper asks his crew. 'Whatever you choose, I'll support you.'

They make a collective decision: they're going home.

The Incident Control Centre at Kangaroo Ground advises them

to go round via Whittlesea; the St Andrews–Kinglake Road is impassable. They look up at The Windies: ten kilometres of treacherous cliffs and hairpin bends, engulfed in fire. But quicker. They all have families, homes and friends up there. And if they can get through, maybe they'll be clearing the way for the ambulances and strike teams that will surely follow.

Dave speaks to Vicfire: 'We're going straight up the Kinglake Road.'

Before they leave, he flicks off the outside speaker of the radio. The news coming out of it sounds bad beyond belief but there's nothing they can do about it. For the next hour they're going to have to focus all their energies on getting up the hill in one piece.

*

Kinglake Tanker Two is also on Jacksons Road when the change sweeps the front over them. Now the crew are becoming intensely worried about their homes and families. They're all desperately trying to call Kinglake, mostly without success.

Crew leader Steve Bell has a quiet word with the strike team leader, comes back grim-faced. 'Just had it confirmed. The fire's hit Kinglake.' Ben Hutchinson looks up the mountain; his house on the outskirts of town will be one of the first to go.

Steve makes the decision to take the crew's phones off them. 'Nothing we can do about it now,' he says. 'We need to concentrate on the job at hand.'

That job is to provide escort for police officers Gary Tickell and Paul Kemezys from Hurstbridge in a convoy travelling through the burnt-out areas. Their mission, as they understand it, is to search for survivors, or victims. A crew of DSE firefighters in a four-wheel-drive takes the lead, their chainsaws running hard.

Along the way they pass several houses engulfed by fire without stopping to intervene, which leads Ben to suspect that they're responding to a specific request. But when they come across a forlorn-looking couple in a ute they pause.

'My house has just caught fire,' the man says. 'Can you help?'

The tanker peels off, rattles up the drive. Comes across a brick house well ablaze and way past saving.

'Can't we help the poor bugger out?' asks Ben.

Steve shakes his head. 'No point wasting the water.'

And that's the way it goes. Some people can be helped, some houses saved. For some there is just nothing to be done.

At one place they find a young girl, about the same age as Ben's daughter Aby. She is terribly injured, the sole survivor of her family.

While they wait for an ambulance Ben tries to keep her conscious and talking. But the ambulance doesn't come. He keeps talking, soothing, encouraging her, and it keeps not coming. From time to time Ben gets up, steps across to his crew leader—'Where's that fucking ambulance?'—until eventually the police decide to carry her out themselves.

Ben wants desperately to go with her, but he's the driver of the truck and can't leave the crew. Somebody from another crew volunteers to go. The two of them pick her up—Ben describes it as the most gentle lift he's ever made—and shift her into the back of the police car.

Ben watches them disappear into the smoke, his heart hurting. He doesn't think she'll make it.

She does, though.

A year later, when Ben Hutchinson is interviewed, the fire looms like a monster in his memory. He's had a hell of a year; he did lose his house and is still living in a temporary accommodation centre provided by the government, unsure when he'll get back into a home of his own. Like a lot of other people wiped out by the fire, he's been hit hard by rising land values and the shortage of builders, among other things.

He managed to retrieve only one object from the ruins of his house: a small, blackened piece of metal that was once his CFA long-service medal. But he has salvaged something else too, and his voice catches when he speaks of it: the knowledge that, in all of that terrible destruction and loss, he and his colleagues helped save the life of that young girl in St Andrews.

YOU HAVE TO KEEP BREATHING

It is firefighter Chris Lloyd from Kinglake West who brings the first of the really bad casualties in to the CFA shed at Kinglake. Having gone home with his partner Debbie to pick up their pets and a few personal belongings, he was trapped by the fire's dramatic arrival. He's managed to save both his own and a neighbour's house; on the way back he comes across a lump on the road that turns out to be a woman who's crawled out of a house in flames. She's terribly burnt. He has no time for first aid: a moment's delay and they'll both be dead, such is the intensity of the blaze coming at them. He lifts her into his vehicle and makes a mad dash for the CFA.

When they carry the woman in, Linda Craske is shocked to find the soles of her feet are burnt off. She is conscious, but in agony. Craske sits her in a chair, cuts away the dead skin, applies crepe bandages. The woman's distress is intensified by the fact that she believes her husband didn't make it out of the house.

One of the volunteers comes in to tell Craske they have another badly burnt patient outside.

'Just pick her up and bring her in,' she says.

'We can't touch her.'

'Why not?'

'Her skin keeps falling off.'

Paul Hendrie, who went out into the town as soon as the front passed, had come across this woman and her husband in a terrible state. She'd managed to drag herself out of the house as it collapsed around her, then realised that most of the occupants—family members and friends who'd been sheltering in another part of the house—were still in there. It was when she tried to get back in and rescue them that she received those appalling burns, covering more than 40 percent of her body.

They wrap her in bandages, try to retain as much of her body moisture as they can. Her friend stays with her, never leaves her side: 'You have to keep breathing,' they hear her whisper, over and over. 'Your family's going to need you more than ever now.'

The scratch medical crew are getting seriously worried. The floor of a crowded back room in a dirty tin shed is no place to treat serious cases such as these. A woman in one of the cars has with her a newborn baby who they fear has stopped breathing; a nurse rushes out and attends her.

Then Lorraine Casey brings in Wendy Duncan. To Trish and Carole, who have given up their friend and fellow CFA member for dead, the sight of her coming through that door is an enormous relief. But few of her colleagues recognise her when she's carried in. She's stooped over, blackened, gasping for air; her lips are blue. All signs Craske recognises as hypoxia. Wendy's running out of oxygen.

Wendy Duncan's was one of the more amazing survival stories of Black Saturday. A barrister by profession, she lived out on Bald Spur Road in a house said to be one of the best-defended in the region: it was equipped with automatic sprinklers and water pumps, double-glazed windows. She'd cleared it rigorously, filled the gutters with water, blocked the entrances.

And the fire swept her defences away in seconds. One moment it was a distant glow in the treetops, next a battery of thrashing horizontal hail. Then, as she puts it, 'the world exploded'.

She'd seen plenty of fires in her ten years with the CFA, but nothing like this. She rushed inside, set about defending herself, threw water around, swatted embers. As the smoke thickened and the heat intensified, the building began to ignite.

'The heat was unbelievable,' she says. 'It was so intense that the woodwork inside the house spontaneously combusted.'

She soon found herself crawling down a smoke-filled corridor searching for a corner of the house that had yet to ignite. She removed a glove, touched a door on the far side of the house from where the fire had come, was astonished when it burned her hand. The fire was everywhere.

Wendy kept her wits about her. Remembering those iconic bush-fire images in which the chimney is the only part of the building that survives, she sheltered alongside hers. She found her phone, put a call through to the CFA, did her best to warn her mates there of how bad the fire was. But her breath was running out, her vision becoming blurred. Finally, when she judged the building was about to collapse, she kicked a metal window frame out with her steel-capped boots. She crawled outside, staggered through flaming air to the road, crumbled into the gutter. Lay there—blistered and burnt, barely able to breathe.

That is, one could almost say, the ordinary part of her story, the part that is repeated by survivors all over the ranges. The amazing part is that she found her phone and managed to get onto a friend over a hundred kilometres away in Gippsland, who relayed the call to another friend, a Kinglake woman named Lorraine Casey. Lorraine immediately set out to rescue her and drove through many kilometres of burning bush to reach her. When the road was finally blocked by falling trees, she did the last few hundred metres on foot, located Wendy, dragged her back up Bald Spur Road into the car and rushed her to the CFA.

Now she's there, and they're worried that she isn't going to make it. Her lungs are so burnt they're afraid she'll suffocate.

A nurse says she needs oxygen. So do a lot of other patients. One of the helpers has worked in the doctor's surgery across the road and says there's oxygen there.

'Break in and get it,' says Trish.

'Don't we need permission to do that?'

'You've got it.'

Wayne McDonald-Price and his wife Jenny run over, do the break-and-enter and return with a tank of oxygen. It helps stabilise some of the casualties, but the situation is grim and getting grimmer. Wendy's breathing is steadily growing more laboured.

The nurses have no medical equipment other than small first aid kits. They are dealing with some fifty casualties, several of them critical.

Trish, as Communications Officer, has been desperately trying to raise outside help all night. She's spoken to Vicfire, emergency 000, other brigades, told them she needed a minimum of twelve ambulances. Earlier on, she'd spoken to Roger Wood, explaining their situation. He'd said he'd see what he could do, but she doesn't hold out much hope. She's received a lot of promises that help was on the way, but they all came to nothing. She gathers there are support teams—ambulances, fire trucks—being assembled at a staging ground at Whittlesea, but the road is still too dangerous to bring them up.

'They told us a strike team was escorting a group of ambulances up from Hurstbridge, and we thought, thank god,' remembers Carole. 'Two minutes later they said it's taken off somewhere else, and Trish and I burst into tears.'

The outside world is yet to comprehend the thoroughness of the destruction wrought here tonight. Again and again, through the long evening, the story is replayed: help is on the way, and then it isn't. The road is blocked, there are trees and fallen power lines everywhere, massive traffic accidents, it's too dangerous to send anybody up.

Dave Cooper, from the CFA vehicle, appears. He sees at once that if they don't get help they're going to have more deaths on their hands. Trish hears him yelling into his radio in frustration: 'They need ambulances! They've got all these people burnt, they're going to die!'

Then Roger Wood and Cameron Caine walk into the building.

UNDERWORLD

For the two police officers it has been a journey through hell.

Wood's sense of time is completely distorted, but he estimates the eight-kilometre trip from Kinglake West takes somewhere between one and two hours.

The CFA crew lead the advance, sawing through fallen trees and power poles. Deputy Group Officer Dave Cooper is in command, Frank Allan is doing the grunt work. He's unsure how many trees he cuts—at least twenty is his estimate, because he has to refuel three times. And this is not your ordinary chainsaw work: he's labouring in the dark with trees still falling, fire everywhere around. Often there are two or three trees twisted into one another; sometimes there are burnt-out cars or power lines inside the mess.

It's hard, hot, heavy work. Frank has already been on the run all day, not to mention being burnt over in Coombs Road; his eyes are aching, his lungs are seared by smoke. As an experienced trainer, he understands exactly how lethal a chainsaw can be and he knows there's nothing like fatigue to amplify the dangers. One slip or kickback could cost him a leg or sever an artery, and out here they are way beyond the reach of the medical professionals.

By the time they make it into Kinglake he can barely stand, let alone operate a chainsaw.

Wood and Caine follow the CFA vehicle, veering off to deal with the myriad jobs that claim their attention as they drive. And struggling to deal with their own emotions. Wood is still terrified that his own family have perished, and what he sees on the road now only intensifies that fear.

Both men are locals. This is their town, their district: their people. They are stunned at the ferocity nature has turned upon them.

'We were just saying fuck—can't believe it—the devastation. There was nothing left. Nothing. Burnt-out cars everywhere. Dead animals. Houses, businesses, bushland, just…gone'

They drive past the Pheasant Creek store, the scene of their earlier rescue, now a nest of twisted steel and black spaghetti, a mangled, smouldering mess. The pine plantation across the road is obliterated. A wash of relief and a silent word of thanks they got those people out when they did.

Kinglake West Tanker One, Karen Barrow in command, catches up with the convoy somewhere near the sports oval. She's trying to get down Extons Road, where they've had a request for assistance from a family trapped in a house. They're all finding the slowness of the journey maddening but with the number of trees on the road, there's nothing they can do about it.

Karen shoots a glance at the hunched, blackened figure ripping a chainsaw into a fallen tree. She looks again, is astonished to realise that it's her partner, Frank.

They notice that the sports stadium is beginning to go up. Karen's crew have little water to spare but they manage to suppress that fire and save the building—a feat that proves invaluable in the following months, when sport looms as one of the crucial supports for the community's recovery.

They turn into Extons Road. A woman runs out, waves them down. Her name is Tess Librieri. She has an injured neighbour in her care. She's called for an ambulance, but none has appeared. Karen goes in to assess the situation and finds the victim, Mick Flynn, has burns to 70 percent of his body. His rescuers are doing all the right things, keeping him in the swimming pool, monitoring his vital signs, but it's a bad situation. She returns to the truck, gets onto Vicfire, reinforces the plea for an ambulance. The operator assures her there's one on the way, so they continue on to their job.

When they eventually reach the call-out, they find the family and the home have survived. They extinguish a fire breaking out in a house nearby and then, heading back, decide to check on Mr Flynn. They're shocked to find the injured man's condition deteriorating and no sign of an ambulance. They try Vicfire again: the ambulances are still down in Whittlesea, unable to travel up the mountain.

The crew improvise a stretcher from a ladder and transport Mr Flynn back to Kinglake West. By this time it's nearing two in the morning, some eight hours since he was injured, and although the ambulances do arrive soon afterwards, Mr Flynn dies later in hospital. Karen is left bitterly contemplating the difference it might have made if she'd been given correct information and ferried him down the mountain earlier.

While all of this is happening, the essential services convoy continues its fitful journey into Kinglake. Roger Wood is worried about the power lines snaking all over the road, but Desi Deas, a volunteer from the State Emergency Service, appears and assures them the lines are dead. He's lost his own property in the fire, but is out on the road straightaway, doing what he can. The fire struck so swiftly and with so little warning that the official SES vehicles were destroyed in their compound, but the SES members have gone out into the community in their own cars.

The coppers spot a group of fifteen or twenty people sheltering in the middle of the oval. The school alongside it is burnt to the ground and Wood realises that these are the people they thought they'd been going to help when they made their frantic dash to the school at Kinglake West.

It turns out most of those on the oval have escaped from the neighbouring hamlet of Strathewen, which has been completely obliterated. They sought shelter in the school. When it burned down around them, they fled onto the oval. Several of them are injured— one has a broken ankle—and they are all shaken, but none of the injuries are life threatening.

Wood, who knows a few of them, moves around checking on their wellbeing. He speaks to Debbie Bradshaw, a fellow parent at

Strathewen school. She fled her home just before the fire struck, came racing up the escarpment. She's had no word from her husband, Darren, who is a CFA volunteer and is still out on a truck. He will come through okay, but when the couple eventually get back to Strathewen they find their home destroyed and a shocking number of their friends dead.

Dennis Spooner, whom Wood also knows from Strathewen, comes over in great distress. 'Roger, I don't know what happened to Marilyn and Damien, they were following us up the hill in the other car and they didn't make it. Can you go and check?' Marilyn and Damien are his wife and son; Damien is another parent at Strathewen school.

'Mate, I'll try,' Wood puts a hand on his shoulder, 'but there's trees down everywhere—don't know if we'll be able to get through.'

The two officers do make a brief sortie down Bowden Spur, the long, narrow track that twists up into Kinglake from Strathewen, but find it's a mess of twisted timber and flame. Impassable.

Anybody who has the misfortune to be down in Strathewen that day is more or less on their own. The tiny CFA crew there are tearing their hair out at the lack of support they are getting. They are reduced to scampering over trees on foot in the moonlight to reach isolated survivors. Other CFA brigades are distressed to hear the Arthurs Creek and Strathewen captain, Dave McGahy, desperately pleading for assistance: 'Will somebody help us? Anybody? I've got critically injured people dying in front of my eyes.'

A year later, McGahy would still be furious at the lack of support his community received in the hour of its destruction. Literally decimated, the town would suffer twenty-seven deaths from a population of around 250. Among the dead were Marilyn and Damien Spooner. Separated from Dennis in their flight, they'd returned to the family home. Their remains were eventually found in the bath.

The group on the oval are hungry and thirsty as well as traumatised. Cameron Caine, who is president of the football club, smashes a window and kicks in the door. 'Drinks in the fridge. Help yourselves!'

They get back onto the road, transfixed by the endless scenes of destruction unrolling before their eyes. Roger Wood stares out the window at the wrecked cars, once metal and glass, now ferocious, fire-spitting distortions. His heart surges with pity for whoever was in there. And he feels the familiar wave of anxiety for his own family.

Again he punches the number: nothing. Who else, who else? He manages to get a radio message through to one of his senior officers, requests that somebody check on his family's wellbeing. The operator says they'll get back to him, but he isn't hopeful. Every police officer in the region is flat out right now.

The CFA crew have pushed on ahead. Frank Allan focuses on the cutting, grimly determined not to look in any of the cars. The policemen don't have that luxury: it's their responsibility to locate victims. They come across numerous vehicles, some they recognise.

Finally they get to the four-car pile-up Wood had been trying to reach earlier that afternoon and find a group of people standing nearby. One of them is leaning into a fence. As they come closer they recognise someone they know well: Rossi Laudisio, proprietor of Cappa Rossi's Pizza Restaurant.

Rossi is weeping. 'Papa,' he's whispering, over and over. 'Papa.'

'Oh no,' Wood murmurs to himself. Rossi's father, Gennaro, is one of Kinglake's most loved characters. Wood grew close to the family the year before, when Rossi's mother died. 'They're great people,' he says. 'Gennaro was one of nature's gentlemen.'

The policemen inspect the accident, confirm what they've been afraid of: a body in one of the cars. The four vehicles have smashed into one another in the whirling chaos of the fire's first attack. The old man had been trapped, his legs pinned. His son stayed with him for as long as he could, until he was forced to seek shelter in a nearby house when the flames swept in and the heat grew lethal. So intense was the fire it melted the mag wheels and engine parts.

For Rossi Laudisio the death of his father is only one part of his personal nightmare. He asks the officers if they've seen his wife and four children. The family had to flee in separate cars and lost each other in the confusion.

Roger and Cameron look at each other: her red Landcruiser is one of the ones they recognised, smashed into an embankment.

Local knowledge coming to the fore, Cameron pulls out his phone and starts making calls. He works his way through the people they've seen on the trip so far, asking everyone about the red Landcruiser. He manages to track down the missing family, finds they've taken refuge at the High Mountain water farm and survived.

Rossi sinks to the ground, overwhelmed by relief.

The two officers have no time for the procedures they'd normally follow at a fatal accident. They have to get through to Kinglake. They place flashing beacons around the pile-up and continue with what's beginning to feel like a journey through the underworld. At one point they come across an open stretch that offers them views all the way to the distant city: a million wheels and jets of flame pierce the darkness. The hills glow with burning stumps and fallen branches. What used to be a manna gum on the edge of the road is a fountain of embers atop a whirling column of fire.

My god, thinks Wood, my family is somewhere down there. How far has the fire got? Has it wiped out half of Melbourne?

They set out once more.

Small things catch the eye, lodge themselves in his memory. Warped images: the cavity where a car-door handle was, now spitting sparks. A red-hot metal chain, a house like a livid skeleton. A sheet of iron wrapped around a steel pole. And the cars; somehow they're worst of all. You know what's been in them. They're scattered at a cacophony of angles: on their sides, in ditches and drains, buckled and blurring into one another. Melted wheel rims. Metal and flesh, fused.

The tension is becoming razor sharp. They're close to the town now, and both men dread what they're about to find. But even before that, they come across one more accident, the very sight of which leaves Wood with cold shivers. Maybe a dozen vehicles, including a motorbike, scattered around the intersection, all of them burnt, many of them crushed by trees. Beneath the front wheel of one car are the charred remains of a dog, its teeth a bitter rictus, its back legs smoking. The scene is weirdly illuminated by light thrown out from the burning bush.

'Jesus,' he whispers to himself. The driver of the first vehicle must have hit the brakes to avoid the dog and been clobbered from behind; other cars rear-ended them both, blocking the road. He imagines the fearful chaos that must have accompanied this carnage: the swathes of smoke, the headlights looming, panic-driven, the squealing brakes, the photos and teddy bears flying.

There are no bodies that he can see, so by the time the fire swept through, the occupants must have scattered. He hopes so.

The CFA crew are still working their way through this jungle. Frank Allan is discovering levels of exhaustion he didn't know existed. He's grateful when a handful of locals loom out of the darkness offering help. Between them they drag the cut-up logs aside, clear a path for the strike teams they hope will be following.

There's one car completely embedded in the tree-jam. A four-wheel-drive appears, and the police prevail upon the driver to help drag the crushed car out of the way. He does so, but not without a massive effort: the heat was so intense the vehicle has sunk into the melted bitumen.

Wood and Caine edge their way round the scene, make the final descent into Kinglake; they cross the last rise.

Roger Wood stares in silence.

The town he last raced through this afternoon is gone. In its place is a lake of fire ringed by a pool of stars. There is no power, of course: Kinglake is illuminated only by the reflected light from blazing bush and raging buildings. Two jets of flame shoot high into the air.

They brace themselves and head down the hill.

SILENT NIGHT

It's the silence that hits the hardest, the emptiness. All along the road to Kinglake they've been coming across little clusters of survivors, often people they know. There's been communication—traumatic communication for the most part, but still something to make them feel they were part of the human race.

Making that first run down the hill, they feel like they're the last men left on Earth.

The wind has settled now, the blood-chilling roar Roger heard before is long gone. There's an eerie hush broken only by the hum of the engine, the crash of the odd falling tree. The flashing red and blue lights enhance the ominous glow thrown out by the fire. Nobody comes running to greet them, no vehicles are moving. Just about every structure on that western approach is gone.

Wood thinks about the death and destruction he's already encountered. Wonders if anybody in Kinglake is left alive. Struggles through a sense of sheer astonishment.

'It was like my eyes were held open with matchsticks,' says Wood. 'I was trying to take it all in—everywhere I looked there was devastation—everything was burning. I'd been up in Kinglake for five years and I knew everything, a lot of people, and everywhere I looked it was, Ah shit, that's gone too. It was overwhelming.'

They enter the main street. The pizza parlour, the hardware store and service station, the vet's. Houses and houses and houses, all destroyed. The mesmerising geysers of flame turn out to be gas venting from the underground gas tanks at the servo. Wood doesn't want to drive too close to that: who knows if it's about to explode?

Amazingly, the police station has survived, although the verandas are beginning to ignite. They extinguish them. There's a Landcruiser and trailer in front of it, still burning, as if some poor bugger had raced up hoping for a last-minute rescue. They drive into Aitken Crescent, where the CFA brigade is based.

The two men catch their breath.

There are hundreds of people there. That explains the emptiness that greeted them as they entered the town. The residents of Kinglake, those of them who are still alive, have come together for solace and support.

It's too crowded to drive through, so they get out and walk.

A man comes up and stares at them. Wood thinks he looks like a stock figure in an old cartoon, the feller who's stuck his finger in the electrical socket: he's black from head to toe, his long hair smoking and standing on end. People are lying on the gravel, staring up at the sky, holding each other. A chubby bloke in a singlet and shorts sits half out of a car, ash-streaked head in hands, an expression of utter weariness—or grief—on what they can see of his face. As they make their way through the crowd, the two officers—the first figures of authority who've made it into town—are bombarded with questions from the crowd.

'What do we do now?'

'What's happening?'

'Is the fire coming back?'

'Where are the ambulances?'

They do their best. Try to reassure people, tell them the fire front has passed, promise ambulances and strike teams will be there as soon as possible.

As they draw closer to the CFA building, the atmosphere becomes more subdued. They see yellow-suited firefighters patrolling the perimeter, keeping an eye out for flare-ups. A tree behind the shed is still flickering. They're disturbed to hear groaning and sobs from within.

'They looked like zombies,' comments Linda Craske, 'the moment they walked in.'

That's about how they feel: they've walked into a horror movie. Where the hell do you start? There are bodies all over the dirty concrete floor. Women are moving among the casualties, giving first aid, applying bandages, fiddling with oxygen tanks and masks, comforting victims who are obviously in extremity. People are crying, holding each other's hands, staring numbly at the ceiling, cradling heads in hands. A boy with tear-stained cheeks is fondling a puppy.

The worst cases have been covered in silver blankets, but it's obvious that the Kinglake CFA and their helpers are struggling to deal with an overwhelming number of injuries with virtually no facilities.

Trish Hendrie and Carole Wilson come over and hug both men. They feel as if somebody has thrown them a lifeline. They've been battling all night, not just the fire, but the maddening fear that they've been abandoned, that the outside world, with its doctors, fire trucks and support systems, has forgotten them. The power is out, the phone lines are down, mobile reception is random and all it delivers is bad news. The CFA radio is so frantic it's impossible to get a word in.

With the arrival of the local cops, they feel as though an intolerable burden has been lifted from their shoulders.

'Oh, when those boys walked in,' says Carole, 'I thought maybe there's hope for us yet.'

'Roger's from St Andrews,' adds Trish. 'He didn't even know if his own family was alive…A lot of lesser people would have said, this is too much, I'm going home. But they were doing their job. Sticking by the community.'

Somewhere in those first seconds, Trish feels the need to clear the air.

'I'm sorry, Rodge.'

'Sorry?'

'We had to break into the doctor's. For oxygen.'

He looks around him at the patients on the floor, realising what a remarkable job these women have been doing.

'Don't worry about it, Trish.' He nods. 'Breaking into the doctor's? That's good.'

He receives a run-down of the situation, and it's deeply troubling. The nurses have prioritised the most critically injured, but some of them will be dead if the ambulances don't get up here soon.

A fire tanker from St Andrews under the leadership of Kaz Gurney has worked its way up the mountain and arrived on the scene. Several of the firefighters on board are friends or neighbours of Wood's. Jeff Purchase, who knows him well, has a quick word. He says later that Wood was so intent upon the tasks at hand that he barely registered his existence.

'He asked how we were,' says Purchase, 'what we were planning to do, but you could see his mind was somewhere else, focused on the job, trying to read the situation. His eyes were scoping the crowd. Working out what to do next. He moved around like a butterfly, talking to different groups of people, seeing how they were going, doing a dozen things at once.'

Wood returns to his vehicle and reports the situation to D24, reinforces the plea for help. His heart sags at the response. Ambulances on hold; the trip is still too dangerous. He sits there for a moment, runs his hands through his hair.

Then he goes back into the CFA and speaks to his colleagues.

'Nobody's coming up. We're gonna have to take 'em down.'

SAVING PEOPLE

Samuel Oliner is an American sociologist. He is also a Polish-born Holocaust survivor who, as a child, narrowly escaped the massacre that killed his entire family. He was rescued by a peasant woman who took him in, gave him a Catholic identity and sheltered him throughout the war. That woman's heroism moved and intrigued him so deeply that he has made the study of heroes his life's work. He has interviewed more than four hundred individuals who rescued Jews during the war in an attempt to understand what it was that made these people do what they did.

What it was *not*, he discovered, was a matter of religion, politics, wealth or whether they had known about what was happening to the Jews in general.

'There is no single explanation for why people act heroically,' he comments. 'It's not absolutely genetic or personality or cultural.'

Among the qualities he could discern were these: rescuers tend to have a strong relationship with their parents, a wide range of friends and a sense of empathy; they feel an inescapable duty to help others. They also tend to have a belief that they can shape their own destiny; they have what psychologists call an 'internal locus of control'. Those whose reactions to disaster are less positive—who stand and watch, or go into their shells—tend to think of existence as something that just rolls over them.

Oliner has found a useful source of information in the records of the Carnegie Hero Fund Commission, which rewards individuals who voluntarily carry out heroic deeds to save others. He found that 91 percent of the rescuers were male—a statistic that may, of course, simply reflect the fact that men held occupations in which they were more likely to be placed in perilous situations. Sixty-one percent of the rescued were male as well.

He also found that the rescuers tended to have trade or working-class backgrounds; of the 283 rescuers interviewed, only two were from high-status occupations. These people are already equipped for the physical demands of the rescue; they are familiar with steel and wood, with equipment. They are used to finding practical solutions quickly. They also tend to know their own strengths and limitations. Another interesting statistic: 80 percent of the heroic acts occurred in rural or small-town America. They happened in places where people knew each other.

In an attempt to go beyond the raw statistics, to find out what inner logic drove these individuals to perform heroic deeds, Oliner interviewed a random selection of them. He found a range of explanations, but the common thread was a sense of empathy derived from their families and their community. The question was not so much why they did what they did, but how they could have lived with themselves if they hadn't.

Male. Rural. Practical. Accustomed to taking control of their own destinies. The picture painted by Samuel Oliner could almost be a portrait of Roger Wood and Cameron Caine. Wood was a fitter before he joined the force, Caine a plumber. Both have strong, supportive families. Both are accustomed to controlling situations.

And both are men with a powerful sense of empathy: active members of their community, engaged and engaging.

They would have had ample opportunity to bow out, to wait for help to arrive. Nobody would have blamed them. Nobody was telling them what to do, nobody was coming up the mountain to assist them. The ambulances, fire trucks, their own commanding officers were all down in Whittlesea. Officially, the road was impassable: trees were burning, still falling. They'd already seen more trauma than most people encounter in a lifetime.

They didn't consider it for an instant.

When Wood was asked, months after the fires, what made him do what he did that day, he seemed momentarily puzzled. He paused, blinked. 'How couldn't I?' he asked. 'They're my community.'

*

One thing Roger Wood knows how to do is drive. Five years of working in this mountain town—of leading search and rescue missions in the ranges, of chasing hoons, of navigating those tortuous tracks and backroads—have honed his ability to handle a four-wheel-drive in tough conditions.

His senior, Jon Ellks, attests to that. He tells the story of a night he and Wood were dealing with a frantic shift in the middle of a ferocious wind storm, racing from one crisis to another. They were miles out of town when they received a report of a violent assault taking place at the medical centre. Wood floored it back to town, lights flashing, careering round the debris that was scattered all over the road, going bush when that was the only option. Ellks hung on to the jesus grip for dear life. They were heading down the final hill when he suddenly spotted a fallen mountain ash hidden in the dip ahead of them.

'Tree!' he shouted.

Wood had already hit the brakes, but it was obvious they were going to collide. To Ellks' horror, Wood instinctively steered into the heavy base of the tree rather than the leafy head. They duly crunched into it at forty kilometres per hour and heard the unmistakable sound of substantial damage being inflicted on the vehicle. Undeterred, Wood backed up, made a quick check of the front end, spotted a local with a heavy winch on his truck. He persuaded the fellow to drag the tree off the road and carried on with their wild ride.

'Why the hell did you do that?' demanded Ellks.

'What?'

'Hit the thickest part of the tree? This vehicle is brand new.'

'Rather kill the car than us,' Wood replied calmly. If they'd driven into the head of the tree, he explained, any of the branches could have smashed through the windscreen, converting a minor bingle into a fatality. Ellks decided that the fellow beside him was cool-headed and quick-thinking—and knew how to handle a vehicle.

In the CFA shed, Wood is discussing the situation with the firies. They decide to organise a convoy. Wood's Pajero will take the lead; following them will be the CFA four-wheel-drive, the police Traffic Management Unit vehicle with senior constables Barron and Liddell, and at least one private car. They allocate the casualties among the vehicles; Wood and Caine take Wendy Duncan in theirs. She's the biggest worry.

Frank Allan helps carry her out. He knows her as a fellow CFA volunteer, but she's so badly burnt, blackened and doubled over with pain that he doesn't recognise her. By this stage there are a lot of things he isn't recognising: he's spent so long on the front line, either fighting the fire or wielding a chainsaw, that he can barely see. His eyes are giving him hell; he's suffering from both smoke inhalation and flash burns. When he eventually makes it down the mountain, he'll be put straight into hospital.

Linda Craske sits with Wendy in the back seat. She's been watching her injured colleague carefully, her concerns escalating by the minute. Wendy has severe internal burns and scarring on the lungs; her breathing is becoming more and more laboured. The fear is that her lungs will soon become so swollen she won't be able to breathe at all.

Wood has been in some tricky situations, but never one like this: leading a convoy in a midnight ride though treacherous, burnt-out terrain with a group of critically injured victims on board.

'Seat belts on!' he orders. It's going to be a rough ride.

CFA volunteer Jim MacLeod, who's been working hard all night keeping the pumps and generators going, is taking a quick breather when he sees the convoy go roaring out into the night.

Speaking months later, he is a man with many criticisms to make of the overall response to the Black Saturday disaster. A forthright Glaswegian—he worked on the docks with Billy Connolly—he isn't afraid to speak his mind. And like a lot of other residents, he's angry at the lack of warnings, the slowness of the official response, the bureaucratic contortions of the recovery process, the arbitrary dictates of many of the outside police who later descended upon the town.

But of his own locals? The Kinglake coppers?

'That drive down the mountain, in the middle of the night,' he comments in his thick Glaswegian accent. 'Everything still on fire? Trees falling?

'Balls of steel, those fellers. Balls of steel.'

DOWN THE MOUNTAIN

Wood takes it slowly at the start. It's not long since they came through, carving a path through the blockages and debris, but the fires are still raging and more trees are coming down. There's thick smoke still over the road, visibility down to ten or twenty metres. They leave the internal lights on so that Linda Craske can keep a closer watch on Wendy.

The patient is conscious and amazingly calm, given her circumstances, but worried. Her breathing is becoming more and more laboured. Linda examines her, desperately hoping to see some signs of improvement; not finding any.

Roger has eyes only for the road. So does Cameron, for the most part: a look-out is crucial on a journey like this. But from time to time he peers into the back and tries to say something reassuring: 'You'll be right, Wendy. Not long to go now.'

But it is long, and they're far from convinced that she will be right. They can see she's struggling for air. Craske is thinking emergency tracheotomies: 'I'd seen them done, but I was thinking, Oh christ, I can't do that.'

Wendy's mouth is burnt dry and she's severely dehydrated. Craske gives her sips of water, but has to restrain her from drinking too much. She's worried Wendy could breathe water into her lungs and drown.

From time to time Linda looks up through the car windows, and she comes to understand the shock she saw on the policemen's faces when they entered the CFA. Huge fires continue to burn on either side of the road. As they climb to the top of the mountain she can peer down into the gullies of the escarpment: it's all ablaze. Images whizz by: burnt-out cars, crazy leaning power poles, a horse with a broken leg struggling through a charred paddock. The odd little untouched miracle: washing on a line behind a ravaged house, a blue plastic pool, a wheelie bin.

They're moving quicker than they did on the way into Kinglake, but they have to balance the need for speed against the disastrous implications of an accident. As obstacles loom out of the smoke, Cameron calls out directions: 'Left! Right! Too far! Watch it!' They duck, dodge and swerve their way down the mountain. They weave their way round dozens of trees, over fallen power lines, off the road and back on again.

They reach the Whittlesea–Yea Road intersection and see something they can hardly believe. This was where Wood set up the roadblock earlier in the day, where he'd had the conversation with Meg, the elderly woman with the shack near the intersection. He'd pleaded with her to leave and she flatly refused.

They're driving past the shack now, and like just about everything else in the vicinity it's burnt to the ground. Then suddenly she's there: Meg, in the middle of the road. Still in her bare feet, bottle in hand, staring at the blazing forest.

Roger has to shake his head. He wonders if he's seeing a ghost. After what he's seen, he didn't think anybody could have survived around here, especially somebody as poorly prepared as Meg. They drive past her, a pale, bewildered figure illuminated by the glowing bush.

'You see her?' he asks Cam.

'Yep.'

'Good. Thought I was losing it.'

They don't have time to dwell on the apparition. Wendy is sounding worse. At one stage, she begins vomiting blood. Then it sounds like she's stopped breathing. There's a long moment of shared anxiety, but the breathing kicks in again and they all sigh, exhaling in sympathy.

Finally they reach the bottom of the mountain. The road is straight, the landscape unburnt.

'Hang on,' says Wood, and puts his foot down.

The night air streams past their windows as they race across the flatlands, reaching speeds of up to 150 kilometres per hour. Roger Wood has already seen too much death today, knows there'll be more to come over the next few days. Doesn't want any more on his conscience.

The flashing lights of a police roadblock appear in the distance. They swing around it, power on into Whittlesea. The world here is as magnesium-bright as the mountain was crimson. A massive bank of lights guides them to the showgrounds, where a staging area has been established. Here are the medical facilities they've been thirsting for on the mountain: rows of ambulances, Red Cross caravans and tents, medical specialists of every description.

Wood slams to a halt outside the biggest tent. A team of emergency medical personnel appear, fifteen, twenty of them: doctors, nurses, orderlies. They swarm round the car, whisk the patient away. Linda follows, rattling out the medical history.

The two policemen settle back into their seats for a moment, close their eyes, breathe deeply. Allow themselves a moment's respite.

Wood takes out his phone again. The reception might be better in Whittlesea. He punches the number, another attempt to call home.

For the first time all night, it's answered.

'Oh Rodge...' Jo's voice is drawn, weary. Enormously relieved. 'I've been so worried about you. Been trying to call you all night.'

'Same here. Worried you were dead.' He blinks back tears. 'Kids okay?'

'They're fine.'

He slumps forward in the seat: the long-held tension slackens like a cut rope, and he's suddenly aware of the terror he's been struggling with for so many hours.

'It was that wind change that saved us.' Jo is still talking. 'It was only seconds away when it turned around.' He is struck by the irony of that. The southerly buster that diverted the fire from St Andrews and saved his own family had driven it up the escarpment to wipe out Kinglake.

'When you coming home, Rodge? Everything's still on fire down here.'

'Soon, honey,' he says. A wrenching need to be there. 'Not just yet.'

'How's Kinglake?'

'Pretty much wiped out.'

A brief silence. 'You do what you have to, Roger.'

'Love you.'

'Yes.'

*

Roger Wood's family had a close shave. They'd spent an anxious day watching the smoke build up in the north, grow stronger as it approached St Andrews. Jo called her father, Ray, who came up from the city to add an extra pair of hands to the defence.

First they were showered with embers and ran around frantically putting them out. The first fires appeared, reached the property across the road; they saw the neighbours out there, attacking it with beaters. It was heading straight for them. Jo went through a rehearsal with the younger kids: they would shelter under a blanket in the bath while she, Ray and eighteen-year-old Dylan fought.

The wind became so wild Jo could barely stand up. The fire accelerated. The horses wheeled in a mob around the paddock, panicking. One broke its neck, another would die the next day from smoke and stress.

She felt a wave of fear, a trembling, teary moment. But that passed. She was a country woman, familiar with pumps and hoses. And she had the kids under her care. She went into action. Tried hosing down the house, but saw the water disappear into steam almost before it hit the wood.

She heard the terrifying roar and looked up reflexively,

commenting that somebody was flying pretty low.

'That's not a jet,' said Ray.

'Oh my god,' she whispered.

She called Roger, the unbearable truncated phone call that sent him into such a spin at Kinglake West.

As the connection went down, it seemed the fire would be upon them in a matter of seconds. There was a moment of stillness. The fire died down, a lull. Then a cool wind came streaming across her shoulders and the flames flared up again, but in a different direction, sweeping up towards the escarpment. The change had arrived.

She watched in disbelief. 'Thank you, Mavis,' she whispered. A prayer of gratitude to Roger's mother, who had died six months earlier and who, Jo knew, was looking after them.

She went inside, got a glass of water from the tap. Almost dropped it as she stared out the kitchen window. Another fire there, to the south, in the bush behind the house. Heading in their direction, driven this time by the southerly change.

'Not again,' she pleaded, as people all over the ranges were doing at that moment. She heard that roaring again, the sound like an aircraft overhead.

But this time it was. The helicrane, the monstrous chopper they called Elvis, came roaring in from the west, hit the fire with a load of water. Refilled at the dam and hit it again. Kept hitting it until the fire was beaten into submission.

The kids came outside, stood watching as the fire rampaged up the slopes to where their father was on duty.

*

Back at Whittlesea, Roger slumps forward in the seat, rests his head on the wheel. Drained. A nurse comes out and glares, insists on giving him and Cameron a check-up. Both men's eyes are stinging from the constant exposure to smoke and fire, their throats are raw. She takes them in and flushes out their eyes. Senior police officers appear, suggest it's time they call it a day, they've done enough. The medical staff concur.

Roger and Cam look at each other, the same response plain on their faces.

Bullshit.

Now that the first proper strike teams and ambulances are ready to tackle the mountain, they know their local knowledge will be needed more than ever. They've been in Whittlesea maybe fifteen minutes. It's time to get back up to Kinglake.

They jump back in the Pajero.

They don't see Wendy Duncan until a few weeks later, when she comes back to thank them for saving her life.

CONVOY

As Wood and Caine race out of Whittlesea they raise their eyes to the ranges: the first chance they've had to observe the scene from a distance. Only now do they realise how widespread the inferno has been. The hemisphere above them is on fire, a livid, swirling tableau; from the rolling foothills to the craggiest heights, everything is ablaze.

Just past the roadblock they catch up with an enormous convoy struggling up the mountain—maybe fifteen ambulances, half a dozen fire trucks—and at last they have a sense that things are stirring. Our wealthy, advanced society is bringing its weight to bear upon the disaster.

Roger and Cam made their rally-cross scramble down this road a mere twenty minutes ago, but already the road is impassable again. The return is a stop-start crawl that makes them aware just how lucky they were to make it down at all. Wood shudders to think what could have happened if they had been stranded on the way down.

In the short time since they made their descent, trees have continued to fall on the road. There are now so many that, even with a backhoe labouring at the front of the column, it takes them over an hour to complete a trip they'd normally do in ten minutes.

The falling of trees—those gargantuan denizens of the Kinglake forest—is a constant backdrop to everything the emergency services personnel do that night and for a long time afterwards. Trees fall for days, weeks. One of the two emergency services personnel who die in the campaign is killed by a falling tree.

(This in itself is remarkable in comparison with previous disasters: that despite numerous burnovers, entrapments and crashes, only two emergency services workers were killed during the entire crisis. The many, many commentators who were to criticise Fire Chief Russell Rees might think about that. It was on his watch that the advances in training and fire-ground practice that saved the lives of so many volunteers were instigated.)

The convoy grinds its way up the mountain. Metre by blackened metre, tree by fallen tree, the kilometre-long column of flashing lights continues its progress, bringing a skerrick of hope to those who see it. Help is on the way.

Roger Wood opens the throttle and overtakes the convoy, comes across a police car at the front: Terry Asquith and Scott Melville, two colleagues from Seymour. The only vehicle ahead of them is a backhoe heaving the burning debris off the road. They watch the heavy machine reef up flaming trees, power lines and poles, smashing a way through, and wish they'd had a few of those available earlier on.

Behind them the convoy stretches off into the darkness.

One of the trucks back there is from Panton Hill and among its crew is a firefighter named Bernie Broom. The Panton Hill tanker has been in the thick of it all afternoon down in St Andrews. They managed to save at least one house and Bernie, tackling his first big fire, thought they'd done pretty well.

Then they enter the fire zone. He and two of his crew-mates are sitting on the back under the roll-over protection canopy. They look back in horror as the vehicle inches its way up the hill, begins to trail past flaming houses and burnt-out cars, the carnage rolling out for kilometre after kilometre.

'Oh those poor fuckers.' Tanya, beside him, shakes her head and gives succinct expression to the emotion they all feel. 'Those poor fuckers.'

Like others, Bernie is struck by the quietness of the mountain: aside from the rumble of their own trucks and the odd crashing tree, there's an unnerving silence drawn over the scene. The stars are shining brightly, parabolas of embers arc from the trees.

They see few signs of life. They're observing one of the features of this disaster: there is a relatively small number of injuries. People either escaped or they died. When the figures are eventually tallied, it is found that there were 173 deaths and only 414 recorded injuries. Many of the houses they drive past now will later be found to have bodies in them.

At one stage, while the loader grinds away up ahead, they pull up close to a burning pile of logs. The crew on the back with Bernie notice, with some discomfort, the heat it is throwing out. Even now, six or seven hours after the fire passed through, it is still blasting out an intense radiant energy. 'Like sitting too close to an electric fire,' says Bernie. 'We stopped there for some obstacle up front and it just glowed—it was white hot in the middle.'

When the convoy reaches Kinglake West, the police officers find themselves in an argument with the leader of the medical team, who has been told to go straight through to Kinglake; Wood insists that they spare some of their number for Kinglake West.

The ambulance officer has her orders and sticks to her guns; she wants to push on. But the argument is resolved when members of the Kinglake West CFA flag them down, say they have casualties and need support. The ambo relents and assigns several vehicles to Kinglake West.

When the rest of the convoy finally crawls into Kinglake proper, the Panton Hill firefighters, like everybody else entering the town that night, are stunned.

'It was like a burning ghost town,' comments Bernie Broom. Then they reach the CFA building, still lit up by the jets from the service station, and there are people everywhere, dogs, cars. They are quiet, still in shock. After a quick conference with Captain Paul Hendrie, they set out to do what they can around the town.

Wood pulls into the police station. The burning utility and its trailer are still sitting in front of the station, and the building has sustained minor damage—a burnt veranda, cracked plate-glass windows—but the generator is still going and the interior lights beckon.

The two cops climb out, stand for a moment watching the emergency services teams swing into action. The paramedics begin treating people, the fire tankers are setting out in different directions.

They both understand that they still have work to do, and traumatic times ahead of them, but, for the moment, it's simply an enormous relief to know that theirs aren't the only flashing lights on the mountain.

Wood has been on the move for over fourteen hours. He thinks maybe a cup of tea is in order. He hasn't eaten a morsel of food all day, and maybe the tannin hit will convince some interior corner of his brain that the world isn't totally off its rocker.

They give themselves ten minutes. Sit alone in the station kitchen, mostly silent. The light from the burning servo casts its flickering glow across them.

Then they get on the road again.

ON AND OFF ROAD

The policemen's radios and mobiles are running hot with messages and requests.

The most worrying is a report of a mini-bus gone into a dam off Parkside Road; multiple fatalities. They cruise along the road, sweeping its smouldering margins with their spotlights. A trail of devastation, but no sign of a mini-bus in any of the dams.

They drive into the last property; everything is still burning viciously, impossible to approach. There's a car sitting there, and a trailer loaded with fire-fighting equipment, both vehicles burnt. They will come to recognise these as ominous indicators. The hoses are laid out, but everything is melted. Whoever was here put up a fight.

They circle the house with their torches, searching for signs of life. Find none. A chilling silence envelops the scene. Nothing to be done, though: whoever was here is either dead or fled.

They drive back out, pause at the corner of Parkside Road to discuss their options and a face suddenly looms in the window. Both men jump: a pair of Indian men are looking at them. They are workers from Singh's, the market garden Wood visited earlier in the day. The beautiful cool farmhouse he was so impressed by is now a smouldering wreck, but the family and their employees fled for the broccoli paddocks and survived. These men have only minor injuries. The policemen direct them to the aid stations being set up in the town.

They resume their patrol, encountering scattered little groups of desolate individuals, offering what support, solace or advice they can. They receive an urgent message that somebody is lighting fires down in the Hawkins Estate, scream down there, find only a group of locals putting out fires with wet hessian bags, conclude that every nerve on the mountain is shot to hell.

On their way back along Glenburn Road they encounter another of the eerie bushfire sights that will lodge in their memories: an abandoned fire truck. They get out and stare at it, bewildered. You don't just get up and walk away from a million-dollar vehicle. They check out the brigade name painted on the door: North Warrandyte. It's about forty kilometres from home. The appliance is badly battered, a windscreen smashed, stuck in a ditch. They poke around, see no signs of life—or death, thank god. Scratch their heads.

*

They have no way of knowing it at the time, but that vehicle is another indicator of how swift and brutal the fire has been. Later they find out that the North Warrandyte tanker, with Rohan Thornton in command, had struggled up the treacherous Kinglake–St Andrews Road when the fire was at its peak; other CFA members describe them as having almost 'surfed' the fire front. They'd come from St Andrews to rescue people trapped in a house, found their escape route back down the hill blocked, Kinglake the only option.

Crawling up the track in virtual darkness, they were battered by flying objects and blasting heat, struggling to see anything other than the lines on the road. Soon their brakes were gone, their driveshaft snagged in power lines. They spotted at least one body on the side of the road. As they reached the top of the mountain, they had to batter their way past the burnt-out vehicles cluttering the road—presumably cars that had tried to get down before the roadblock was set up.

Suddenly two cars came careering out of the smoke, panicky drivers at their wheels: they avoided one but T-boned the other. Wild fire surging in front of them, they managed a crazy turn by bouncing off a farm gate and drove back the way they'd come. A tree crashed; dodging sharply to avoid it, they plunged into a ditch with an impact so severe it broke Rohan's back. Immobilised, they put out a mayday as the fire swept over them; they turned on the crew protection system and lay sprawled out in the cabin. Gasping for air, blasted by radiant heat, slipping in and out of consciousness. When their crew protection water ran out they thought they were dead.

Incredibly, another truck, from Wonga Park under the leadership of Andrew Wright, managed to respond to their mayday. They followed the same nightmarish path, battering trees out of the way, inching through that blackness, ultimately locating their colleagues and bringing them back down the other side of the mountain.

Some residents of the ranges were angry that there were no tankers on hand when the fire struck. They felt they had been abandoned; that perhaps the town's destruction might have been less complete if the trucks had been there. Volunteers from Kinglake West report being abused, and the Flowerdale CFA was graffitied by locals annoyed that the truck was away.

The fate of the tanker that Wood and Caine found deserted like the *Marie Céleste* in Glenburn Road encapsulates why, even if the local tankers not been down the hill trying to defend their hometown against the fire coming up from St Andrews, their presence on the mountain would probably have had minimal effect. Indeed, many of the firefighters interviewed suggest that if they had remained on the mountain, they would most likely have died somewhere along the top of the escarpment as they struggled to intercept the fire.

It's hard to imagine a more dramatic illustration of the fact that, if you are going to make your home in a fire zone, the only person you can rely upon in an emergency is yourself. Like most country towns, Kinglake had hundreds of houses, and only two tankers to defend them. As was seen again and again, from Kilmore East to Kinglake West, from Steels Creek to Marysville, even the best-equipped, state-of-the-art fire appliance is struggling to save a single house when it is under attack from a fire the size of the Black Saturday inferno.

The CFA does its most important work in attacking minor outbreaks before they become conflagrations. Despite the shocking loss of life on Black Saturday, it could have been a lot worse. Around the state there were some five hundred outbreaks that day, and the vast majority of them were suppressed before they did much damage. Experienced firefighters speak with great admiration for the gutsy work done by their colleagues in suppressing a fire in Ferntree Gully in Melbourne's outer east that, had it got away, could have devastated the heavily populated Dandenong Ranges.

*

Wood and Caine climb back into their vehicle and continue their ghostly patrol, with the reported mini-bus playing on their minds: they never do find it, but they find a lot of other things, most of them in flames.

They're troubled by the dearth of survivors. What the death toll is going to be they have no idea. The number of people who found shelter at the CFA gives them some hope, but the forbidding silence that hangs over the burnt-out properties they inspect chills them to the core. And they know it will only get worse. The deaths they've already seen are but a forerunner. There will be many, many more and, as the local police officers, they'll play a critical role in uncovering them. But that will be over the next few days. Right now, most buildings are still too dangerous to approach.

They make a short run down the St Andrews road, but it's completely impassable: they get about a kilometre down the road before they're blocked by falling trees. Roger Wood sits staring at the road thinking about his family, somewhere down there on the other side of that inferno.

They're alive, that much he knows. Or they were a couple of hours ago. But there are still fires burning along Buttermans Track, on the edges of his property. Who knows what the hell's happening anywhere tonight? Those ruined houses and burnt-out cars are playing havoc with his nerves.

They turn the car around and get on with it; but some time around 4.30 am they get a call from their boss, Senior Sergeant Laurie Parker, in Seymour. He knows about Wood's situation, orders him to knock off, to get home and see his family. There are other officers on the way up, they can take over.

Wood relents. The urgency of the work to be done here is ebbing, and this driving round in the dark magnifies his feeling of helplessness, his feeling of insignificance in the face of the monstrosity. Time like that, family's really all you've got. His fears about them have been biting away at him all through the emergency. He's been on the go for eighteen hours and there isn't much more he can do right now.

It's time to go home.

He assures Cameron he'll be back later in the day and sets off in his private car. It has been sitting in the station garage all day and turns out to be unscathed.

Cam takes the opportunity to check up on his family too. He drives back to the Kinglake West CFA, where they are still sheltering; joins Laura for a cup of coffee. While he's there, Des Deas from the SES comes over and casually asks what happened to Cam's own house.

Cam looks at him blankly. 'Dunno, mate. Gone, I guess.' But he has no idea. In the chaos of the past few hours, he hasn't given it a thought. They drive round to have a look. Many of the nearby houses are gone, the fences and trees are still alight, but the Caine house is pretty well untouched.

Roger Wood, meanwhile, continues his solitary journey down the mountain. Because of the blocked road, he takes the roundabout way, back down through Whittlesea.

He drives, once more, through livid orange forests, past fire trucks and ambulances; reaches Whittlesea, takes the road that goes the long way to St Andrews.

The sun is coming up as he drives along the curving dirt track to his property. On the left-hand side, to the north, there are scorched paddocks and slopes. On the right, where his home is, the land appears untouched. His family—himself, really—have been saved by the same wind change that turned the fire around and drove it up into Kinglake.

He pulls into the drive. Jo is still awake, as are most other adult residents of St Andrews. All too nervous to close their eyes in case the fire comes back.

She looks up at him, smiles wearily.

'Kids?'

'In bed,' she says.

Arm in arm, they walk into the children's rooms, where he stands for a moment, watching them, lost in the gentle murmur of their breathing. Then he bends and kisses their sleeping heads.

BITTER HOMECOMING

When Dave Hooper and the crew of Kinglake Tanker One crawl back into what's left of their home town, they look around with the same feeling of disbelief that everyone has experienced.

'It was just...fuck, what do we do now? I mean, give us a fire and we'll put it out, but what do we do with this shit?'

They're barely back in the station when they head out on patrol, trying to see if there's anything left to rescue in their tormented town. Much of Kinglake is gone, but there are large sections that remain unburnt and with so many fires still raging close by, they have to remain on their guard.

When they're driving down his own street, Sycamore Avenue, Dave spots the familiar wicked glow near his house and comments, almost casually, 'There goes my joint.' But he's mistaken. The fire has taken out his fences and sheds—and his much loved Harley Davidson—but by some quirk of nature the house survives. He searches for his dogs, is relieved to find them still alive. He runs them down to the station, then they resume their patrol.

Later they will be able to identify only one Kinglake house they can be sure they saved that first night, but given the amount of burning debris and vegetation they extinguished, indirectly there would have been many others.

*

The crew of Kinglake Tanker Two also spend the rest of the night at work, battling the fire, saving houses, witnessing death and destruction. Gradually working their way back home. The

St Andrews–Kinglake Road is blocked again, so they make their way around the mountain. Through Christmas Hills, up the Melba Highway, cutting through back tracks and burning roads. It's around two in the morning when they limp back into town.

At the CFA Ben Hutchinson runs into a neighbour who tells him his house has been destroyed. He'd half-expected it, but it's a blow nonetheless. Trish Hendrie asks him what's wrong.

'Me house has burned down.'

'You're not alone there, mate,' she says with that growling Australian humour. 'So's Carole's, Phil's, Wendy's; Steve's too. Half the town's gone.' Later, when the losses are tallied up, they will find that among all the CFA brigades across the ranges, some twenty-five volunteers have lost their own homes.

For now, hearing that bleak list reminds Ben that he's part of a team. The crew catch a quick drink—they've been on the job for ten hours—then climb back onto the tanker to see if there's anything they can do to prevent further destruction.

The convoys from Whittlesea have arrived by now, so they have support, but there's no shortage of jobs to choose from. They patrol the town, extinguishing whatever they can. They hose down a plastic tank they find burning furiously next to a house—it would have taken out the building if they hadn't got to it in time—and they're reminded of 'normal' fire fighting.

'A good clean save,' Ben calls it, wryly. 'That's the way it's supposed to go.'

Sometime during the night, Ben suddenly realises he's so exhausted he can barely stand. The fire-lit roads are wobbling in front of him. He needs to knock off. Other CFA members relieve them, take over the truck.

Ben goes back to Barry Byrne's house and collapses onto the couch—covered in ash, eyes stinging, throat aching. It's still not safe out there: there are fires burning almost up to the veranda and trees crashing in the distance.

Ah fuckit, he thinks, and falls asleep. Some inner voice assures him that, after what he's seen that day, the fires won't touch him and he'll wake up with the dawn. Which he does.

*

First thing in the morning Ben makes the sombre journey back to his own home and trawls through the ruins, astonished by the thoroughness of the destruction. The massive redgum beams supporting the upper storey have simply vanished; the engine block of his car is melted.

When he goes to check on his neighbours, a middle-aged couple, he's disturbed to see their Magna still in the driveway, burnt out. He inspects it anxiously, but to his relief there's no sign of bodies. He checks the property; still nothing. He recalls hearing that they'd been planning to leave in the event of a fire, so maybe they hitched a ride out to the Melba Highway?

A few days later the Disaster Victim Identification Team discover their incinerated bodies in the house.

Ben goes back down to the CFA, jumps onto a truck and works non-stop for days. Keeps going until his superiors order him to stand down. 'Felt like telling them to bugger off,' he comments. 'What else was I supposed to do? Not like I had a home to go back to.'

For most of the CFA volunteers, it is simply not possible to stand still. They just want to keep going. If you stop, thoughts come flooding in. Better to exhaust yourself, dull the pain, hope that the waking nightmare will be less vivid than the ones that await you in your sleep.

Virtually every member of the brigade will spend the next few weeks on the go, putting out spot fires, organising food and emergency supplies, assisting with enquiries from the public. CFA members who hadn't been there on the mountain—John Stewart, who was in India, Darryl and Michelle Lloyd, who were in Sydney, Trish McCrae, down in Melbourne—come racing back and get stuck into the job, even though all of those just mentioned lost their homes.

They can't stand still. It's the adrenaline, the shock. The guilt: the creeping, unshakable, completely unjustified feeling that it was somehow their fault. That they'd failed.

NIGHTMARES

Roger Wood's day dawns grey, distasteful, dreadful. His hair is full of ash, his nostrils full of smoke. His mind is full of death. His eyes are killing him, he has the mother of all headaches and an ache in his neck that he doesn't like the feel of.

He tries to get some sleep but the phone begins ringing early and the news is all bad. About as bad as it could be, really, particularly from Strathewen, where the kids go to school and where he and Jo have many friends. A terrible number of those friends haven't made it.

Having experienced tragedy in their own lives, with the loss of their first child, Jo and Roger feel the pain of their friends and community all the more. 'I felt I knew what people were going through,' explained Jo.

Wood returns to Kinglake that afternoon, where the mopping-up continues and his colleagues are frantically struggling to cope with a battery of aftermath activities. The most ominous are the euphemistically named 'welfare checks'.

Wood began the previous day with a welfare check: an anxious father wanting to know his daughter was okay. She was fine, but he knows that the requests he's getting now aren't going to be so happily resolved.

This is one aspect of the job that people who get their idea of country policing from cosy rural soap operas would not appreciate: the cops have to find the bodies.

Victim identification teams and army personnel will eventually move in and take over, but that doesn't happen for some time. Even when the outside experts do arrive, they still need to make use of the Kinglake police. So many distraught relatives and friends want 'somebody local' to search for their loved ones. It seems the closest you can get to a personal touch in this monstrous business. Because of Sergeant John Ellks' policy of community involvement, many residents have the officers' numbers in their phones; they make their calls for help directly.

Then there is the simple practical problem that many of the street signs, house numbers and other markers have been destroyed. The outsiders might receive the request, but they need the locals to come along and help out.

Usually the locals can indeed help. And sometimes they know the people whose bodies they're uncovering. It all adds to the mounting trauma: the next few days are a procession of soul-shattering tasks for all of the police officers involved.

This is a job nobody should have to do, particularly somebody who knows the victims. Nobody should have to do it, but somebody does have to, and it is upon the weary shoulders of the local cops— and of the CFA, who are in a similar situation—that the task falls.

At one stage Wood is walking into a burnt-out property when he receives a call from Mandy Crowley, an old friend from the Mounted Branch.

'Rodge,' she says, 'just calling to check that you're all right.' She's working in the Command Centre at Victoria Police. 'I'm recording all the bodies that are discovered; where and when. Who by. Your name keeps coming up, so, you know...Just wanted to see if you're okay.'

'Thanks, mate.' He stares into the charcoal landscape and thinks about it for a few seconds. 'I'm right.'

For Cameron Caine and Sergeant John Ellks, the permanent officer in charge of the region, the darkest moment comes early on the Sunday after the fire. Ellks has come back to Kinglake at first light. He was on leave and has been fighting all night to save his own property in Whittlesea, then reported back for duty as soon as he was able.

The two officers meet at the site of the crash that claimed the life of their friend Gennaro Laudisio. Cam gives his senior a sad debriefing from the night before.

They spend the morning doing more welfare checks, often with the CFA—sifting and searching through gutted homes. Whenever they find bodies, they cover them with a blanket, try to afford them some dignity. But often there's very little left: a skull, maybe a few bone fragments. Sometimes what they believe to be two bodies later turns out to be four.

They reach the house in Reserve Road where they make the discovery they've both been dreading: the Buchanan children, Macca and Neeve, as well as Bec's brother Danny, and family friends Penny and Melanie Chambers.

'It was a terribly emotional experience,' says Ellks of that period. 'We all broke down occasionally.'

*

Roger Wood arrives back in Kinglake that afternoon, gets straight back into the grim task.

The police have been ordered to exercise caution: work in teams and restrict their searches to the daylight hours. The houses are still smouldering, and sifting through a building reduced to rubble or dragging aside sheets of twisted corrugated iron is not a task for a couple of cops working with their bare hands.

But they're under enormous pressure: they have grief-stricken friends and relatives on the phone begging for information, struggling to deal with the agony of not knowing. Most searches are carried out during the daylight hours, but such is the pressure they are under that they sometimes have to stretch the rules. By the second day there are more officers on the mountain, though still not as many as the Kinglake staff would like. Late that night Wood receives a call from a mate asking if he could check up on some family friends.

It's after midnight and he's due to knock off; he'll be going against orders. But there's a family somewhere, racked, desperate to know, hanging onto a sliver of hope. He decides to do this one last job.

He goes out with Mark Williams, one of the constables who was rostered on for that Saturday night but hadn't been able to get up the mountain; he worked instead at Whittlesea.

They get an address and drive out to the lonely ridgetop road, but the house numbers are destroyed. Wood rings back to get a better description of the property and the vehicles. Finds the place; is troubled to see that all three cars are in the driveway, incinerated. He's come to know what that means.

He takes a torch, walks around the house, beam sweeping. Nothing. There's no structure left, just a pile of smouldering rubble and roofing iron, the odd lick of flame drifting up from some persistent material, the odd shadow running over scorched ground. He pulls some timbers aside, a sheet of iron, a length of twisted steel. Still nothing.

One last piece of iron.

And there they are, huddled together in what might have been the living room. Two adults, two tiny children cradled in their arms.

He trails back to the car, sits in the driver's seat and covers his face with ash-covered fingers. Gives himself a moment. The image won't leave him, though; hasn't yet. Never will.

He and Mark ring the house with blue police tape, marking it for the victim identification officers who'll be following.

Wood is an Aussie bloke; he tends to keep his deepest emotions close to his chest. Jo recounts the story of their coming home after the death of the baby, Jesse. Roger's response, heartbroken as he was, was to throw himself into the farm work and spend long hours on the tractor or fixing fences.

But now the pain mounts up. There are so, so many deaths.

A few days later Wood pulls up outside the house of a good friend, a fellow parent at Strathewen school. He's come to say good-bye. Garry Bartlett died that Saturday, along with his wife, Jacinta, and their youngest daughter, Erryn.

He sits in the car, staring at the devastation. He thinks about the times they had together; a school working bee just the weekend before. Garry was a landscape architect, a local legend for the amount of work he put into the environment and the community. They were beautiful people.

Wood finds himself slumped against the car window, weeping. Not just for this one lost family but for all of them, all the poor souls in the district who died on his watch.

'We did our best,' he tells himself. 'We all did: me and Cam, the firies and DSE crews. It wasn't enough.'

Soon afterwards he and his station colleagues get together, resolve to go to every one of the funerals. And, over the next few weeks, that's exactly what they do.

BUSHFIRE BRAIN

When the sun rose on the Sunday from hell, the residents of the ranges crawled out of their shelters and hideaways, ash-covered and stunned. Bedraggled, staring out into a post-apocalyptic world.

All was black and smoking as far as the eye could see. No power, no water, no communications, no word of loved ones other than those within eyesight. Charred remains littered the earth: small birds, wallabies, power poles and cars; people. They commenced the nerve-shattering business of discovering who'd survived and who hadn't.

All too often, the news was bad. There were 173 deaths overall, 120 of them from the Kilmore East fire. Of the 2000 homes destroyed, 1200 of them were in this region.

As the magnitude of the disaster sank in, outside help began to arrive. The CFA became the focal point of the relief effort, dishing up meals, dispensing emergency supplies, acting as first port of call for the incoming organisations: Red Cross, army, Centacare, Salvation Army. Politicians and pop stars, cricketers and camera crews, they came and went. Some stayed longer than others, some kept in touch afterwards.

And then there were the funerals. The professional advice was only to go to those of people you knew well, otherwise the accumulated burden became too heavy. But many residents found themselves turning up to a dozen or more heartbreaking ceremonies. Again and again, at churches and centres all over the region, the melancholy ritual was repeated: the flowers and photos, the treasured objects— footy jumpers, teddy bears, battered guitars—the weeping relatives and weak tea. The casket, or caskets; the long black cars.

People moved through it all in a state of shock.

Then, as the disaster receded, they set about rebuilding their lives. Some, maybe 40 percent, left the community. Whether or not that decision turned out to be wise varied enormously. Some said they felt like aliens down in the 'burbs and returned as often as they could; they missed the shared experience, the solidarity. Others were glad to be out of the place.

Demolition crews and insurance assessors moved in, builders and bureaucrats followed. The quality of the builders—variable at best—and the pedantry of the officials charged with issuing everything from building permits to lost documents became hot topics of conversation.

People were making life-changing decisions, but often they were in no state to do so. The experts called it post-traumatic stress; the locals had a more vivid expression: 'bushfire brain'.

The world seemed disordered, adrift, not quite real. Residents were on edge, forgetful, insomniac, frustrated by minor obstacles. There were individuals who threw their belongings into the car and left the mountain, unable to face filling in another form.

Some turned to drink or drugs to ease the pain; the police found more and more of their time taken up with domestic violence and drink-driving.

*

The human desolation was mirrored in the devastation of the natural environment, which had been what drew people there in the first place. There was a general fear that the bush was beyond repair, that it would never recover its former glory. Even to an experienced professional like Tony Fitzgerald, the destruction was deeper than anything he'd ever imagined.

'Fire like that,' he says, 'all bets were off. We weren't sure what would come back, if anything. Our worry was that we'd be left with just scorched ground.'

The magnificent stands of mountain ash that had been his working day's delight were obliterated, the massive trunks that remained staring out over the land like monuments to dead kings. The hundreds of hectares of the Everard block had formerly been covered with a thick storey of banksias—a pyrophiliac species if ever there was one. Normally in a fire their wafery seeds would fly out of the cones and waste no time re-establishing themselves in the ash bed. After Black Saturday Fitzgerald and botanist colleague Cam Beardsell were shocked to find the trees totally destroyed.

'Even the cones were burnt,' he says. 'You'd find a blackened stump, thick as your thumb. That was it.'

After hours of searching, they came across a single tree that had survived through some quirk of physics or topography. Determined to hang on to any symbol of hope in those dark days, they immediately threw a protective barrier around it. Took cuttings, replanted them at the nursery.

But they were worried. There'd already been twelve years of drought. If the rain failed for one more year there would be unimaginable changes in the landscape. A Burnt Area Emergency Response team carried out a geomorphological study of the region and made a startling discovery: there'd been a shift in the very composition of the earth. The soil to the south side of the park, with its high clay content, had been burnt so deeply it was now glazed, like pottery fired in a kiln.

As Fitzgerald and his crews worked away in the charred landscape, they were chilled by the silence that lay upon it. The sounds that normally formed the soundtrack to their working day—the birdsong and the screeching insects, the thumping kangaroos—were gone.

The bigger birds might have fled before the flames, but the smaller species—the fragile wrens and robins, the treecreepers and silvereye—had been wiped out. Larger animals such as kangaroos would normally outrun a fire, but in this all-consuming blaze they had been trapped. He'd seen it on the day: they'd flee to what they assumed was an island of safety, only to find themselves over-whelmed as the fire swept in from every direction at once.

Stella and Allan Reid ran an animal sanctuary named Wildhaven, on the road to Kinglake. Stella, out on a CFA truck when the fire struck, watched from a distance as her life's work—and her home, and very nearly her husband—were incinerated. Touring the prop-erty afterwards, she was devastated by what she found: 'Hundreds and hundreds of animal bones: kangaroos, wallabies, possums, echidnas, their little teeth lying in the white ash. Between our home and Kinglake few survived, millions died.'

The rangers made spotlight walks, searching desperately for signs of life and came up with nothing. They found the bones of kanga-roos wedged into wombat holes where they tried to shelter. They stared up into the scorched crowns, wondered how anything—any sugar glider or koala—could have survived.

*

Roger Wood was no exception to the general mood. In the weeks following the fire, he threw himself into the recovery operation with the slightly manic energy shown by all the emergency services personnel, a determination to do whatever they could to alleviate the despair. And there were moments of light amid the over-whelming blackness. He came across friends he'd feared were lost, was the occasional bearer of news that was good rather than bad, was able to find some satisfaction in putting his local knowledge to good use.

On one of his trips down the mountain, driving past the ruined house of his good friends Drew Barr and Angie O'Connor, he was amazed to spot Chaz, the dog they thought they'd lost. He was sitting faithfully by the photo album Drew had soaked as they fled. Roger arranged for the CFA to take the album and the dog down to St Andrews, and the photo of Angie's joyful reunion with the family's lost pet was flashed around the world.

Even that little incident had its downside, though. 'I just about got killed trying to save that album,' said Drew. 'Then I opened it up and found that it was an old one of Angie's—and the photos in there were mostly of her bloody ex-boyfriend!'

Between recovery work, funerals and the post-disaster tension in the town, it was a hectic time for Wood. But within a few days it became apparent that something was not quite right. What started out just after the fires as a nagging pain in his neck became, over the next few months, a searing agony that left him barely able to move. There were strange shooting pains up the length of his arms, too. He'd never had such problems before. The doctor suggested that the huge adrenaline overdose of Black Saturday would have had a lot to do with it.

A series of tests showed the pain in his arms to be carpal tunnel syndrome: no picnic, but curable with an operation. The neck was the real worry. The diagnosis was severe damage to the upper vertebrae, with bulging discs at C3 and C4. Prospects of recovery were reasonable, but there were no guarantees. There was every chance that his career was over, even that he'd end up in a wheelchair.

When he was given the news, Wood's mind ran through the events of Black Saturday and zeroed in on the incident at the Kinglake West school: leaping the high cyclone-wire fence as the fire closed in, crash-landing on his back.

He was forced to take leave from the job that had defined him, uncertain whether he'd ever be able to go back.

As the days grew short and the winter wind came scything down the slopes around St Andrews, his situation grew progressively bleaker. This fit, powerful man who could spend all day breaking horses or splitting wood was laid so low he could barely lift a screwdriver, let alone an axe. He spent slow, frustrating hours staring out the window at the blackened slopes; taking the long walks the doctors had suggested might help the injury.

None of it did much good. By October he knew that surgery was his only chance. Even more frustrating than his personal situation was his inability to help the Kinglake community. Cameron

Caine was on long-term leave as well. Now, more than ever, people needed to see a familiar figure in the uniform. They'd gone through the nightmare side by side; it seemed only right that they should go through the recovery together.

He could still drive. He and the family would often pile into the Pajero of an evening and drive up to Kinglake, share a meal with friends at one of the community venues that had sprung up after the fire. An essentially positive person with a strong family to support him, Roger Wood never succumbed to the depression that afflicted so many others in the wake of the fire. But his head was full of dark memories, haunting images. A counsellor told him he was suffering from post-traumatic stress. Its most potent manifestation was guilt.

'Survivor guilt, I suppose you'd call it,' he says; we're talking in his living room, months after the fires. 'Still can't get it out of my brain, things we did that day. What we saw, keep going over it. Every decision I made. Made 'em on the run, had no choice; but you keep asking yourself, Did I do the right thing?' He picks up his mug of tea and contemplates the far wall. 'We did our best, me and Cam, but Jesus there were a lot of poor buggers didn't make it.'

If there is a single emotion that runs like an electric current through the minds of just about everybody touched by Black Saturday, it is guilt. I interviewed dozens of survivors and almost all of them manifest it in some way; scratch the surface and it's there. It's like an infection that keeps breaking out.

One of the firefighters was moved to comment: 'Geez, I lost my own house, just about lost me life. I know we saved a few people. Why the fuck do I feel so guilty?'

Some feel it because they survived and their friends didn't. Some because the neighbours lost the house and they didn't. Emergency workers feel guilty because so many people died: their primary responsibility was to save lives, ergo they must have failed. Parents feel guilty for putting their children through that terror. Many kids even feel guilty for not being able to help as their parents fought the fire. Some feel guilty because they stayed, others because they left late and were nearly killed. Just about everybody feels they should have been better prepared.

Dr Paul Valent, a psychiatrist and Holocaust survivor, commented on the second anniversary of the fire:

> Something major has happened that's implanted in the brain. It's like a big, dark gravitational force. Everything has imploded in there. It's invisible but it's got enormous energy. You can't think about it, you can't talk about it, and you don't have words for it. It's overwhelming.

Disaster survivors, he says, can

> ... disconnect parts of their minds: emotions, thoughts. But when you kill off parts of yourself, you can't negotiate what you kill off. If you kill off guilt, you also kill off love. If you cut off from fear, you experience psychic numbing. You can't be loving and creative and whole any more.

What Valent is saying is that those with the richest emotional lives—people who are by nature caring and empathetic, the very people most likely to find themselves at the forefront of a disaster—are the most likely to suffer from negative feelings such as guilt and sadness in its wake.

*

Mid-winter, the snows arrived. Scattered all over the region were people huddling over tiny radiators in shacks and caravans, the denuded earth around them slushy with ash and mud. Many an anxious glance was cast at the incinerated bush, the grieving neighbours, the mounting bills.

People were horrified by the expense of rebuilding: the new Bushfire Attack Level regulations could add anything from $100,000 to $150,000 to the cost of building a house in the flame zone. In some cases it might have doubled the cost—and the increased costs meant most people found themselves underinsured. Many, maybe 30 percent, were not insured at all. The fire was a financial as well as human disaster.

People wondered whether they'd ever again own the roof over their heads. Nothing raised the hackles as much as somebody outside the burn zone asking, 'Things getting back to normal up there yet?'

Many a soul in the Kinglake Ranges wondered if things ever would get back to normal.

RESURRECTION

The seeds of the recovery were there all along. They'd been planted by various members of the community, whether they realised it or not, almost as soon as the roar died down. It was just that the results, like mountain ash germinants, took time to emerge from the ashes. Outsiders came in to help, and they were important, but the real driving force to the community's recovery could only come from within. And it did.

Out of a hundred possible examples, here are a handful.

The Strathewen school burned down on the Saturday night. The principal, Jane Hayward, and her colleagues didn't know whether their own houses were still standing but they spent the Sunday organising a new school for the shell-shocked kids, half of whom had lost their homes, all of whom had lost friends. The new school opened a couple of days later in nearby Wattle Glen, and young survivors scattered all over the area were able to link up with their mates and help each other through the recovery.

A group of local women—Jemima Richards, Kate Riddell and Arwyn Taylor—set up a relief centre that morphed into an organisation called Firefoxes and went on to provide an astonishing range of support activities for families in the district.

A woman named Lesley Bebbington, who had lost her own home to the fires, recognised that the young people of the region were experiencing a trauma of their own. She organised a youth group, supported with her own funds, that soon had a hundred teenagers turning up at the centre.

Barely a week after the fires, with the bush still smouldering all round him, Cameron Caine addressed a meeting of the Football and Netball Club and asked whether they could form a team. The response was an overwhelming, 'Bloody oath we can!' The entire district would follow the fortunes of the Lakers that season. Sport was one of the poles around which recovery revolved.

Art was the other. A manna gum near the bridge at Strathewen came to be known as the Poetry Tree. That blackened stump was a lightning rod for the storm of emotions that swept through the region: songs of love, death and memory were plastered all over its scorched bark. A community choir called the Phoenix Singers rose out of the ashes. Blacksmiths forged leaves for a steel memorial tree; they received contributions from all around the world. Local musicians sang alongside artists such as Paul Kelly, Lee Kernaghan—even retired-rocker-turned-politician Peter Garrett—at concerts throughout the district. There was barely a painter, poet or songwriter in the ranges whose work was not shot through with bursts of crimson.

The twin poles—art and sport—came together one blustery afternoon in September when local muso Ross Buchanan, whose children Macca and Neeve died, got up at the local football grand final and joined Prime Minister Kevin Rudd in a performance of the national anthem. The emotional resonance was extraordinary. There is a tribe in New Guinea, the Kaluli, who hold that music is a form of communication with the dead; there were those on the oval that afternoon who felt, fleetingly, the same thing.

As the people of the community found the resources within themselves to rise from their near-death experience, so did the environment.

Tony Fitzgerald found cause for hope in fleeting images of resilience: a koala spotted trundling along near the Strathewen school, a lace monitor that must have buried itself as the storm passed over it. His greatest thrill came the day he flew over the ghostly remains of the mountain ash at Wallaby Creek and spotted flashes of green among the sea of brown.

He pinpointed the spot on a map, made a closer inspection on foot and found that maybe as many as fifty trees had survived. Some were even sending up epicormic shoots. In both cases, they were breaking the rules: mountain ash will not normally survive a cranking fire like this one, and, unlike other eucalypts, they don't make use of epicormic growth.

The long-term survival of the many of the drought-stressed trees was still dependent upon rain. The rainfall that winter was reasonable, the next it was incredible, the wettest year the state had ever known. The CFA found themselves rescuing people from floods, not fire. Fitzgerald went into the forest, marked out a couple of metre-square plots, counted around two hundred mountain ash germinants springing through the chocolate soil.

'That was a breath-taking moment,' he says. 'They were coming back. I might be standing in a cemetery of big dead trees, but the forest was recovering.'

It wasn't just the mountain ash, of course. Botanist Carl Just found that the combination of fire and rain was doing astonishing things to the bush. He identified some fifty species—among them tall shaggy peas, bluespike milkwort and long-style bitter-cress—that had never been recorded in Kinglake. The orchids were amazing, tiny medallions of colour amid the black and green: locals had never seen them in such profusion.

There were still heavy loses. A significant stand of old-growth myrtle beech rainforest at the headwaters of the Plenty River, for example, was totally cooked. A handful of mountain ash survived, but thousands died.

'After the rains,' said Fitzgerald in March 2011, 'most areas of the park have now got good, solid vegetation, with 80 to 100 percent covering. But on some of the dry ridges it's still at around 50 percent.' The bare, scorched earth is becoming badly eroded, with vicious gullies cutting into the slope, rock falls common. Its long-term prospects are unknown.

*

As so often happens, what's happening in the environment is reflected in the residents. You hope you've turned a corner, but it's a dicey business at best: sometimes you run into a brick wall.

'The State Emergency Response Plan dictates that the infrastructure of communities that have been struck by disaster should be better than it was before, and by and large that's happening,' says Colin French, a member of the Community Recovery Committee. 'Schools, the church, the tennis courts, the Building Advisory Centre, the National Park Visitors' Centre, the Youth Space, they're all coming along.' As is the Wilderness Camp he and his wife Michelle have been working furiously to rebuild. 'But inside people's heads, it's a different matter. Some are coping. An awful lot aren't.'

Michelle recently returned from a women's weekend get-together at Mansfield. 'I'd thought most of us were getting on top of things,' she comments. 'But when you sit down and talk, heart to heart, you see that a lot of survivors are still grieving, still deeply scarred.'

The scarring expresses itself in many forms: people can be quick to anger or tears, frustrated by the smallest things. It's an emotional rollercoaster, according to Carole Wilson. 'There's been a lot of marriage break-ups, suicides,' she says; local medical professionals report a sharp increase in stress-related illnesses.

'I look at other disasters differently now,' says Di MacLeod. 'Earthquakes in Japan, floods in Queensland. You understand what people are going through.'

Perhaps the most troubling long-term manifestation of the scarring is among the youth of the community. 'The fire brought about a fundamental change in the relationship between kids and their parents,' says Lesley Bebbington. She recounts the story of a teenager screaming at his mother as the house was engulfed, 'Are we going to die?'

'I don't know,' she yelled as she dashed back to the fire.

Lesley comments: 'They've seen that their parents are not infallible.' The result is a sharp increase in family stress and breakdown, as well as adolescent risk-taking behaviour of every description: alcohol, drugs, promiscuity. There are stories of children sneaking anti-depressant pills to their parents in the hope that it will make things right. 'One mental health youth worker told us he had seventeen kids in a critical condition,' says Bebbington. 'In a population this size, he'd normally expect one.'

Two years after the fire less than half of those hoping to rebuild their homes have managed to do so; most remain in rented accommodation, many in shacks and caravans.

All of them view the countryside now through the filter of fire. A crimson sunset or a mystic valley can make you shiver. The wind will keep you awake at night. Houses are no longer assessed for their architecture or views, but for their vulnerability.

The survivors' world will never be the same.

A REFLECTION

We no longer have roots, we have aerials.
McKenzie Wark

Some years ago I lived for a time with Warlpiri people in Central Australia, and spent many an evening watching them sing to the elemental forces that kept the country whole. Prominent among those forces was fire. They respected fire as one of the shapers of country, they understood it, they feared and respected it. Ceremonies were always performed by firelight, with the participants often running a gauntlet of flaming brands. The embers that floated off into the night sky merged in their myths and in their minds' eye with the constellations whirling overhead. Fire inevitably entered the dreaming. Walk into any collection of Aboriginal art and chances are there'll be a fire painting on the wall.

These dreamings are not trivial. They are not abstract philosophy to be buried away in books, or cute stories to be told around a campfire. They are lessons about how to live in the land, truths that have evolved over tens of thousands of years. They determine the behaviour of every individual, from the infant to the elder. To Aboriginal people, they are raw power.

So how does contemporary Australia respond to the dilemma of fire?

With lawyers.

On February 13, 2009 Premier John Brumby appointed Justice Bernard Teague to head the Victorian Bushfires Royal Commission with the announcement that it would 'leave no stone unturned'. And after daily media reports of 154 days of evidence from more than four hundred witnesses, the Victorian public must surely have felt that had been the case.

A REFLECTION

The Royal Commission, as is usual with Australian government inquiries, was conducted by that profession whose primary function is to find somebody guilty or innocent. The question of how things—systems, organisations, training—can be improved to stop the calamity happening again is also central, but the blame game always appears to be more so, at least in the eyes of the media.

In this case the main villain of the piece was held to be CFA chief Russell Rees who, as the *Age* reported on the day of his resignation, 'copped severe criticism in the commission's interim report, which concluded he failed to take a direct management role on Black Saturday "even when the disastrous consequences of the fires began to emerge"'.

The heads of the other emergency services involved—the police, the DSE—were also criticised.

When the Royal Commission released its final report in July 2010, prominent among its sixty-seven recommendations were those calling for an overhaul of the 'stay and defend or leave early' policy, an increase in the amount of fuel-reduction burning, the replacement of overhead power lines and a buyback scheme for dwellings in dangerous locations.

The recommendations are sensible and practical, along the lines of the sensible recommendations made whenever there's a disaster and a commission or inquiry is constituted to stop it happening again. Where they are adopted, they will most likely save lives.

But one of the dispiriting features of these inquiries is the assiduity with which those recommendations are ignored once the trauma has passed. In 1939, after Black Friday, the Stretton Inquiry's recommendations included: reconstruction of the relevant fire authorities, reallocation of resources, establishment of refuges, an increase in controlled burning. Seventy years later, years in which our society's wealth, science and communication capabilities have increased immeasurably, Justice Teague and his colleagues were forced to cover much of the same ground.

Sometimes, through sheer intelligence or perhaps because of the emotions generated in a jurist who has peered into the abyss, there are flashes of wisdom. Justice Leonard Stretton, who headed the 1939 Royal Commission, coined one such insight with the comment: 'They had not lived long enough.'

He meant that his fellow Australians were living in an environment into which they had not had time to evolve. Unlike the Warlpiri, they were strangers in their own land. They—we—shot first and asked questions later.

If we had not lived long enough in 1939, it seems that seventy years later we still haven't. Indeed, it could be argued that we've gone backwards: 71 people died on Black Friday in 1939, 173 on Black Saturday 2009. Of course the population has grown, but so have our defences. The victims in 1939 had no idea what was coming until they saw the inferno surge over the hill. Now we have aircraft, radio, radar, the internet, a well-equipped fire-fighting force and a vastly greater understanding of how fire works. But still, the devastation was terrible.

What's gone wrong?

More miles on the clock we well may have, but our cultural awareness of the environment has not kept pace. Some would argue that it is slipping backwards: 'As we've become more addicted to the trappings and technologies of the virtual world,' comments fire scientist Nic Gellie, 'we are losing our awareness of the natural one.' Technology can be a snare for the unwary. One of the images that recurs from that day is of people who perished because they were staring at a screen and not at the sky. Others seemed to assume that, because there were a couple of fire trucks in town, one would necessarily be propped in front of their own house when the blaze came.

People involved in the emergency services shake their heads in despair as they drive through their own communities: they see overgrown houses in dangerous locations, woodpiles on back verandas, gutters stuffed with leaves. Whenever there's a crisis, they have people rushing up at the last moment and asking, 'What are we supposed to do?'—as if the CFA had not spent years trying to tell them exactly that. As John Handmer said at the Royal Commission, some people were 'in denial of the fire threat to the last, purposefully ignoring—in some cases, mocking—the advice of friends, relatives or agencies'. These people, he said, 'had made a conscious decision to take no action'.

Then, when the unthinkable occurs, we search for scapegoats: it's all the fault of the CFA, the DSE, the local council, the tree changers, the police, the greenies. It's always somebody else. The accusing finger sweeps out, searching for a target. Only rarely does it turn back towards its owner. We blame the government for insufficient preventative burns—but what is government if not a reflection of the people it governs? Most of the land around Melbourne is privately owned, and landowners almost universally lack the knowledge (and, rightly, the confidence) to put match to fuel. It simply sits there, accumulating energy, salting away firepower.

Our failure to engage with fire is a failure of our culture. The lesson of how to live with our environment has yet to sink into our bones. Rather than adapting to our environment, we are isolating ourselves from it, building barriers of plastic and steel between ourselves and the real world.

But environments don't just go away because you ignore them. They need to be worked at, handled with care, respected; and if they are not, they can come back and savage you. Empires from the Mayan to the Egyptian have collapsed because this adamantine truth was disregarded.

Now, looming like a spectre behind these considerations, is the question of global warming. As the planet heats up, scientists predict that temperatures and rainfall will increase. These make a deadly duo: rainfall will increase the fuel load and heat will bring it closer to ignition. Future fires will be worse than ever.

Modelling by the Commonwealth Scientific and Industrial Research Organisation forecasts that the number of fire-prone days will increase dramatically. By 2050, days of very high to extreme fire danger for southern coastal cities such as Melbourne will increase from the present five to ten per year to between ten and fifteen. Further north, the situation worsens: high-danger days will rise from twelve up to seventeen a year for coastal communities such as Sydney. The residents of inland cities such as Canberra or Bendigo will face catastrophic conditions: twenty to thirty-five dangerous days a year.

What will rural Australia look like a hundred years from now? Conceivably, a procession of dying towns and jungly thickets from which frequent fires erupt and lash the dwindling population. Fire one year, flood the next, each giving a fillip to the other.

Town dwellers will be affected too, and not just the millions who live along the city's edges but all urban residents. Even a city of steel and stone is in many ways a reflection of its environment. Its occupants need drinking water, and fire can do terrible damage to a city's water supply. They need the green lungs of the forest to purify the air they breathe. They need food. As the smothering blanket of global warming descends and the oil runs out, our cities are going to have to become more self-sufficient, and that will be made vastly more difficult if they're located in an environment fraught with fire. And fires, like floods, rip massive holes in the economy: they destroy homes, businesses, livelihoods.

Such concerns seem to have been largely absent from the trophy-hunting convolutions that surrounded the Black Saturday Royal Commission. So eagerly were barristers and journalists circling for a kill—why did the Police Commissioner go out to dinner that night? What happened to the missing map?—that there was little attention left, it seemed, for an examination of the nation's soul.

There were few headlines about people's lack of preparedness. Nobody was questioning cultural conditions such as rampant expansionary consumerism or a political system in which any attempt to reduce carbon emissions can be exploited as a chance to arouse fear and win votes.

The Royal Commission's recommendations mostly depended

on government action: burying power lines, increasing prescribed burns, creating community refuges, instituting a stronger emphasis on warnings and a more unified approach to fire management. These outcomes may affect some of our thinking for a time. But they'll be worth precious little if they do not also change us, heart and soul, in the way that music or art or raw emotion can change us—if they are not accompanied by a fundamental shift in attitude, one that stretches from the halls of power to the family weekender in the bush.

There are many things we can do as individuals to reduce risk: develop a fire plan, join the CFA, install a pump or a bunker, organise a local fireguard group. We need to assess our own situations, understand the risks, remove them if we can, remove ourselves if we can't. More than anything else, we need to educate ourselves. But some things are beyond the powers of any one person.

Consider, as an example, the question of arson. We have a critical problem in our midst and it's not going away any time soon. Even in the summer of 2009–10, after all the devastation and despair the state had witnessed, some 750 fires were deliberately lit across the state.

If you were to ask the average resident of the burnt-out areas what to do about firebugs, the answer would probably include hempen rope and good strong branches. The very word tends to raise the hackles, and understandably so: that some whacko could deliberately inflict such trauma upon his fellow creatures just about defies belief.

But a response based purely upon the desire for retribution will simply not work. Arson is a manifestation of complex societal problems, and it can only be resolved by society-wide responses—a comprehensive program, for example, targeting at-risk communities and supported by all relevant agencies: fire and mental health services, police, justice and social welfare. The teacher delivering after-school programs or the youth worker providing interventional counselling will arguably have more impact on the prevention of arson than a fleet of fire trucks.

Perhaps there is also a case to be made for a more interventionist legal approach. South Australia has an apparently successful program called Operation Nomad in which known, or even suspected, arsonists receive close police attention on blow-up days. Victoria has recently introduced a program called Operation Firesetter, which will increase police patrols in fire-prone areas, although it doesn't appear to be as proactive as its South Australian counterpart in that the cops don't go banging on suspects' doors. Some commentators go further, suggesting that surveillance aids such as electronic bracelets should be mandatory for anybody with a history, even a suspected history, of arson.

There is a debate here that we need to take on. Both approaches raise questions about civil liberties, about infringements of an individual's legal rights. That we are innocent until proven guilty is one of the foundations of our legal system. But legal rights must seem the flimsiest of apparitions to a parent watching her family die by fire.

Another example of wider thinking that offers a promising lesson for the future comes from a small community near Castella, in the heavily timbered eastern part of the ranges. By rights, the twenty or so houses near Castella shouldn't still be standing. They were struck by fire as intense as most other places in the ranges, and yet they survived.

How did they avoid the general destruction? It was a combination of factors. In the first place, the DSE had carried out carefully targeted burns, totalling around 450 hectares, in the years before Black Saturday. But just as importantly, the community was actively involved in its own defence. There was a strong fireguard group, so the residents were there to inform and support each other. Two farms in particular were well prepared: they had cattle grazing right up to their houses and four-wheel-drives with mounted fire-fighting units. When the fire came they fought collectively, as a community, and they won.

Whether this modest example can provide a model for society is a big question. The broader scenario is of course much more complex;

there will always be a range of individuals with different levels of experience and knowledge; governments will come and go, their priorities often determined by factors that appear to have little to do with rural Australia. But surely it is a question we have to tackle. The consequences of not doing so are too serious to ignore, and the thousands of Melburnians who had a close escape on February 7 might not be so lucky next time.

*

If there's a glimmer of light in the terrible story of Black Saturday, it emanates from the dozen or so individuals featured in this book—and not from them alone, for there were thousands of others like them. Coppers racing around trying to save lives; firies scrambling on foot in the moonlight to reach endangered properties, forcing their chainsaw blades into one more tree; women who put aside their own suffering to help rebuild the community. Most moving of all, the parents who sacrificed themselves in the attempt to save their children.

These deeds are testament, all, to the power of the human spirit. We can do amazing things when we see a need. There is a need now. If we can turn that fitful glimmer onto our future, if we can absorb something of its energy, then there'll be a way forward. We may acquire the strength to make decisions, the sense to take precautions, the wisdom to develop, like the Warlpiri, fire ceremonies of our own.

If we do those things, then 173 souls will not have died in vain.

If we fail to, there will be many more to join them.

*

It is a cool night in August, 2010. Many residents of Kinglake are enjoying the deepest laugh they've had all year as they gather to watch *Paydirt*, a rattling musical comedy written by Ross Buchanan. It is the ultimate bravura performance, a heart-rending manifestation of the healing power of art and music.

A few metres from the hall, the bush is stirring. Tendrils twist and creep, triffid-like, buds are bursting, seeds are responding with astonishing alacrity to the twin forces of fire and water. The growth this year has a wild profusion most observers have never seen.

'Looks like an oil slick to me now,' comments firefighter Di MacLeod as she surveys the lush new growth. 'Year or two, the fire threat'll be worse than ever.'

In millions of homes across the country, residents switch off the television, adjust the air con, kill the lights and slip into bed. Some on the fringes of the city might spare a thought for the looming summer and its threats, but few will do much about it.

Really, what are the odds?

UPDATE

A quick survey of some of the individuals who have contributed their stories to this book:

Drew Barr and Ange O'Connor stayed with their in-laws in nearby Cottles Bridge. They briefly considered moving to Queensland, but decided they were too close to the community to leave it, and purchased a house in nearby Wattle Glen. Like a lot of survivors, Drew found his brush with death made him reassess his goals in life. He resigned from the superannuation industry and is undertaking a permaculture design course. Drew has joined the CFA. 'We realise we were incredibly lucky to survive,' says Ange, 'but we can't undo the girls' trauma.'

Tim and Linda Huggins remain in Kinglake, where the newspaper Tim edits, the *Mountain Monthly*, has become an important local voice. 'Still on the warrior path,' he says wryly—he recently added a sixth Australian tae kwon do title to his collection—but the words have assumed a new dimension for him in the wake of the fire.

Di MacLeod resigned from her position with an import business. 'They just didn't understand,' she says. 'Within three days of the fire, they were ringing me up saying, "When can you come back to work?" While we were still out fighting fires!' After a period of unemployment, she obtained a job in the local childcare centre. She is undertaking a degree in counselling.

Phil Petschel purchased a new house in Kinglake. He's found it hard to get used to having neighbours after the splendid isolation of Bald Spur Road, but he's doing okay. Two years down the track, Carole Wilson and Trish Hendrie remain in temporary accommodation, while Ben Hutchinson has recently completed his new house.

All remain active members of the CFA, as do John Grover, Frank Allan, Karen Barrow, Karyn Norbury, Paul Lowe and Dave Hooper. Karyn Norbury is at present the captain of the Kinglake West CFA; her family and farm survived. Kelly Johnson has gone to university, where she is studying international development; she has spent time working as a volunteer in the third world.

The CFA brigades have had a small increase in their number of volunteers, but no more than that: members are still reduced to standing around at markets with collection tins in hand to raise the funds they need to carry out their vital role.

Tony Fitzgerald suffered a number of health problems after the fire, something he suspects was due to the stress of the disaster. His situation was aggravated by a local resident's complaint that his last-ditch backburn added to the intensity of the fire. He had to live with that hanging over his head for a year, but his actions were completely vindicated by forensic fire scientists at the Royal Commission. He still works as a ranger, but has decided to take a break from the stressful fire-management aspect of the job. He and his family have purchased a house in the nearby suburb of Hurstbridge.

Aaron Redmond remains a member of the DSE crew. While some of his colleagues resigned after the fire, Aaron found it a life-changing experience of a different kind. He plans to enhance his skills and training in the field of fire management. (Like much else in Kinglake, the fire was something of a family affair. Aaron's mother is Kerrie Redmond, the CFA volunteer who helped save Drew and Ange; Jane Hayward, the Strathewen school principal, is his aunt.)

Wendy Duncan made a strong recovery from her injuries and returned to her legal practice, but has left the community. She now lives on the south coast, where she shares a house with her rescuer, Lorraine Casey.

Mike Nicholls has left the region to take up a new position as Professor of Psychology at Flinders University in South Australia.

Cameron Caine threw himself into the recovery effort and emerged as one of the community leaders. Particularly important was his role as president of the Football and Netball Club. He returned to the team himself, booted some sixty goals and in that first season saw the Lakers through to the grand final. His days were filled with furious activity, but his nights were haunted by images of the fires. Finally he was forced to take time off the job. He stood as a candidate in the 2010 federal election; he didn't win, but did use the campaign as a platform to speak out on behalf of the bushfire victims. At the time of writing he has returned to active duty as a senior constable at the Kinglake police station.

Roger Wood underwent the operation on his neck at the Epworth Hospital in February 2010. Everything went well. After a slow, painful recuperation period, he returned to work on light duties in June 2010 and was fully operational by October.

In October 2010 Roger Wood and Cameron Caine were presented with Victoria Police's highest award, the Valour Award, for their actions on Black Saturday. The four other officers mentioned in this narrative, senior constables Alexander Barron, John Liddell and Paul Kemezys and Leading Senior Constable Gary Tickell, were awarded the Medal for Courage.

NOTES

FIRE PLAN

p. 12 Fire plan figures are from Whittaker and Handmer.

ARSON

Most of the information on **pages 44–5** is from a Monash University (Melbourne) symposium called 'Collaborating for change: Symposium advancing bushfire arson prevention in Australia'.

Specifically: Maclean, A. (2000:11) Wildfire arson in Victoria: Analysis of crime patterns to assist the development of specific prevention and enforcement strategies. Unpublished, University of Melbourne. Cited in: Cozens, P. (2010) Overview: *Environmental criminology and the potential for reducing bushfire arson.*

A report by A. Tomison: *Bushfire arson: Setting the scene.*

Additional information concerning arson from the report of the symposium, entitled: *Advancing Bushfire Arson Prevention in Australia*, edited by Janet Stanley and Tahl Kestin, MSE Report 10/3, June 2010. Monash University, Monash Sustainability Institute.

p. 45 Statistics on arson rates among CFA members are from Danielle Clode, *A Future in Flames*. The information on arsonists' motivations is from Janet Stanley and Tahl Kestin, quoted in Clode.

RED FLAG

p. 67 Stephen Pyne, *Burning Bush*, p. 38.

p. 68 Clive Countryman, *Fire Whirls, Why, When, and Where*, p. 7.

p. 69 Quote from William Kininmonth obtained in conversation.

SURVIVAL ARC

pp. 108–13 Disaster stories, and the quote from Gordon Gallup, taken from Amanda Ripley, *The Unthinkable: Who Survives When Disaster Strikes and Why.*

p. 113 Percentage of victims who perished in the bath from Whittaker and Handmer, *Review of Key Bushfire Research Findings.*

p. 115 The London tube story and the quote from Massad Ayob are both from Ripley.

SNAPSHOTS

p. 141 John Handmer quoted in the *Age*: 'Most fire victims fail to prepare' by Karen Kissane, April 28, 2010.

FIRE: AN ILLUMINATED HISTORY

p. 148 Stephen Pyne, *Fire: A Brief History.*

p. 150 The major study mentioned in para 2 is Davidson, Close and Jones, *The Decline of the Eucalypt.*

p. 152 John Stokes: *Discoveries in Australia...* p. 228.

pp. 152 and 154 Rhys Jones, 'Fire-stick farming'.

p. 153 Ernest Giles, *Australia Twice Traversed*, p. 111.

p. 153–4 The Arnhem Land elder is Yibarbuk, quoted in Phil Zylstra, *Fire History of the Australian Alps.*

p. 155 A. P. Elkin also quoted in Zylstra.

p. 156 Banks quoted in Pyne, *Burning Bush*, p. 150.

p. 156 Zylstra, *Fire History*, p. 26.

Robert Clode is quoted in Paul Collins, *Burn*, p. 55.

p. 158 Pyne, *Burning Bush*, p. 224; the quote from D. M. Thompson is on p. 208.

Old timer quoted in Eric Rolls, *A Million Wild Acres*, p. 247.

p. 159 Information from Neil Davidson obtained in conversation, February 2011.

p. 161 Figures on the social impact of bushfire trauma from Catherine Caruana's article in *Family Matters*, 'Picking up the Pieces'.

p. 162 Demographic information from Chen and McAneney, pp. 1–4.

Phil Cheney quoted in Danielle Clode, *A Future in Flames.*

SAVING PEOPLE

p. 199 Samuel Oliner quoted in Ripley, p. 189.

BUSHFIRE BRAIN

p. 232 Stella Reid quoted in Jim Usher and Mac Gudgeon, *Footsteps in the Ashes*, p. 67.

p. 235 Paul Valent's quote is from an article by Karen Kissane, 'Embers of pain stir in young hearts', *Age*, January 5, 2011.

A REFLECTION

p. 243 'CFA chief Russell Rees resigns', *Age*, April 23, 2010.

p. 245 CSIRO modelling on fire-prone days forecast is from *Bushfire Weather*, Lucas, Hennessy et al.

p. 247 *Age*, November 20, 2010, p. 14.

p. 248 Castella information obtained in conversation with DSE ranger Tony Fitzgerald.

REFERENCES

Australian Bureau of Meteorology (2008) *Climate of Australia,* Australian Bureau of Meteorology, Melbourne.

Caruana, C., 'Picking up the Pieces: Family Functioning in the Aftermath of Natural Disaster', *Family Matters*, no. 84, 2010.

Chen, K. and McAneney J., 'Quantifying Bushfire Penetration into Urban Areas of Australia', *Geophysical Research Letters*, vol. 31, no. L12212, 2004, pp. 1–4.

Clode, D. (2010) *A Future in Flames*, Melbourne University Press, Melbourne.

Collins, P. (2009) *Burn: The Epic Story of Bushfire in Australia*, Scribe, Melbourne.

Colls, K. and Whittaker, R. (1993) *The Australian Weather Book*, National, Brookvale, NSW.

Countryman, C. (1971) *Fire Whirls, Why, When, and Where*, Pacific Southwest Forest and Range Experiment Station, US Forest Service Berkeley, Calif.

Davidson, Close and Jones, 'The Decline of the Eucalypt', *Fire Update*, no. 20, May 2007, Bushfire Cooperative Research Centre.

De Villiers, Marq (2006) *Windswept: The Story of Wind and Weather*, Walker and Company, New York.

Giles, E. (1889) *Australia Twice Traversed: the Romance of Exploration, Being a Narrative Compiled from the Journals of Five Exploring Expeditions into and through Central Australia and Western Australia from 1872 to 1876*, Sampson Low, Marston, Searle and Rivington, London.

Hunter, J. to the Duke of Portland, June 10, 1797, in *Historical Records of New South Wales*, 1797, vol. 3, p. 220.

Johns, David (2009) *A Day Like No Other*, D. & B. Johns, Kinglake.

Jones, R., 'Fire-stick farming', *Australian Natural History*, September 1969.

Kissane, K. (2010) *Worst of Days*, Hachette Australia, Sydney.

Latz, P. (2007) *The Flaming Desert: A Fire-shaped Landscape*, Peter Latz, Alice Springs.

Linacre, E. and Geerts, B. (1997) *Climates and Weather Explained*, Routledge, London and New York.

Lucas, C., Hennessy, K., Mills, G., Bathols, J. (2007) *Bushfire Weather in Southeast Australia: Recent Trends and Projected Climate Change Impacts*, Bushfire CRC.

Luke, R. and McArthur, A. (1986) *Bushfires in Australia,* Australian Government Publishing Service, Canberra.

Mitchell, T. L. (1848) *Journey of an Expedition into the Interior of Tropical Australia in Search of a Route from Sydney to the Gulf of Carpentaria*, Longman, Brown, Green, London.

Mountain Monthly Cooperative Ltd (2009) *In Our Own Words*, Kinglake.

Pyne, S. (1982) *Fire in America: A Cultural History of Wildland and Rural Fire*, Princeton University Press, Princeton, N.J.

—— (1991) *Burning Bush: A Fire History of Australia*, Allen & Unwin, Sydney.

—— (1997) *Vestal Fire: An Environmental History, Told through Fire, of Europe and Europe's Encounter with the World*, University of Washington Press, Seattle.

—— (2001) *Fire: A Brief History*, British Museum, London.

Ripley, A. (2008) *The Unthinkable: Who Survives When Disaster Strikes and Why*, Random House, Sydney.

Rolls, E. (1984) *A Million Wild Acres*, Penguin Books, Ringwood.

Schultz, D. (ed.) *Fire on the Savannas: Voices from the Landscape*, Tropical Savannas CRC, Darwin, 1988.

Stokes, J. (1846) *Discoveries in Australia with an Account of the Coasts and Rivers Explored and Surveyed during the Voyage of HMS Beagle in the Years 1837–38–39–40–41–42–43*, T. & W. Boone, London.

Usher, J. and Gudgeon, M. (2010) *Footsteps in the Ashes: The Story of St Andrews and Strathewen in the 2009 Bushfires*, community publication.

White, M. (1990) *The Nature of Hidden Worlds*, Reed Books, Chatswood.

Whittaker, J. and Handmer, J. (2010) *Review of Key Bushfire Research Findings*, Centre for Risk and Community Safety, School of Mathematical and Geospatial Sciences, RMIT University, Melbourne.

Zylstra, P. (2006) *Fire History of the Australian Alps, Prehistory to 2003*, Australian Alps Liaison Committee.

ACKNOWLEDGMENTS

My first and greatest debt is to those members of the community who have shared their stories in what has been a terrible time for us all.

Phillip Adams

Frank Allan

Drew Barr

Karen Barrow

Lesley Bebbington

Debbie Bradshaw

Bernie Broom

Andrew Brown

Dom Bourke

Cameron Caine

Steve Chapman

Danielle Clode

Linda Craske

Debbie Donald

Wendy Duncan

Jon Ellks

Tony Fitzgerald

Colin French

Michelle French

Steve Gormley

John Grover

Trish Hendrie

Dave Hooper

Tim Huggins

Ben Hutchinson

Cathy Lance

David Lance

Paul Lowe

Sarah McAloon

Di MacLeod

Jim MacLeod

Michelle Marshall

Bruce Newport

Mike Nicholls

Karyn Norbury

Angie O'Connor

Phil Petschel

Jeff Purchase

Aaron Redmond

Kerrie Redmond

Jim Usher

Lisa Waddell

Carole Wilson

Jo Wood

Special thanks to Roger Wood, whose story forms the heart and soul of this book.

As tends to be the case with my work, I've been harassing scientists all over the country in an attempt to make up for my own short-comings. A special thank you to:

Tony Bannister	Neil Davidson
Liam Fogarty	Nic Gellie
Kelsy Gibos	William Kininmonth
Andrew Stacey	Philip Zylstra

Two experienced CFA captains have taken time from their busy volunteering activities to look over this manuscript and make help-ful comments: John Schauble and Laurie Steel. My sincerest thanks to you both. I'd also like to acknowledge the friendship and words of advice from my colleagues at the St Andrews CFA; many of the insights—and sometimes even the language—you've all given me as we bounce around the back roads of St Andrews have worked their way into this narrative.

Parks ranger Tony Fitzgerald has been a constant source of wisdom and encouragement.

Kind thanks as well to Senior Sergeant Pete Sambell and Sergeant Sven Koernig from Victoria Police, and to John Sylvester for help with the contacts.

Thanks to Greg Bailey, for the Indian mythology.

I would like to acknowledge the influence of the great fire historian Stephen Pyne. His *Cycle of Fire* suite has delivered a new element—fire—into our literature, and underpins much of my discussion of the role of fire in our culture and landscape.

Amanda Ripley's *The Unthinkable: Who Survives When Disaster Strikes and Why* is a brilliant study of how people behave in times of crisis.

Danielle Clode was another source of inspiration, and her book, *A Future in Flames*, is warmly recommended.

Thanks to Lisa Jacobson for permission to reproduce her beauti-ful poem, 'Girls and Horses in the Fire'.

ACKNOWLEDGMENTS

Special thanks to my colleagues at La Trobe University, especially Susan Bradley-Smith, Lucy Sussex, Catherine Padmore, David Tacey and Clare Williams.

Thanks to my agent, Mary Cunnane.

Again, thanks to the mob at Text for their faith in my work. A special thanks to Mandy Brett for the editorial masterstrokes.

Thanks to Stan, Helen and crew at the St Andrews pub for 'the office' and the coffee.

As always, the last word and the deepest expression of gratitude go to my beautiful girls, Kristin, Sally and Siena.